Jewish Continuity
and Change

JEWISH POLITICAL AND SOCIAL STUDIES

Daniel J. Elazar and Steven M. Cohen, Editors

Center for Modern Jewish Studies
BRANDEIS UNIVERSITY

Jewish Continuity and Change

EMERGING PATTERNS IN AMERICA

Calvin Goldscheider

INDIANA UNIVERSITY PRESS • *Bloomington*

Manufactured in the United States of America

Library of Congress Cataloging in Publication Data

Goldscheider, Calvin.
Jewish continuity and change.

(Jewish political and social studies)
Bibliography: p.
Includes index.
1. Jews—United States—Social conditions.
2. United States—Ethnic relations. I. Title.
II. Series.
E184.J5G6265   1985   305.8'924'073   84-48746
ISBN 0-253-33157-9

1 2 3 4 5   89 88 87 86

CONTENTS

Figures

Tables

Preface

One of the conspicuous features of American society has been its complex, pluralistic religious and ethnic structure. Ethnic differentiation is associated with family patterns, socioeconomic characteristics, residential concentration, and community institutions. Changes over time have diluted some of the structural and cultural distinctiveness of ethnic communities. The general issue of ethnic continuity in modern societies can be subdivided into two sets of questions: First, what are the distinctive features of ethnic communities which mark them off from others, and how have these changed over time? Second, how do these distinctive patterns relate to ethnic assimilation or group continuity?

For the question of distinctiveness, we need to make systematic and detailed comparisons among ethnic groups, examining relative changes over time. We need as well to disentangle the sources of distinctiveness to evaluate the question of continuities. It is critical to know whether the sources of distinctiveness are temporary and transitory or whether they are embedded in the social structure. In investigating the question of the consequences of these patterns for ethnic cohesion, we need to study the multiple dimensions of group cohesion, i.e., patterns which reflect the strength of community. These include the variety of spheres of activity where interaction occurs—families, neighborhoods, jobs, and school, as well as in cultural and social contexts. These questions are at the very core of social-scientific analysis—social differentiation, group cohesion, intergroup relationships, and social change.

Thus, the investigation of the sources of ethnic group distinctiveness and their consequences for group cohesion focuses on two analytically distinct issues, not one. Change or the lack of distinctiveness does not automatically or necessarily mean ethnic assimilation. The relationship between ethnic distinctiveness and ethnic cohesion is an analytic issue, not an inference. There has been a widespread assumption in the social science literature that ethnic change is necessarily linked to a decline in ethnic group cohesion. Increases in residential integration, secularization, educational attainment, and occupational achievement, reductions in family size, and intermarriage between ethnics have all been *assumed* to mean declines in the salience of ethnicity and decreases in interactions among ethnics in their communities. We take that set of assumptions as one of our core research questions, rather than as a logical conclusion from the changing distinctiveness of groups.

The Jewish experience in America exemplifies issues of distinctiveness, social change, and cohesion at the community level. The analysis of the American Jewish community illustrates the tension between ethnic group distinctiveness and assimilation; between social change and ethnic continuity; between social-structural and cultural sources of distinctiveness. Thus, our focus on Jews is illustrative of social processes for ethnic groups in general.

We examine Jews in the context of their community. Our focus is on social and demographic processes—marriage and family formation, residence and mobility, social class, lifestyle, religious and ethnic communal affiliation, identification, and behavior. We analyze the links between these processes and determine: (1) Are Jews different from others, and why? If so, (2) What are the consequences of these differences for ethnic cohesion or assimilation?

To focus on Jewish cohesion is to examine the extent and variety of intragroup

xii

interaction. The studies in this volume examine three sets of issues which form the basis of a detailed analysis of one American Jewish community: (1) interaction or Jewish cohesion among those at the margins of the Jewish community—the inter-married, recent migrants, and those in integrated neighborhoods; (2) generational and demographic bases of group continuity, including marriage, family, and repro-duction; and (3) issues of quality, including occupational concentration, educa-tional resources, and the generational transmission of socioeconomic status, as well as religious, ethnic, and institutional bases of continuity.

These themes build cumulatively upon previous research, refining and includ-ing new variables and documenting systematically patterns observed more casu-ally. For example, the analysis of marriage patterns documents the strong family orientations of Jews and explores the trade-offs between education and marriage for men and women. Evidence on fertility confirms the low fertility of American Jews and identifies important relationships between labor force participation of women and family size expectations. The Jewishness of the intermarried, the non-married, and migrants is examined, and patterns of socioeconomic concentration are investigated. New areas of inquiry, previously unexamined with systematic empirical evidence, are pursued. These include an analysis of household structure and family extension, intermarriage norms and attitudes, residential concen-tration and measures of Jewish density, and patterns of self-employment of men and women. In each of the chapters the findings are placed in broader theoretical and substantive contexts. While the dominant theme throughout is the analysis of social-structural and Jewish continuity, each chapter attempts to probe in depth specific issues associated with a particular theme.

The analysis shows that the transformation of the American Jewish community involved some overall convergences between Jews and non-Jews. There has been a reduction of differences in terms of family, marriage, and childbearing patterns, as well as in social class, residence, occupation, education, and culture. Neverthe-less, a detailed, systematic examination of the evidence points to the unmistakable conclusion that American Jews are different on every one of these dimensions. These differences do not mainly reflect, and cannot be understood as, the lack of integration of Jews in America or discrimination against them. The distinctiveness of Jews does not seem to reflect mainly specific Jewish values.

The distinctiveness of American Jews in part reflects their background social and economic characteristics. Yet some of the differences between Jews and others remain unexplained. Jewish distinctiveness means more than the absence of as-similation. The distinctive features of American Jewish life imply bonds and link-ages among Jews which form the multiple bases of communal continuity. Ties are structural as well as cultural and are deeply embedded in major social processes—family, education, jobs, and residence patterns. They are reinforced by religious and ethnic communal behavior and cemented by shared lifestyles and values.

We focus on one body of empirical evidence, the Boston Study of 1975, incor-porating where appropriate findings from the 1965 survey. These data were col-lected and organized by others, and the methodologies have been documented (see Fowler 1977 and Axelrod, Fowler, and Gurin 1967). They were originally de-signed as community reports and were largely descriptive. The data used in this book address analytic issues associated with recent changes among Jews and the continuation of Jewish distinctiveness. We therefore do not describe the Boston Jewish community or its institutions. The secondary analysis of these data illus-

trates the richness of the material available awaiting exploration. Much more remains available. The extraordinary value of the Boston study is the detailed
information collected on representative samples of Jews and non-Jews.[1] No previous analysis using these data has focused on the systematic comparison of Jews
and non-Jews or examined the issues covered in this book.

The oversimplified assimilation framework predicting the continuous erosion of
Jewish cohesion in modern American society is inconsistent with the empirical
evidence and has distorted the approach to the sociology of American Jews. We
argue throughout for a pluralistic framework which identifies a variety of sources
of cohesion within the Jewish community. Family ties, economic networks, social-
class bonds, educational backgrounds, and residential patterns are linked to lifestyles, interaction patterns, and ethnic-community associations. In turn, these
forms of cohesiveness are related to Judaism and new ways of expressing Jewishness in America. We focus on the numerous junctures of social structure and
Jewish continuity between generations and among age peers. Our approach is to
analyze these generational patterns directly with longitudinal data constructed
retrospectively and to compare systematically Jews and non-Jews.

On both quantitative and qualitative grounds, the evidence reveals a dynamic
picture of an extensive and intensive Jewish community. Contemporary American
Jews are clearly different from those of the past; so are their communities. To
describe them only in terms of demographic decline or assimilation is not only to
miss the complexity of social life but to obscure the major sources of cohesion
which characterize the community. Jews continue to be distinctive relative to non-
Jews, and their differences have crystallized and widened over time. There is
every indication of Jewish continuity in America in a transformed community.

The reorganization of the data from the Boston studies began as a demonstration
of the value of Jewish community studies for examining variation and change
among American Jews. The grander idea was to begin to put some order into the
chaos of Jewish community studies of the past and to help shape the quality of data
collected in the future. That remains the ideal toward which we should strive. To
demonstrate the utility of such an approach, we began the analysis of these data to
explore themes untapped by previous research and expand on questions already
investigated. Our hope was to generate new questions in the process of building
cumulatively on past research.

The occasion for thinking about these ideas and organizing some of the previous
research was a conference held in October 1979 at Brandeis University. I was
invited, along with others, to prepare a background paper for the development of
a Center for Modern Jewish Studies. (These papers were published in Sklare
1982.) Subsequently, I accepted a two-year appointment as visiting Professor of

1. The Jewish sample consisted of two parts: (1) sampling from lists of the Combined
Jewish Philanthropies of Greater Boston and (2) a household sample from a random survey of
the entire area. The two samples were combined by weighting procedures which yielded "an
unbiased sample" of the Jewish population (Fowler 1977, pp. 3–9). We use only the weighted
sample in this analysis, as it is the only basis for a representative sample of the total Jewish
community in the area. The non-Jewish sample was derived from the general household
survey of the entire area. In 1975, there were 934 cases of Jews (weighted to 2,133 cases) and
1,043 cases of the total population of the Boston area. No data are reported when there were
less than 10 cases in the original unweighted sample. In all the tables reporting these findings, an asterisk (*) is used to designate too few cases for analysis.

Contemporary Jewish Studies in the Department of Near Eastern and Judaic Studies at Brandeis as part of the establishment of the new Center for Modern Jewish Studies. It was during this appointment that I prepared the data and wrote the analysis of material in this volume. Marshall Sklare, the director of the center, was instrumental in bringing me to Brandeis and involving me in the initial development of the center's program. He has supported this research in every way and has made available to me the resources and staff of the center. The completion of this project owes much to this support. Marvin Fox, the head of the Lown School of Near Eastern and Judaic Studies at Brandeis, has always been supportive and encouraging. I am indebted to both for the opportunity they provided me during this period of time.

The studies appear in this volume for the first time and have not been published before. The background review, evaluation of the literature, and identification of the major analytic themes for the demographic questions examined were prepared for the 1979 conference (see Goldscheider 1982). The theoretical issues on household structure and self-employment draw on continuing research carried out jointly with Frances E. Kobrin, focusing on ethnic variations and change (Kobrin and Goldscheider 1978; Goldscheider and Kobrin 1980; Kobrin and Goldscheider 1983). Over the course of this project, I have consulted regularly with her on statistical and methodological problems, as well as on substantive analysis. She provided important insights which led me to think in new ways about a whole series of issues connected with this research. Her fresh perspective and challenging questions pushed me beyond the routine analysis I had planned. She read through the entire manuscript, critically and constructively, under the pressures of time and competing obligations. The successful completion of this project is in no small measure a reflection of her contribution.

During the period of time I was working on this project, I was completing a comparative-historical overview of Jewish society and politics in the last century with Alan S. Zuckerman of Brown University. The insights into the broader theoretical issues associated with Jewish survival in the modern era which emerged out of that collaboration have been useful in sharpening my perspective about the future of American Jewry (Goldscheider and Zuckerman 1984, especially chapters 10 and 11). Although he has not been involved directly in this project, his research on the broader issues has stimulated and clarified my research on American Jews.

The data analysis could not have been carried out without the full and generous cooperation of the Combined Jewish Philanthropies of Greater Boston. Bernard Olshansky and David Rosen saw to it that the data were made available. Floyd Fowler carried out the survey, organized the data, and prepared the computer file that was the dream of any researcher. If the data have value, it is because Jack Fowler prepared them in a way which could be analyzed by others. The project is indebted in the most fundamental way to these persons and their institutions and staffs for carrying out their part expertly.

The data were reorganized and analyzed at Brown University in cooperation with the Population Studies and Training Center, the Social Science Data Center, and the sociology department. All the costs for the computer time were covered by my continuing appointment as Adjunct Professor of Sociology and Judaic Studies at Brown University. I am grateful to the director of the center, Sidney Goldstein, and the chair of the department, Alden Speare, Jr., for their full cooperation and support.

The Center for Modern Jewish Studies of Brandeis, established with the aid of the Charles H. Revson Foundation, provided funds to cover the preparation of this volume. The statements made and views expressed, however, are solely the responsibility of the author.

At Brown, Deborah A. Abowitz and W. Ward Kingkade provided invaluable research assistance, working under the pressures of time and my schedule. I knew I could count on them to do a first-rate job, and I was not disappointed. At Brandeis, Sarita Goldberg and Alena Strauss provided indispensable administrative assistance. I am grateful to both for being cheerful and cooperative at a time when I was less so. I was fortunate to find at Brandeis two graduate students who were a source of stimulation and inspiration to me, Gerry Showstack and Shelly Tenenbaum. In conversations about their own research in the sociology of American Jews and in courses with me on ethnicity, I learned much from them. They helped make my stay at Brandeis a rewarding intellectual experience. Carol Walker at Brown typed the final drafts of the manuscript expertly, efficiently, and with a charming sense of humor.

Sidney Goldstein read through an earlier draft of the manuscript with his customary critical eye. His comments were helpful in sharpening and clarifying the analysis. Steven M. Cohen read through an earlier version as well, raising questions and making suggestions for revisions. His own work, in part based on the Boston data, focuses on related themes in the sociology of American Jewish life. Conversations with them in Providence, New York, and Jerusalem encouraged me toward greater analytic precision. I am indebted to both for their advice and assistance.

The volume is dedicated to my teachers in the sociology and demography of the Jews with humility and respect for their scholarship, friendship, and concern for me.

Calvin Goldscheider

Jewish Continuity
and Change

ONE

Transformation and Jewish Cohesion: The Analytic Issues

Over the last century, the Jewish community in the United States has been transformed. Whether judged by population growth, educational attainment, occupational achievement, residential distribution, marriage and family patterns, religious behavior, or organizational structure, the American Jewish community in the 1980s is radically different from the immigrant community of Jews in late-nineteenth-century America. The patterns of change are well documented; the impact on the Jewish community, however, is less clear. Does the transformation imply the assimilation of Jews, the decline in communal cohesion, and the erosion of Jewish life in America? Has the transformation of American Jewry weakened the Jewish community, threatening its vitality and survival?

There is a widespread assumption that "change" automatically and necessarily results in a decline of ethnic group cohesion. Indeed, residential integration, the secularization of Judaism, increases in educational levels, reductions in family size, intermarriage with non-Jews, and the attainment of middle-class managerial and professional occupations have been repeatedly cited as signaling the weakening of Jewish life in America. To study transformation, however, requires an investigation of the social-cultural patterns which are emerging. We cannot simply infer the consequences; the new patterns need to be examined directly. Our focus is, therefore, on the contemporary Jewish community that has developed.

The cohesion of a community depends on the extent and depth of solidarity of its members. In its most fundamental sense, Jewish cohesion means the variety of ways, and the various spheres of activities, in which Jews interact with other Jews. In the specific area of religious activities, for example, Jews obviously interact with one another. That may, however, not be the only or necessarily the most significant context. Jews interact with other Jews in families, neighborhoods, and schools, at work, and in organizations and political activities. Similarly, while Jews may share basic cultural values associated with their Jewishness, of equal importance they may share broader lifestyles, aspirations, and other status concerns. The strength of the Jewish community reflects the number and intensity of in-group interactions. The more the bases of interaction and the greater its intensity, the more cohesive is the community. Taken as a whole—fam-

1

ilies, jobs, schools, residences, sociocultural activities—the community is a network of interactions. These structural features of the Jewish community are therefore of major importance in shaping Jewish cohesion.

Our questions can now be formulated more precisely: Does the transformation of the Jews imply moving away from cohesion, or might it not generate new patterns of cohesion as well? Do the new patterns emerging in America mean weak levels of Jewish cohesion? Does transformation result in fewer bases of Jewish cohesion and less-intense levels? Previous research has assumed that these changes have resulted in assimilation and lower levels of group cohesion among third- and fourth-generation American Jews. We take that assumption as our research question.

THE GENERATIONAL CONTEXT

The pattern of transformation of American Jews needs to be understood in comparison to the patterns of other white ethnic-religious groups and as part of the broader historical context of American society. Jewish immigrants to the United States were part of a larger and continuing stream of migrants to America. How different was the transformation in America for Jews compared to other ethnic groups? What are the sources of cohesion among contemporary American Jews?

American society has long been characterized by the arrival of immigrant groups from diverse countries of origin. Ideologically, America supported the integration of immigrants, the preservation of religious and ethnic diversity, and the extension of political rights to all its citizens. The power of industrialization and the scope of modernization in America transformed the streams of immigrants and their communities.

Jewish immigrants responded in many ways to the process of becoming Americans. They were socially and geographically mobile, became college-educated, entered the middle class, and adapted their religion. Indeed, America has become a major test case for the survival of Jews as a minority group in a relatively free and open, pluralistic society with a developing economy and expanding opportunity structure. (For a comparative-historical analysis of the variety of Jewish communities, see Goldscheider and Zuckerman 1984.)

To understand the relationship between social change and Jewish continuity, we need to sketch briefly some background context. The formation of the American Jewish community was conditioned by the timing and rate of population growth. At the end of the eighteenth century, there were approximately 1,200 Jews in America. The Jewish population increased to about 50,000 in 1848 and to slightly less than 250,000 before the mass immigrations from eastern Europe in the 1880s. As a result of high rates of net immigration and natural increase, the Jewish population in the United States increased to over 1,000,000 by the turn of the twentieth century and to over 4,000,000 by the mid-1920s. By 1950, the American Jewish population numbered approximately 5,000,000—(a 100-fold increase in a century (Goldscheider 1982; Goldstein 1981b).

The level of Jewish immigration from eastern Europe declined substantially with the quota restriction in the 1920s. Fertility levels of second-generation Jews plummeted to replacement levels during the economic depression, and rates of population growth declined. The number of American Jews was estimated at 5,775,000 in 1970–1971, with a margin of error of almost 250,000 on either side (Lazerwitz 1978). It is likely that the size of the Jewish population of the United States had not attained the 6,000,000 mark by 1980. Taking into account the whole range of demographic processes (mortality, fertility, immigration, emigration, conversions to and from Judaism, and net changes due to outmarriages), the Jewish community hovers at a zero population growth rate. Because this rate has been slower than that characterizing American society, the proportion of Jews out of the total American population has declined to less than 2.7 percent. That is the lowest proportion Jewish since the first decade of the twentieth century.

The relative decline of Jews in America and their continuing slow rate of population growth have led to concerns about the shrinking population size of American Jewry. In turn, inferences have been drawn about the political significance of reduced size and connections made to the absence of vitality in the Jewish community. There are, indeed, important links between demographic processes and the quality of American Jewish life. Nevertheless, American Jews have never constituted a numerically large segment of the population, nor has their political or economic power been a simple function of population size. America is the world Jewish demographic center. It is not likely that it will be overtaken by another Jewish community in the world—including Israel—for the rest of this century (cf. Schmelz 1981; DellaPergola 1980; Bachi 1976). The future demography of American Jews depends on a complex combination of marriage and fertility patterns which may not be as negative for Jewish cohesion as some have suggested. High rates of migration and low levels of Jewish residential density may also not have negative implications for Jewish cohesion.

Jewish immigrants who arrived in the United States around the turn of the twentieth century did not transplant the world of their origins. America was different, and so were the immigrants. They left the old world behind, not all of it to be sure, to become part of the new society. Their Jewishness was conspicuous in their background, culture, and social structure. What the sources of their children's Jewishness would be, however, was not clear. How they would convey their traditions was set aside as they struggled to survive in America.

Residential segregation, occupational concentration, and family centrality characterized the communities of the Jewish immigrants settling from eastern Europe. Alliances and cleavages were formed among Jews from towns and villages of origin. These resulted in the development of

new communal institutions and organizations, generating patterns of interaction and family life that reinforced Jewishness.

In a relatively short period of time following immigration, Jews changed
in ways which reduced their obvious separateness. They shed their ethnic
language and foreign dress, moved to new residentially integrated areas,
and attended public schools, colleges, and universities in unprecedented
numbers and proportions. In schools and neighborhoods, Jews interacted
with non-Jews. Moving away from working-class occupations within selected industries and restrictive job opportunities, Jews became professionals and managers. In their social mobility, they have become affluent.
Poverty and unskilled occupations are largely uncharacteristic of contemporary American Jews.

These occupational, educational, and residential changes were accompanied by shifts in the relative importance of families. Like others under
similar circumstances, Jewish families experienced reductions in size and
stability. They became less traditional in religious practice than earlier
generations, and Judaism has become less central in their lives. As religious authority declined and ritual observances shifted away from the traditional, alternative religious institutions and new secular organizations
were forming, creating American ways to express Judaism and Jewishness.

In short, industrialization, urbanization, modernization, and secularization transformed the Jews of America. Indeed, every indicator reveals how
Jews have become modern, secular, and American in the 1980s. They
exemplify the power of achievement, the success of meritocracy, and the
value of individual liberty in American society. The transition to an Americanized third- or fourth-generation ethnic group has been the master
theme in the study of contemporary American Jews. In the 1980s, approximately 80 percent of the American Jewish population is native-born, and
half are at least two generations removed from the immigrant experience.
Given the depth of the transformation from earlier generations, the central analytic question becomes: What are the contemporary bases of
American Jewish cohesion?

THE THEORETICAL CONTEXT

Why have people assumed that changes such as those experienced by
American Jews would necessarily reduce cohesion? The association of extensive change with ethnic group assimilation and the erosion of ethnic
communal cohesion results from the application to American Jews of a
major theoretical model of social change. This model has in the past
shaped the questions which have been asked about American Jews and
the interpretations offered for the empirical patterns uncovered. Other
theories of social change and ethnicity either have not been appropriate
for understanding Jewish communites or have never been systematically
applied to the Jews.

The model which has been most applied to the Jews may be referred to as the theory of modernization and assimilation. It posits that societies based on ethnicity are poorly adapted to the requirements of modernity. Elements of modernization, such as the spread of a national economy, polity, mass culture, and bureaucracy, entail universalistic criteria which cut across ethnic statuses. Increasing similarities in how ethnic groups live replace traditional ethnic attachments with social class and political cleavages (cf. discussions in Leifer 1981; Nielsen 1980; Glazer and Moynihan 1975; Gordon 1964). Following this logic, any maintenance of ethnic cultural forms is partially an attempt to preserve a backward lifestyle. If modernization means achievement and progress, then it is concluded that ethnic continuity implies resistance to change. While there may be some ethnic remnants less affected by modernization, time and institutions (e.g., education), so it is argued, minimize their differences.

Ethnic persistence, therefore, is viewed as an aberration, a cultural lag, an unexpected feature of modernity to be explained away. Searching for a core basis to account for the continuous presence of ethnic groups experiencing economic and social assimilation, some have emphasized that religion and ideology become anchors of identity for individuals (cf. Herberg 1960). Others have suggested limited political interests, primordial "tribal" attachments, or the desire for group survival as the basis for continuity. Others view ethnicity as a reflection of nostalgic cultural traits of no depth or consequence (cf. some of the essays in Glazer and Moynihan 1975). The fundamental argument remains the same: modernization of the Jews or any other ethnic group leads to their demise as a separate community.

Even when the theoretical model emphasizes the multiple dimensions of ethnic assimilation, beyond culture and religion to social structure and identity (e.g., Gordon 1964), similar assumptions have been made about the association of change with ethnic decline. Thus, for example, college education, social mobility, residential integration, and marital "assimilation" are thought to be interrelated. Hence, change in any one leads to the others and to a weakening of the ethnic community. While these links may have characterized earlier generations of immigrants, when conflict and change between the foreign-born and their children were conspicuous, it is not clear whether these correlations characterize contemporary ethnic communities.

A second set of theories emphasizes intergroup conflict and economic discrimination as the basis of ethnic continuity. These have rarely been applied to Jews. One argument, for example, has been made that the changes associated with modernization result in ethnic conflict, discrimination, and racism. In turn, ethnic communities symbolize the continuity of economic disadvantage and deprivation. Thus, it follows, the core of ethnicity in modern societies is class conflict and competition based on the overlap between ethnic groups and social class (Hechter; Smelser;

Stone). The conspicuous mobility of American Jews and their class structure, educational attainment, and occupational concentration hardly fit
models of deprivation and discrimination.

Moreover, the implication of this theoretical model is that ethnic solidarity weakens as economic mobility occurs. With increasing educational
levels, occupational mobility and diversification, higher levels of income,
and residential integration, the strength of community cohesion based on
ethnicity declines. For Jews, therefore, this prediction would be the same
as with the previous model: without extensive discrimination, forced residential exclusion, and economic exploitation, and with the attainment of
middle-class status, Jewish cohesion should weaken.

A third theoretical model focuses on networks of social relationships
within the community as the basis for ethnic continuity. This "network-
cohesion" theory has not been applied systematically to the study of the
contemporary Jewish community in America. It views the strength of ethnic communities in terms of the number of social-structural bases of cohesion. Emphasis is placed on the overlap of ethnicity with a variety of
statuses—family, social, cultural, political, residential, and economic. The
economic base of ethnic cohesion includes a wide array of factors, from
occupational distinctiveness to lifestyle, social class, and educational levels. Inequality, disadvantage, and economic deprivation are not the only
sources of overlap between ethnicity and economic factors. Competition
and occupational networks are powerful sources of ethnic cohesion (Bonacich; Nielsen 1980; Leifer 1981; Zuckerman 1982). While group boundaries may become relatively more open and fluid (Barth 1969), alternative
family, economic, and residential bases emerge (Yancey et al. 1976).
Hence, ethnicity is neither an ascribed nor a transitional characteristic.
Ethnicity can also emerge with modernity and is not only a cultural legacy
of the past. While modernity transforms ethnic groups, new patterns may
emerge which strengthen the kinship, residential, occupational, class, and
cultural networks of ethnic communities. These networks, so the theory
argues, are the bases for ethnic continuity in modern society. Moreover,
links among members of an ethnic group may be reinforced by broader
international bonds of identification. These include concerns about related groups in a national homeland or in other countries.

The network-cohesion model alters the questions we ask about ethnic
groups in modern society and changes the prediction about their future.
It forces us to reevaluate assumptions of ethnic erosion and decline. We
shall use this theoretical orientation to focus on the structural sources of
Jewish cohesion. The emphasis on the structural bases of Jewish continuity moves the analysis toward the selected features of Jewish communities associated with families, occupations, residence, and religion. It
views these bases as the foundations of ethnic cohesion. Social-psychological dimensions of ethnic identity, cultural consensus, political ideologies,
and anti-Jewish attitudes and prejudices are the consequences of these

structural processes, not their determinants. Hence, our focus is on the structural foundations which have emerged in the Jewish community in America.

THE RESEARCH CHALLENGE

There have been few studies of contemporary American Jewry which have examined the links between social change and Jewish cohesion, in part because the theoretical model used assumed that the links were there. In addition, the data available were not designed to examine these links. Much of what is known about the sociology and demography of American Jews is based on evidence of uneven quality. Methodological limitations, particularly biased samples, inadequate coverage of the community, and problems of comparability among communities, have prevented systematic research. Most of these surveys have been designed as reports to the Jewish community. As a result, they have not included comparable non-Jewish groups; they tend to be descriptive rather than analytic. (For a recent evaluation of the current state of the field, see the various essays in Sklare 1982; for an evaluation of data sources, see Goldstein and Goldscheider 1968; Goldstein 1973a.) We have, therefore, not gone beyond the documentation of the transformation to ask more comprehensive questions about connections between these transformations and Jewish cohesion.

We focus in this volume on one Jewish community of medium size, Boston. It is not a representative Jewish community: there are none. Indeed, the absence of comparative Jewish community research in the United States prevents us from knowing what possible sources of biases characterize any one community study. Is community size related to Jewish cohesion? Is its ethnic composition, geographic location, date of settlement, pattern of residential dispersal, structure of economic opportunities, relative population size, or proximity to other locations where there are larger Jewish communities correlated with Jewish cohesion? We do not know. Whatever biases may characterize the Boston Jewish community, they are not known. Its attractiveness from a research point of view rests with the availability of comprehensive, detailed survey data collected in 1965 and in 1975 which have been largely unexplored.[1] These data allow us to answer new questions about social change and Jewish continuity and to address old questions in new ways. In particular, we focus on three major analytic questions which emerge from previous

1. Two community reports were prepared from these studies, Axelrod, Fowler, and Gurin 1967 and Fowler 1977. Steven M. Cohen was writing a comprehensive analysis of American Jews based in part on the Boston surveys while the studies in this volume were being prepared. His focus and emphasis were different. He used other data sources and examined other themes. His analysis revolved around the Jewishness and politics of American Jews, and no systematic comparisons to non-Jews were included (Cohen 1983).

research: (1) Do Jews continue to be different from non-Jews? What are the sources of these differences, and have they diminished over time? (2) What have been the patterns of change among young Jews growing up in the 1960s and 1970s? Have there been major shifts away from Jewishness and Jewish continuity in the recent period as social changes have occurred? (3) What are the sources of variation within the Jewish community? Have these widened or diminished in the recent period, and more so for Jews than non-Jews?

We apply these questions to several major realms of potential ethnic cohesion: (1) intermarriage, migration, and residential concentration, reflecting issues associated with contacts and relationships with non-Jews; (2) marriage, family, and life cycle, exploring patterns of reproduction, household structure, and thereby group continuity; (3) socioeconomic transformations and self-employment patterns for men and women, which relate to the quality of Jewish life and the ethnic networks associated with lifestyle and social class; and (4) religiosity and ethnic-community attachments, addressing directly patterns of cohesion in the Jewish community. In the process, we expand the analysis of issues which have been investigated in previous research and explore new areas which require further research.

We compare Jews to non-Jews and to specific religious and ethnic subgroups of non-Jews. We place the specific empirical findings on Jews in the context of what is generally known and what may be learned from previous research on the sociology and demography of Jews. Our objective is not to locate universal Jewish patterns, since we expect variations related to particular social and economic contexts. Jewish communities will reflect the broader communities of which they are a part, as well as particular features—structural and cultural—common to Jewish communities.

The specific questions we ask and the particular themes we investigate are fundamental to understanding and evaluating two core issues associated with Jewish American continuity: (1) demographic continuity through family-reproduction, generational changes, intermarriage, and, at the community level, migration; (2) the quality of American Jewish life as reflected in the stratification and family ties of Jews, as well as religious and ethnic sources of cohesion. These core issues are, as we shall illustrate in the chapters that follow, interrelated.

The complex dynamics associated with economic position, education, migration, family formation, employment, and Jewish continuities are most clearly observed at the level of community. Indeed, it is in the community, rather than at the national level, where links and networks are most conspicuous. Community studies can clarify in depth the complex factors involved in ethnic continuities and change and can untangle the web of relationships, particularly when the focus is on cohesion and networks.

Community studies per se cannot fully clarify national issues. Some communities are growing, while others are declining in size; some are gaining in-migrants, while others are losing out-migrants. Neighborhoods and geographic areas change in composition and are sometimes renewed. Research focused on one or several communities is by design more localized and less generalizable in specifics. The studies in this volume, therefore, are not oriented toward the description of the Boston Jewish community. Our focus is on analytic issues, connecting social change and variation among Jews and making comparisons to non-Jews.

Emerging from our detailed analysis is a portrait of Jewish continuity through transformation. There are powerful indicators of socioeconomic and community networks which go beyond arguments about assimilation, socioeconomic change, or ethnic revival. These emerging forms of Jewish cohesion require continuous research focused on the complex interplay of social change and Jewish continuity in America.

TWO

Intermarriage Norms and Attitudes

Intermarriages between Jews and non-Jews symbolize, as perhaps no other indicator, the conflict between universalism and particularism, between assimilation and ethnic continuity in American society. High rates of out-marriage threaten directly demographic survival of small minority populations. Most important, marriages between Jews and non-Jews reflect the core of communal cohesion. Since marriages are a major form of intensive and extensive interaction, changing levels of ethnic intermarriage imply alterations in group cohesion. Demographically, socially, and symbolically, intermarriage patterns are, therefore, of critical importance in assessing social change and Jewish continuity in America.

Until the 1960s, the Jews in America had been accurately described as the classic illustration of voluntary group endogamy, i.e., most married other Jews. Social scientists had hardly a basis for questioning Jewish group continuity when intermarriage rates were low and the intermarried were marginal to communal life. Evidence of increasing levels of Jewish out-marriages began to accumulate in the early 1960s, and the intermarried have become a conspicuous concern of the American Jewish community.

What do these rising rates of intermarriage mean for Jewish continuity? Are intermarriages part of the larger picture of demographic erosion among American Jews? Do intermarriage patterns reflect a desire for assimilation and loss of ethnic identity? Is out-marriage a product of higher education and the complex effects of universalistic values and Jewish–non-Jewish contacts in colleges and universities? Are the Jewish intermarried characterized by alienation from Judaism and the Jewish community? These questions guide our analysis of the quantitative and qualitative aspects of Jewish intermarriages.

JEWISH INTERMARRIAGES: QUANTITATIVE ISSUES

The evaluation of the demographic consequences of Jewish intermarriages in the United States is hindered by the absence of systematic and reliable evidence. Official data sources, censuses, and marriage records have no information on Jewish intermarriages.

Although some data on religion are available in the marriage records of two states (Iowa and Indiana) and from the 1957 Current Population Survey, these data have limited value for any detailed analysis of Jewish intermarriage rates (see Rosenthal 1963; Glick 1960; Goldstein 1973a.)[1] The major source for an analysis of trends and differentials in intermarriage is Jewish community surveys. While allowing for the inclusion of details on the background characteristics of intermarried couples, these surveys often do not fully cover marginal Jewish households and the nonaffiliated.

A brief overview of findings on changes and variations in Jewish intermarriage levels in the United States reveals the following patterns (cf. the review in Goldscheider 1982; Waxman 1982). Overall, Jewish endogamy is high and intermarriage rates are low relative to those of larger American ethnic-religious groupings.

An examination of intermarriage rates by age and generation, as well as of general levels of intermarriage between different time periods, reveals an unmistakable pattern of increase in the level of Jewish intermarriage. Some scattered evidence and impressions suggest that disproportionate shifts in the rate of intermarriage have occurred in the 1960s and 1970s among young Jews of the third and fourth generations (cf. Farber and Gordon 1982; Farber, Gordon, and Mayer 1979).

The systematic evaluation of the quantitative significance of increasing intermarriage levels is incomplete, since the level of conversions to Judaism is not well documented. Nor do we know the eventual Jewish commitments of the children of intermarried couples. The general impression from selected community studies and the National Jewish Population Study of 1970–1971 is that the level of conversion to Judaism has increased, and significant numbers of intermarried couples, usually over 50 percent, raise their children as Jews. Thus, it is impossible with the data available to know the extent to which current rates of Jewish intermarriage affect the size of the American Jewish population or have longer-term demographic consequences for the size of generations yet unborn. It is also clear that not all Jewish intermarriages imply the loss to the Jewish community of the Jewish partner or the children of the couple. To the contrary, substantial evidence shows that the Jewish community often gains rather than loses members through intermarriage, conversion, and the Jewish socialization of the children of intermarried couples. The limited evidence suggests that there are no simple connections between increases in intermarriage levels and demographic erosion of the American Jewish community.

The level of Jewish intermarriage varies considerably among commu-

1. Since so much has been written about the 1957 study, it should be noted that fewer than 75 Jewish intermarried couples nationally were included in the sample. There are fewer than 45 cases a year in Iowa (1953–59) and fewer than 100 cases a year in Indiana (1960–63). In total, around 400 Jewish intermarriages of all ages and generations were included in the National Jewish Population Survey.

nities, because of variation in the size and composition (generation and socioeconomic status) of their Jewish populations, as well as related factors such as the age of the community and the extent of its institutional structure. It is not clear, therefore, whether communities with higher intermarriage rates foreshadow what will come to characterize in the future the Jewish American population as a whole, or whether because of their size or composition these communities are exceptional.

In addition to the complexity of the demographic issues associated with intermarriage, methodological considerations raise questions about the value of previous research. We have already noted the coverage biases of Jewish community surveys. In addition, as samples of the Jewish community as a whole, these surveys include all ages and generations, limiting the analysis of small segments such as the intermarried. In general, community surveys tend to be snapshots of the population at a point in time, while intermarriage analysis requires a dynamic, longitudinal design. Hence, the systematic evaluation of the demographic implications of intermarriage requires different study designs, not simply more data. It requires particular focus on the process of marriage and the links between generations. The centrality of the intermarriage issue for the Jewish community has not led to attempts at systematic research.

These limitations of past research cannot be overcome with the Boston data. Moreover, no questions were included about conversions to Judaism or the religious identification of children. Some data were obtained on the "current" religion of adults in the household, which can be compared to those on the religion in which they were "raised." Comparisons between the levels of intermarriage between 1965 and 1975 show some increases, particularly among younger, third-generation American Jews. Nevertheless, the overwhelming impression is the relatively low level of intermarriage characteristic even of the younger cohorts of the 1975 study. Since age at marriage averages 25 years for Jewish men and 22 years for Jewish women, the recent data refer to those born in the 1950s. We know neither the patterns of current marriages in the 1980s nor the cycle of marriage and intermarriage among those born in the 1960s.

QUALITATIVE ISSUES OF INTERMARRIAGE

Even if intermarriages result in some demographic erosion because the net statistical balance of out-marriages, conversions, and the religious-ethnic socialization of children is negative, a series of questions remains about why Jews intermarry and about the Jewishness of the intermarried. It has often been assumed, for example, that intermarriage reflects an assimilationist ideology among Jews and a desire to reject their ethnic identity. The inference has often been made that intermarriage represents a qualitative erosion of Jewish life. These assumptions and inferences will be examined with detailed data on the extent of the acceptance of the intermarried among Jews, ideological and normative factors in intermarriage, and the Jewishness of intermarried households.

The value of the Boston study for the study of intermarriage rests on a series of in-depth attitudinal questions on intermarriage which allow us to extend our understanding of Jewish intermarriage beyond issues of the demographic level and variation. Three broad areas of intermarriage attitudes and norms were the focus of these questions: (1) feelings about intermarriage ("If a child of yours were to consider marrying a non-Jew, how would you most likely feel about it—very negative, somewhat negative, would make no difference at all, or would you feel positive about it?"); (2) actions about intermarriage ("If a child of yours were to consider marrying a non-Jew, which would you most likely do—strongly oppose it, discourage it, be neutral, wouldn't mind, accept it?"); (3) concerns about intermarriage ("There are a number of concerns Jewish parents express about their child marrying a non-Jew—even those who could accept it. Which of these issues, if any, would concern you? Would you be concerned that by marrying a non-Jew (a) your child might be contributing to the decline of the Jewish people; (b) you might not be close to your child and his family; (c) your grandchildren might not be raised as Jews; (d) your child might be rejecting Jewish principles and beliefs; (e) your child might be rejecting you—the things you believe in and what you did as a parent; (f) your child would be less likely to have a happy marriage?").[2]

An examination of these questions shows that the most frequently expressed concern about intermarriage is that grandchildren might not be raised as Jews (59 percent); the respondents' areas of least concern are about their closeness to their children (20 percent) and personal rejection (25 percent). Concerns over the effects of intermarriage on the "decline of the Jewish people" or on the rejection of religious beliefs and principles were expressed by 45 percent of the Jewish community; the effects of intermarriage on the "happiness" of the couple, a common argument expressed by religious and community leaders, is not a concern of about two-thirds of the Jewish community.

Underlying the formulation of these questions were assumptions about the possible fears and issues which concern American Jews. Conceptually, these might be divided into two dimensions—issues of family or personal concerns, and community–Jewish continuity considerations. Are there empirically two dimensions to the concerns about intermarriage? A statistical technique, factor analysis, was used to determine how many factors could be separated out of the six questions about concerns. The results indicated clearly that people do not differentiate systematically between

2. These questions were asked without dealing directly with conversion. Hence, we have no idea how people responded relative to that qualification. It is not clear whether the acceptance of the intermarried is associated with a presumed conversion. The data are analyzed with this limitation in mind.

family and community concerns. As a result, we combined these six measures into one index which would reflect the intensity of concern. The index ranges from those who were not concerned at all about intermarriage (ranked low-intensity) to those who indicated concern about at least five out of six issues (ranked-high intensity). The remainder were included in a middle category.

These data provide for the first time a basis for learning in detail, for a large representative sample, changes and variations in the feelings and acceptance of the intermarried and in the concerns and fears about the consequences of intermarriage.

To the extent that there is increasing acceptance of the intermarried within the Jewish community, the simple association of intermarriage rates and community erosion can be challenged. The incorporation of the non-Jewishly-born within the Jewish community implies that intermarriage per se does not automatically result in the weakening of Jewish cohesion.

ACCEPTING THE INTERMARRIED

Theoretically, we have argued that an increasing level of intermarriage is imbedded into the structural and cultural conditions of American Jewish life. Yet there are powerful norms which have reinforced the particularism and endogamy for Jewish continuity. The balance of these pressures is reflected in the empirical data (table 2.1). More than half (58 percent) of the respondents expressed some negative attitudes toward intermarriage, and very few see intermarriage as positive. While the majority have clear negative feelings, few indicate that they would interfere with their children's intermarriage by opposing it (14 percent) or discouraging it (21 percent). Indeed, fully 65 percent would accept the intermarriage. Even among those who expressed negative feelings toward intermarriage, 41 percent would accept the intermarriage rather than oppose or discourage it. In addition, few have high levels of concern about the effects of intermarriage on their family, their community, or Jews in general. Over one-fourth express no particular concerns at all about the impact of intermarriage; half have some concern. Comparing the data on intermarriage attitudes in 1965 and 1975 reveals a growing acceptance of intermarriage. That is particularly the case among third and later generations and among the younger age cohorts.

More detailed data show remarkably consistent patterns of age variation in intermarriage attitudes. The older population has much more negative attitudes than the younger population: 43 percent of those age 60 or over have very negative feelings about intermarriage, compared to 5 percent of those age 18–29; three-fourths of the older generation have some negative feelings, compared to about one-third of those age 18–29. Nevertheless, the less negative feelings of younger Jews have not resulted in a positive

TABLE 2.1
Indicators of Intermarriage Attitudes by Age

	Total	18–29	30–39	40–59	60 +
Feeling about Intermarriage					
Very negative	23	5	22	32	43
Somewhat negative	35	32	39	41	32
No difference	38	58	35	26	21
Positive	4	5	4	1	5
	100	100	100	100	100
Action about Intermarriage					
Strongly oppose	14	3	17	17	28
Discourage	21	13	24	28	24
Accept	65	84	59	55	48
	100	100	100	100	100
Intensity of Concern					
High	18	7	17	20	37
Medium	54	50	58	63	45
Low	28	43	25	17	18
	100	100	100	100	100

NOTE: In this and subsequent tables, percentages may not add up to 100 percent because of rounding.

endorsement of intermarriage. Rather, there has been a growing indifference to the religious upbringing of spouses—from 21 percent among older Jews to 58 percent among younger Jews.

Similar patterns of variation characterize what people say they will do if their child intermarries. While 28 percent of the older generation would strongly oppose intermarriage, and another 24 percent would discourage it, only 3 percent of the younger generation would strongly oppose it, and 13 percent would discourage it. Fully 84 percent of those 18–29 years of age would accept the intermarriage of their children; less than half of the older people would accept the intermarriage. Similarly, there is an increase in the lack of concern about the implications of intermarriage (from 18 percent to 43 percent) and a decrease in intensive concerns (from 32 percent to 7 percent).

The data do not allow us fully to disentangle the effects of life cycle from those of generation. Will the younger generation have attitudes similar to those of the older generation as they age? Did the older generation have attitudes similar to those of the young thirty to forty years ago? While age

variation often reflects life cycle factors, it is likely that the major implication of the age variation is that intermarriage attitudes have changed over
time and generationally. Comparisons of one attitudinal question in the
1965 and 1975 studies support this interpretation. Moreover, those born
before 1915 are not likely to have the same attitudes in 1975 as they had
when they were growing up or when their children were growing up.
Attitudes are more likely to change as the experiences of aging *and* the
social context change.

The very large increase in the proportion who feel indifferent about the
religious upbringing of their children's spouses suggests that there is no
deep-rooted ideology favoring outmarriage. There is no evidence that intermarriage is the result of an increase in the values of assimilation or
specific norms encouraging marriage between Jews and non-Jews. In
large part, these data suggest that ethnic-religious background per se is
not among the major considerations involved in the values associated with
marital choice. The absence of specific negative or positive intermarriage
norms and the increasing indifferent feelings about the ethnic upbringing
of spouses fit in with the different ways younger and older Jews perceive
the consequences of intermarriage. Older persons tend to view the consequences of intermarriage as threatening to the family and the community. As such, there is a basis for developing negative attitudes toward
intermarriage. On the other hand, young people do not express much
concern about the consequences of intermarriage for family or community
continuity. Therefore, they have no basis for negative attitudes toward
intermarriage. On the other hand, there is no basis for positively valuing
intermarriage as a desirable goal in and of itself. Hence, the attitudes
expressed are indifference to the intermarriage of children. This indifference should not be interpreted as either to the Jewish family or to
Jewish continuity. It seems to be related to an assessment of the implications of intermarriage for Jewish continuity. Among the young, fewer see
the connection between intermarriage and total assimilation. Hence, they
express less alarmism and greater acceptance of those intermarried.[3]

EXPLAINING INTERMARRIAGE PATTERNS

There have been few systematic attempts to explain intermarriage trends
and variations (cf. Farber and Gordon 1982). Most research has tended to

---

3. If intermarriage attitudes by age reflect mainly life cycle factors, the argument could be
made that as young people age and gain more experience with marriage, childbearing, and
childrearing, they will become less sanguine and more negative toward the idea of intermarriage. Perhaps the young can express more acceptance of their child's intermarriage, since it
is far removed from the reality of their experience as parents. For reasons noted above, there
is doubt that age reflects solely life cycle variation. Moreover, while removed from the immediate reality of their children's experience, intermarriage is closer to their own experience
and that of their friends and neighbors. Data presented in the final section of this chapter
suggest that the perception of the consequences of intermarriage among the young comes
closer to reality than the perception of the older generation.

associate intermarriage with "marital assimilation" (Gordon 1964). At a simple level, the argument is that intermarriage is the end point of the assimilation process. Once ethnic or religious minorities marry into the majority or with each other, the structural and cultural distinctiveness of the ethnic community disappears. Whether it is a melting pot, conformity to the majority, or some other form of assimilation, intermarriage is viewed as the response to, and the determinant of, broader patterns of assimilation.

The marital assimilation framework implies four specific themes, parts of which can be tested empirically. Briefly, these themes are: (1) Intermarriage reflects a general desire to assimilate. If there are some who intermarry more than others, we may infer that the desire to assimilate varies accordingly. (2) Educational attainment is one of the major sources of changing desires for assimilation and for intermarriage. Particularism is inconsistent with the liberal values associated with university education. Interaction among persons of different backgrounds, the development of universalistic values, and the greater independence from the constraints of family and community of origin should lead to higher intermarriage rates and more positive intermarriage attitudes among the more educated. (3) A second source of intermarriage norms relates to the decline of particularism as reflected in religious values. Secularization results in the development of attitudes and norms which are universalistic. In turn, these result in greater ethnic assimilation through intergroup marriages. (4) A final direct implication of the marital assimilation framework relates intermarriage directly to measures of group continuity. Rather than focusing on norms, the argument is that the intermarried in their behavior and commitments are less identified with the Jewish community than the non-intermarried.

We shall examine each of these implications with data from the Boston community. In the process, an alternative to the equation of intermarriage with marital assimilation emerges which seems to fit the evidence more consistently and suggests new avenues of research.

Does variation in the level of intermarriage reflect variation in the desire to assimilate? One way to investigate this theme is to examine sex differences in intermarriage norms and attitudes. Previous research has indicated that Jewish men tend to marry out more often than Jewish women, although recent evidence suggests a narrowing of these differences. In part, this tendency has been explained in both the popular and the scholarly literature as the "shiksa" complex. Jewish men are attracted to non-Jewish women as sex symbols and sources of status and assimilation. In contrast, Jewish women tend to be more protected by the family environment. Recent convergences in the sex differential in intermarriage have been postulated to result from changes in the protection of women by their family of orientation, their liberalization, and their greater independence.

An alternative hypothesis places the study of intermarriage in the broader context of marriage choices, not assimilation. Sex differences in intermarriage rates, like sex differences in marriage rates, relate primarily to the number and characteristics of men and women in a population eligible for marriage, i.e., the conditions of the marriage market. Marriage markets (and in turn marriage and intermarriage rates) are affected by a complex set of demographic and sociological factors. These include changes in reproductive patterns of an earlier generation, immigration, sex-selective mortality and migration, overall marriage rates, ages at marriage for men and women, and dissolution rates (divorce, separation, and widowhood). Marriage markets are very difficult to measure for ethnic groups in local communities. Questions about who is included within the boundaries of the group and rates of in- and out-migration by age and sex add to the complexity. One argument has been that increasing rates of intermarriage, in general, and the changing level of intermarriage rates among men and women reflect changing structural conditions associated with marriage markets (cf. Goldscheider 1982).

The argument that sex differences in intermarriage rates reflect the greater desire of men to marry out and the greater protection of women by the family implies that men and women should have different attitudes about intermarriage: men should be more accepting of intermarriage than women, have more positive attitudes, and express less concern over the implications of intermarriage for Jewish continuity. However, if differences in the rates of intermarriage between men and women are the result of structural-market constraints, few systematic sex differences in attitudes should be observed. Fewer women may marry precisely because more men have married out, creating market shortages (see chapter 5). Viewed in another way, the pervasiveness of the acceptance of the intermarried should extend to both sexes, if no different values or norms are involved.

Overall, the evidence points to small sex differences in intermarriage attitudes, with no statistically significant patterns. A detailed examination of sex differences within age groups reinforces this overall pattern (table 2.2). For most age comparisons, there are no systematic differences between men and women in their feelings, actions, or intensities of concern about intermarriage. The largest difference appears in the 30–39 age group, where women were much less likely than men to have negative feelings about intermarriage and somewhat more likely to be accepting of the intermarried.

To further examine the structural argument, we explored the relationship between marital status and intermarriage attitudes. The data show (table 2.3) that the never-married among the young have the least-negative attitudes toward intermarriage and are most likely to be accepting of the intermarried when compared to the ever-married. This pattern characterizes both younger age groups. For the older age cohorts, the patterns are not clear. A higher number of the never-married have nega-

TABLE 2.2
Indicators of Intermarriage Attitudes by Age and Sex

	18–29		30–39		40–59		60+	
	Male	Female	Male	Female	Male	Female	Male	Female
Feeling about								
Intermarriage								
Very negative	4	6	26	16	31	34	40	45
Somewhat negative	34	31	42	35	45	37	33	31
No difference	61	57	27	45	24	28	21	20
Positive	2	7	5	3	1	1	7	4
Action about								
Intermarriage								
Strongly oppose	3	3	20	14	17	17	36	24
Discourage	12	14	24	23	28	29	19	27
Accept	85	83	56	63	56	55	45	50
Intensity								
of Concern								
High	10	4	23	10	21	19	39	35
Medium	45	55	49	69	56	69	49	43
Low	45	41	28	21	23	12	12	22

tive attitudes, strongly oppose intermarriage, and express high levels of concern about the implications of intermarriage. However, the older never-married by age 40–59 represent a small, select group within the Jewish community. These patterns are not characteristic of those 60 and over. Hence, it appears that there is much greater acceptance of intermarriage among those who are most likely to be in a situation of pressure to marry and facing a shortage of potential eligibles within the Jewish community. Perhaps the never-married are no longer part of the marriage market and express negative feelings rooted in their exceptional marital status.

These data on sex and marital status differences in intermarriage norms are the first clues that ideological factors are less important as determinants of intermarriage than structural conditions. This theme can be further examined by looking at the role of secular education and religious particularism in shaping intermarriage attitudes. Is the growing acceptance of intermarriage among the young a consequence of educational attainment (and hence a general liberalization of values) and secularization (and hence a general disaffection from religious values of endogamy)? Is it a more pervasive feature of the American Jewish community, characteristic of a wide range of socioeconomic levels? If educational liberalization is the key, we would expect a positive relationship between educational attainment and the acceptance of the intermarried. Similarly, if secularization is an important factor in intermarriage, we would expect a disproportionate concentration of negative attitudes toward intermarriage among Orthodox and Conservative Jews compared to Reform and non-denominational Jews. We would also expect a sharper increase in the acceptance of intermarriage among the Reform and nondenominational.

Data on the three intermarriage attitudes for various educational levels are presented in table 2.4. For older men and women, the variation by educational levels tends to confirm the hypothesis that those with higher educational levels have a higher proportion who are indifferent to intermarriage. For example, about 40 percent of the women age 60 and over with some college education indicated that it would make no difference to them if their children intermarried, compared to 19 percent of those with a high-school education. In addition, 70 percent of the women who completed college would neither oppose nor discourage their child's intermarriage, compared to 42 percent of those with a high-school education. While 30–40 percent of the older women who completed college indicated no particular concerns for the implications of intermarriage for family or community, only 16 percent of the high-school-educated expressed no concerns.

However, the relationship between education and concern over intermarriage is weaker for middle-aged persons and does not appear at all for young men and women in the sample. More-educated women express more-negative attitudes, while levels of acceptance are somewhat higher among the least educated. Similar reversals occur among men. Hence, the association of more liberal, accepting attitudes among the more educated is an older pattern that has attenuated or even reversed among the younger ages. While it is clear that there is no greater acceptance of intermarriage among more-educated younger people, it is not clear why the least educated have less-negative feelings about intermarriage. Perhaps the least-educated young Jews are threatened by the high educational levels of the Jewish group. As such, they may be viewed (or view themselves) as deviant from the overall educational norms. More important, the concentration of young Jews in high educational levels places the least educated in a smaller marriage market. There are simply very few young Jews who have only a high-school education (see chapter 8). Hence, the choice among the least educated is to face a very limited Jewish marriage market of equal educational level, not to marry, or to marry out. In this context, it is not surprising that the least educated have the most accepting attitudes toward intermarriage. Nevertheless, it is clear from these data that changes in the educational level of men and women have not been the major source of more-accepting attitudes toward intermarriage.

These data are consistent with earlier research which showed that intermarriage levels are not systematically related to educational attainment or occupational achievement (Goldstein and Goldscheider 1968). As such, the concern seems unfounded that with increasing levels of education,

TABLE 2.3
Indicators of Intermarriage Attitudes by Age and Marital Status

	18–29		30–39		40–59			60+		
	Ever Married	Never Married	Ever Married	Never	Currently	Formerly Married	Never	Currently	Formerly Married	Never
Feelings about Intermarriage										
Very negative	5	5	21	25	29	53	42	49	42	25
Somewhat negative	51	21	40	31	43	29	38	21	40	47
No difference[a]	44	74	38	44	28	18	20	30	18	28
	100	100	100	100	100	100	100	100	100	100
Action about Intermarriage										
Strongly oppose	7	1	17	22	16	7	41	37	23	12
Discourage	17	11	26	6	26	69	7	19	30	27
Accept	75	89	57	72	58	24	53	44	47	61
	100	100	100	100	100	100	100	100	100	100
Intensity of Concern										
High	5	8	19	9	18	11	73	29	50	33
Medium	52	49	55	75	63	87	7	55	39	27
Low	43	43	26	16	19	2	20	16	11	40
	100	100	100	100	100	100	100	100	100	100

a Includes a small percentage positive

TABLE 2.4
Indicators of Intermarriage Attitudes by Age, Sex, and Education

	Women			Men		
	Feelings	Action	Concern	Feelings	Action	Concern
	Percent no difference	Percent accept	Percent low intensity	Percent no difference	Percent accept	Percent low intensity
18–29						
High school	87	88	59	*	*	*
Some college	55	91	43	70	90	36
College graduate	54	80	53	48	70	45
Postgraduate	53	78	29	52	83	43
30–39						
High school	50	75	45	43	81	33
Some college	45	52	35	63	77	63
College graduate	12	53	15	37	80	37
Postgraduate	56	56	12	36	42	13
40–59						
High school	31	58	21	16	60	24
Some college	18	46	9	17	42	3
College graduate	19	64	12	29	57	15
Postgraduate	56	58	38	35	57	23
60+						
High school	19	42	16	25	44	14
Some college	40	50	19	20	40	8
College graduate	41	71	31	33	26	17
Postgraduate	38	70	39	46	59	14

rates of intermarriage will systematically rise. The relative increase of intermarriage among the young is not the direct result of a process of liberalization associated with higher education or with the correlation of liberal intermarriage norms with educational level.

A key finding of previous research has been that Jewish particularism is associated with low levels of intermarriage. Intermarriage rates tend to be lowest among those who are more committed religiously and have higher levels of intensive Jewish education. The data on intermarriage norms and attitudes (table 2.5) support this finding. There is a relatively consistent pattern for each age group of higher proportions indifferent, accepting, and unconcerned about intermarriage among Reform and nondenominational Jews.

Orthodox and Conservative Jews of the older generation and Conservative Jews of the younger generation[4] are more likely to express nega-

TABLE 2.5

**Indicators of Intermarriage Attitudes by
Age and Religious Denomination**

	Feeling about Intermarriage	Action about Intermarriage	Intensity of Concern
	Percent no difference	Percent accept	Percent low
18–29			
Conservative	38	49	20
Reform	72	92	43
Other	76	97	57
30–39			
Conservative	21	25	4
Reform	57	70	37
Other	33	80	38
40–59			
Orthodox	5	7	5
Conservative	16	33	10
Reform	28	70	7
Other	52	86	58
60+			
Orthodox	25	30	6
Conservative	10	42	5
Reform	45	61	25
Other	60	82	78

4. This pattern probably characterizes the Orthodox young generation as well, but the number of cases available on Orthodox young persons is too small for reliable analysis.

tive attitudes toward intermarriage, would discourage or strongly oppose, rather than accept, the intermarriage of their children, and express high levels of concern about the implications of intermarriage for family and Jewish continuity. In short, Jewish particularism is associated with norms and attitudes favoring in-group marriage.

INTERMARRIAGE AND JEWISH CONTINUITY

The evidence pointing to the association of Jewish particularism and more-negative intermarriage norms and attitudes raises a key question in the study of the qualitative implications of Jewish intermarriages: How Jewish are the intermarried? A basic assumption of the marital assimilation argument is that those who are intermarried are removed from the ongoing activities of the Jewish community, cease to identify with things Jewish or with Judaism, and are disassociated from Jewish values and culture. The issue, of course, is not the "loss" of the non-Jewish spouse to Jewishness, since there is a basis for postulating only "no gain," not a loss. Rather, the concern is over the discontinuity with Jewishness and Judaism of the Jewish spouse in an intermarriage.

We have already documented the changing perceptions of the consequences of intermarriage among young adults. Here our question focuses on the intermarried per se. Are they more or less identified with the Jewish community, in all its various dimensions, than the nonintermarried? While there has been scattered research on the Jewishness of converts, no previous research based on a total community has focused on the Jewishness of Jews in intermarried compared to nonintermarried households. The analytic question does not focus on individuals who are Jews by birth or by conversion (formal and informal). Rather, we compare those who are in households where all the members are Jewish with those in households where some members (but not all) are non-Jewish. That is a restrictive definition of intermarriage, since a household was defined in terms of current religious identification. Formal and informal conversions are thus included among those classified as homogamously born Jewish. Thus, in focusing on the Jewishness of intermarried and nonintermarried households, any differences will represent the extreme patterns.

The data in table 2.6 allow us to answer three critical questions: (1) Are the intermarried less "Jewish" than the nonintermarried? (2) Do variations by age suggest a pattern of greater or lesser differences between the intermarried and the nonintermarried over time? (3) Do the overall patterns of Jewishness among the young intermarried imply disaffection from Judaism and the Jewish community?

Without exception by age, and for each measure,[5] those in intermarried

---

5. The specific measures are described in chapter 10. Suffice it to note here that the range of items includes associational, religious, ritual, and community-ethnic ties.

TABLE 2.6

Measures of Jewishness for Households where All Members are Jewish and Those with Intermarried Persons by Age

	Total		18–29		30–44		45+	
	All Jewish	Intermarried	All Jewish	Intermarried	All Jewish	Intermarried	All Jewish	Intermarried
Percent mostly Jewish friends	89.3	62.4	77.6	59.3	95.0	65.7	93.2	64.5
Ratio		1.43		1.31		1.45		1.44
Percent mostly Jewish neighbors	51.0	28.3	46.8	39.4	48.6	19.2	53.3	16.1
Ratio		1.80		1.19		2.53		3.31
Regular synagogue attendance	35.9	11.1	19.9	8.8	48.6	16.4	39.1	6.4
Ratio		3.23		2.26		2.96		6.11
Percent denominational	80.9	58.2	67.8	53.6	84.3	73.1	85.7	39.7
Ratio		1.39		1.26		1.15		2.16
Percent synagogue member	43.9	6.9	14.1	1.1	59.7	14.9	53.5	6.5
Ratio		6.36		12.82		4.01		8.23
High Jewish values	66.1	37.2	55.6	38.5	57.7	38.8	76.3	30.0
Ratio		1.78		1.44		1.49		2.54
Personal ritual	28.7	5.8	16.4	0.0	26.0	14.9	36.4	3.2
Ratio		4.94		*		1.74		11.38
Family ritual	74.0	48.7	65.9	65.9	77.5	28.4	76.6	41.9
Ratio		1.52		1.00		2.73		1.83
Community-ethnic	35.2	10.6	27.8	8.8	33.0	14.9	39.4	6.5
Ratio		3.32		3.16		2.21		6.06

households are less associated with Jewishness and Judaism than those in nonintermarried households. There is a range of variation among the indicators. For example, differences between the intermarried and nonintermarried are largest for formal synagogue membership, regular synagogue attendance, personal religious ritual, and measures of communal-ethnic activities (reading Jewish periodicals and visiting Israel). Differences are much less pronounced for the percentage who have mostly Jewish friends and neighbors, who identify with one of the three religious denominations, who express Jewish values, and who are involved in family-related religious ritual.

A second, more significant feature of the data points to the clear reduction of these differences among the young (see figure 2.1). With but minor exceptions (synagogue membership and personal ritual), there is a consistent pattern of convergence in the expression of Jewishness between those in intermarried and nonintermarried households. For those age 18–29, only minor differences appear in associational ties to other Jews (friends and neighbors who are Jewish), and there are no differences in family religious rituals. The large difference in synagogue membership is partly related to life cycle. However, examining those age 30–44, the level of synagogue membership is four times higher among nonintermarried than intermarried households. That represents a reduced ratio compared to those age 45 and over (where it is over eight times higher). However, while only 15 percent of those in intermarried households (age 30–44) are synagogue members, fully 73 percent identify themselves as Orthodox, Conservative, or Reform Jews. Thus, while the level of membership is four times higher among the nonintermarried than the intermarried, the level of denominational identification is only 15 percent higher. Moreover, while the proportion denominationally identified among the nonintermarried was relatively constant for the 30–44 and 45 and over age groups, it increased from 40 to 73 percent for the intermarried households. The increase from 7 percent to 15 percent of the intermarried who are synagogue members (for these age groups) is also high. Nevertheless, the discrepancy between religious denominational identification and synagogue membership suggests an important gap for organized religious institutions.

The convergence patterns show some of the different paths to the growing similarities among the young. For example, the closing gap between the intermarried and nonintermarried in Jewish friendship is the result mainly of changes among the nonintermarried. In contrast, changes in the percentage with mostly Jewish neighbors reflect the sharp increases among the youngest age group of the intermarried. A third path of convergence is illustrated by the percentage with high Jewish values, which is the consequence of declining levels among the nonintermarried and increasing levels among the intermarried.

This overall convergence in the Jewishness of intermarried and nonin-

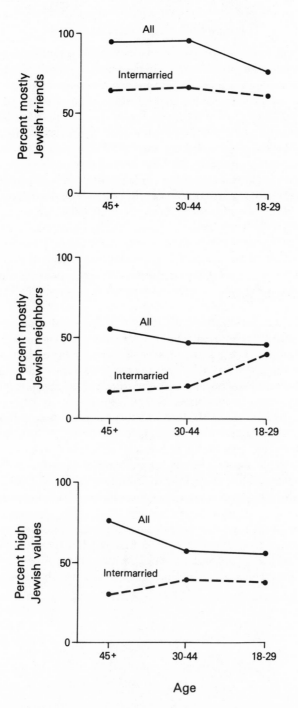

2.1 Convergences in Measures of Jewishness between Jewish and Intermarried Households

termarried households is consistent with convergences shown in previous literature in socioeconomic, family, and demographic characteristics of intermarried and nonintermarried persons (Goldscheider 1982). Together, these data fit in with the more general notion that intermarriage is no longer a marginal or deviant phenomenon in American Jewish life. Convergence implies further the absence of an ideological base for intermarriage and the lack of major socioeconomic and demographic selectivity for those who out-marry compared to those who in-marry.

The final point these data address relates to an overall profile of the Jewishness of the intermarried. The data indicate strong Jewish communal and identificational ties for the intermarried. It is difficult to argue that young intermarried households are disassociated from Jewish communal life and the networks of the Jewish community when 60 percent say that most of their friends are Jewish, 40 percent say that most of their neighbors are Jewish, 54 percent define themselves into established religious denominational categories, and almost two-thirds observe religious family rituals.

Taken together, these data point strongly to the growing acceptance of intermarriage and the intermarried into Jewish life. Perhaps as a cause, or maybe as a result, there is an increasing similarity between the intermarried and the nonintermarried in measures of Jewishness. There is a relationship between intermarriage and Jewish discontinuity, but it is weak and growing weaker. These data show that intermarriage is not necessarily the final step toward total assimilation. Powerful forces within the Jewish community, informal as well as formal, have resulted in the continued (perhaps reinforced) Jewishness of the intermarried. Concerns over the demographic implications of Jewish intermarriage for survival of the group seem exaggerated. The strong Jewish continuity of those who are supposedly on the fringes of total assimilation forces us to revise accepted theories and explanations of intermarriage. Much more research needs to be done to focus on the relationships among attitudes, norms, and intermarriage patterns for younger Jews. Research efforts to monitor systematically changing levels and norms over the life cycle are needed, since marriage and intermarriage issues are the heart of Jewish American continuity.

THREE

Residential Concentration and Jewish Cohesion

Where Jews reside, and the Jewishness of those neighborhoods within the broader community, are major aspects of Jewish cohesion. In particular, the greater the density of Jewish settlement, the more likely it is that Jews will interact with other Jews in schools, as neighbors, and as friends. Moreover, residential concentration maintains the visibility of the Jewish community for Jews as well as for the society as a whole and, thus, may be viewed as a critical factor in fostering and strengthening ethnic bonds. The ethnic factor is likely to be most pronounced when ethnics are clustered residentially. In turn, residential clustering represents a core mechanism for the continuity of the community (see Yancey et al. 1976; Lieberson 1963; Lieberson 1980; Kobrin and Goldscheider 1978).

It follows that the reduction of ethnic residential clustering would be associated with group assimilation. Indeed, it has often been assumed that the changing residential location of ethnic groups has been toward residential integration and that the new areas are characterized by low levels of ethnicity.

Research on the residential segregation and dispersal of white ethnics in America has shown the process to be more complex. First, initial segregation levels of immigrant groups in late-nineteenth- and early-twentieth-century America were high. Indeed, they were higher than for blacks. Over a relatively short period of time, the levels of segregation declined sharply for white immigrants, and much greater dispersal occurred within metropolitan areas and in new areas of settlement (Lieberson 1963; Lieberson 1980). Despite these changes, a second feature of contemporary American society is the continuous concentration of white ethnics in neighborhoods of metropolitan communities and in regions of the country (Kantrowitz 1973; Kobrin and Goldscheider 1978). It is unclear whether residential segregation differences between blacks and white ethnics are mainly a matter of degree or represent fundamentally different structural and cultural processes (cf. Kantrowitz 1973; Glazer 1971; Lieberson 1980). Nevertheless, the key finding is indisputable: white ethnics are not randomly distributed among regions or among neighborhoods within the metropolitan area.

More specifically, recent research on contemporary white ethnics has demonstrated that changes in residential concentration have been from high to medium levels, rather than to low levels, of concentration. While the young, more educated, and middle-class are less likely to reside in areas of high ethnic concentration, ethnic residential concentration is not a pattern solely of older immigrants, the less educated, or lower classes. While changing over time, ethnic residential clustering has continued to be one of the major structural sources of ethnic continuity (see especially Kobrin and Goldscheider 1978, chapter 4). Nevertheless, other contexts for interaction seem to be replacing the neighborhood in late-twentieth-century America. Hence, we would expect residential concentration to be less central for ethnic cohesion.

JEWISH RESIDENTIAL CONCENTRATION

Analysis of residential concentration of Jews has been conceptualized in much the same way. The earlier theoretical and empirical work on Jewish immigrants in America viewed residential concentration as a carry-over of old-world patterns of ghetto segregation. Over time, second- and third-generation American Jews were expected to move away from areas of first settlement toward greater assimilation and integration in American society (see in particular the classic work of Wirth 1928). Residential integration was associated with lower levels of Jewishness. In turn, residential concentration was identified with the foreign-born, the lower-class, and the unacculturated. Living in an area of low Jewish density, in contrast, was assumed to be characteristic of the third and fourth generations—young, middle-class suburbanites. As such, Jewish residential concentration was viewed as a reflection of initial immigrant adjustment and related to cultural peculiarities of the first generation.

Empirical research on the residential segregation of Jews is relatively weak. Since few studies have included both Jews and non-Jews, there is little basis for knowing the relative residential concentration of Jews compared to that of white ethnics. Census data have been the major basis for an analysis of residential concentration but are not very useful for studying contemporary Jews. Research on the initial residential segregation of Jewish immigrants has been carried out, and the changing neighborhood patterns of their children have been studied. However, there is no firm empirical base for assessing the residential patterns of younger Jews of the third and fourth generations. We know by observation and some local studies that the residential clustering of Jews in the 1970s and 1980s is different from that of earlier periods, but we do not yet know the extent of residential transformation or the costs to Jewish continuity. Nor have we studied whether there is any connection between residential concentration and Jewish values.

Community studies have also been severely limited in clarifying residential concentration issues. For the most part, samples have been obtained which overrepresent Jews in areas of greater Jewish concentration. Hence, the resulting distribution of Jews often undercovers those in areas of low Jewish density and of greater residential integration.

Two general models of residential change emerge from previous research on the Jews. The first model posits that Jews moved away from areas of first settlement to other areas of Jewish concentration. These new "golden ghettos" were more in harmony with patterns of socioeconomic mobility and neighborhood changes. Along with the transformation of their jobs and education came residential changes, which nevertheless retained a disproportionate number of Jews. A second model argues that the move out of areas of first settlement was toward greater residential integration and assimilation. Particularly in suburban areas and among third-generation Jews, the density of Jewish settlement decreases. Residential integration influences, and is influenced by, broader patterns of Jewish assimilation.

These models have rarely been systematically tested. Some research in the 1960s demonstrated how new areas of both residential concentration and residential integration developed in the same metropolitan area. In turn, these residential options were associated with different patterns of Jewishness (Goldstein and Goldscheider 1968; Kramer and Leventman 1961).

Two general issues of residential concentration will be explored with the Boston data: (1) What are the residential concentration patterns of young, third-generation Jews? Are areas of greater Jewish density characterized by the foreign-born, poor, and less educated? (2) Are levels of Jewish cohesion related to the residential concentration of Jews?

Two potential indicators can be used to measure residential concentration: (1) an objective measure estimating residential concentration of Jews in census tracts; and (2) a subjective measure of Jewish neighborhood density.

Since census data do not have any information which allows us to identify Jews, we constructed a crude measure of census tract concentration by allocating each of the sample households to a census tract in the Boston metropolitan area. The weighted distribution of Jews in the sample should represent a relatively unbiased areal distribution, since the sample design included both Jewish and non-Jewish households. There were 229 census tracts covered by the sample in 1975. Those which had 20 or more sample cases were designated as areas of high Jewish density; those with fewer than 4 sample cases were designated areas of low Jewish density. The middle cases were subdivided arbitrarily, based on the distribution: 11–19 sample cases were categorized as medium-high; 5–10 sample cases were classified as medium-low.

There are no obvious ways to evaluate this census tract measure. External checks are not available. Two internal checks suggest that the measure has some validity. An examination of the distribution of cases in the weighted and nonweighted samples indicates that the weighted sample is considerably less concentrated in census tracts which were classified as high Jewish density.[1] That is as expected, if the weighted sample picked up less-affiliated Jews in areas of lower Jewish densities.

Another internal validity check relates to a subjective question about the perception of Jewish neighborhood concentration. A question was included in the survey: "How many of the people who live in this neighborhood are Jewish—all, most, about half, a few, or almost none?" This question used a neighborhood reference point, which is likely to be a smaller unit than the census tract, although census tracts are designed to approximate relative homogeneous areas or neighborhoods of an average of 3,000 to 6,000 persons (cf. Shryock and Siegel 1973, p. 132). Moreover, perceptions are often distorted in terms of the ethnic composition of neighborhoods (Farley, Bianchi, and Colasanto, 1979). Nevertheless, the constructed measure of census tract residential concentration is very highly correlated with the subjective measure of Jewish neighborhood density ($r = .69$), and it is relatively stable by age. (Among the youngest age cohort, the correlation is 0.77.) Thus, despite the different units of reference and differences between objective and subjective realities, the high correlation between the measures provides greater confidence in the validity of the census tract measure. It seems unlikely that both measures are biased in ways that distort their validity as indicators of residential concentration.

A more detailed examination of the relationship between residential concentration and the perception of Jewish density reinforces the overall high correlation (table 3.1). Of all those who lived in census areas defined as high Jewish concentration, fully 94 percent perceived their neighborhoods as at least half Jewish, and almost 60 percent perceived their neighborhoods as all or mostly Jewish. At the opposite end of the continuum, almost 85 percent in the census areas designated as low Jewish residential concentration perceived their neighborhoods as having few or almost no Jews. The proportion living in areas of low Jewish residential concentration who perceived their neighborhoods as having almost no Jews was over twice as high as the proportion of those in areas defined as medium-low levels of Jewish concentration and over ten times higher than the proportion of those in areas defined as medium-high or high levels of Jewish concentration.

Overall, the data indicate that most Jews (65 percent) live in census tracts classified as medium Jewish concentration, with twice as many in areas of low Jewish concentration as in areas of high Jewish concentration. Twenty percent of the sample perceive that all or most of their neighbors are Jewish; a similar number perceive their neighborhood as having almost no Jews. Again, most are in the middle—28 percent perceive that half of their neighborhood is Jewish, and one-third say few are Jewish.

1. See fn. 1, to the preface to this book. See also Fowler 1977.

TABLE 3.1

Census Tract Jewish Density by Perception of Neighborhood Jewish Density

Census Tract Jewish Density	Perception of Neighborhood Jewish Density				
Classification	All or Most	Half	Few	Almost None	TOTAL
High	57	37	3	4	100
Medium-high	35	45	18	3	100
Medium-low	10	22	49	19	100
Low	3	13	39	45	100
TOTAL	20	28	33	19	100
High	30	14	1	2	11
Medium-high	49	46	16	5	31
Medium-low	18	28	53	34	34
Low	4	12	31	59	25
TOTAL	100	100	100	100	100

The high correlation and general empirical equivalence of the census tract and perception measures of residential concentration allow us to focus on either measure. In general, the detailed patterns and correlates were identical. Our focus will be on the census tract measure of Jewish density; we shall include findings from the neighborhood perception measure when they provide additional insight for particular issues. Our first objective is to examine whether living in areas of relatively high Jewish density is associated with demographic and socioeconomic variations among Jews. Secondly, we shall explore the implications of residential concentration for Jewish continuity.

WHO LIVES IN AREAS OF HIGH JEWISH DENSITY?

We begin our analysis of the residential concentration of Jews with an ecological question, focusing on the census tract as the unit of analysis: What are the major characteristics of areas where Jews are more and less densely settled? Are high-density Jewish areas characterized by older, foreign-born populations of lower socioeconomic status?

The evidence in table 3.2 clarifies these issues. Areas of high Jewish density are disproportionately young. Almost half of the Jews in high-density census tracts are 18–29 years of age, compared to about 35 percent in other tracts. There is also a slightly higher proportion of persons who are 60 years of age and older in areas of high Jewish density, but differences among areas in the proportion of older Jews are small. Clearly, census tracts defined as high Jewish concentration do not consist only of

TABLE 3.2
Age, Migrant Status, Family Structure, Education, and
Income Characteristics of Jews
in Census Tracts Classified by Jewish Density

| | Census Tract Jewish Density | | | |
	High	Medium-high	Medium-low	Low
Age				
18–29	49	39	38	34
30–39	11	15	15	20
40–59	17	28	30	25
60+	22	18	18	20
Total %	100	100	100	100
Percent Foreign-Born				
All ages	16	11	11	12
18–29	13	0	3	5
30–39	23	1	6	2
40–59	13	19	9	5
60+	20	40	34	41
Percent of Nonnuclear *Living with Relatives*				
All ages	19	11	18	8
18–29	13	4	21	6
60+	47	17	18	8
Percent Males with Less *Than High-School Education*				
All ages	27	24	20	25
18–29	11	1	8	11
30–39	6	4	1	15
40–59	33	35	23	24
60+	61	67	63	63
Percent Family Income *Less Than $10,000*				
All ages	51	30	31	31
18–29	72	44	54	37
30–39	54	3	8	18
40–59	5	9	7	8
60+	19	56	43	66

older people. These data do not imply that most young people live in areas of high Jewish density. To the contrary, most young people (and older people as well) live in a wide range of areas of different levels of Jewish concentration. Only 14 percent of those age 18–29 live in areas of high Jewish density; 12 percent of those 60 years of age and older live in areas of high Jewish concentration. Nevertheless, the data indicate clearly that areas of high Jewish concentration have a disproportionate number of young people.

These data do not suggest any clear patterns of change in residential density over time. The age data are much more reflective of life cycle variations and housing-employment markets at a particular time period than indicative of generational change. Therefore, the age data cannot be viewed as indicators of real cohort change, where the residential patterns of young persons will continue into the future. Thus, the fact that younger people are more likely than older people to live in areas of lower Jewish density and perceive their neighborhoods as having fewer Jews (compare table 3.3) should not be interpreted as the pattern which foreshadows the future. These younger people will move to new residential areas as they complete their educations, marry, take on new jobs, and have more resources to acquire housing. Their residential choices, both for remaining in the Boston metropolitan area and for the Jewish character of their future residences, are not known. Perhaps they are unknown to them as well, as broader societal forces will shape and reshape their choices.

How are patterns of residential concentration related to the immigrant composition of areas? Does residential clustering characterize mainly the foreign-born? The data show that areas of greater Jewish residential concentration also have a larger proportion of foreign-born: about one out of six Jews in high-Jewish-density census tracts was not born in the United States, compared to about one out of nine in tracts of lower Jewish density. This pattern is characteristic of those age 18–39, but not of those age 40 and over. Census tracts of lower Jewish density have a higher proportion of foreign-born Jews 60 years of age and older than the high-density Jewish tracts.

It should be stressed that most of the adult Jews living in areas of high Jewish density were born in the United States, and there is no simple relationship between extent of Jewish density and age or foreign-born status. There is, therefore, no support in these data for the argument that the higher the Jewish density, the higher the proportion of older and foreign-born Jews.

What other factors may be associated with variation in residential concentration among Jews? Are features of the housing available, its costs, and the socioeconomic character of the neighborhood related to residential clustering? Or does residential clustering simply reflect the desire of Jews to live in their ethnic neighborhood? An analysis of the characteristics of residential areas where Jews live—household composition, education, and income—shows clearly that no simple pattern associated with relative assimilation can account for the distribution of Jews in the metropolis.

We start with an examination of the relationship between education and residential concentration. The assimilation argument leads us to expect that as levels of education increase, the extent of Jewish residential concentration should decrease. Put in another way, areas of high Jewish density should be characterized by relatively higher proportions of lower-educated Jews. The evidence does not support that argument.

There is no relationship between the Jewish density of areas and the level of education attained by the Jewish population. Areas of greater Jewish concentration are not disproportionately areas of lower education, even within age groups. Viewing these educational patterns in terms of the residential characteristics of persons with different levels of education (rather than the educational characteristics of areas of high and low Jewish densities) leads to similar conclusions. For example, about 7 percent of those age 40–59 with a high-school education live in areas of high Jewish density, similar to the proportions of those with a graduate school education. About 20 percent of this age group who are high-school or college graduates live in areas of low Jewish concentration. Among older persons, the proportions of high-school and college graduates who live in areas of low Jewish concentration are identical, while a slightly higher proportion of college than high-school graduates lives in areas of high Jewish concentration. Similar conclusions emerge from the data on perceptions of Jewish neighborhood density (table 3.3).

In contrast, areas of high Jewish density seem to have a disproportionate number of Jews in the lowest income category. About half the Jews in areas of high Jewish density have low incomes, compared to 30 percent of those in areas of lower Jewish density. However, that is characteristic only of the younger population (i.e., below age 40). The opposite relationship prevails among Jews age 60 and over: family income is higher among those in areas of higher compared to lower Jewish densities. Both age groups reflect the complex life cycle dynamics relating residence to socio-economic and family status. For the younger ages, particularly those below age 30, the relationship between income and residential concentration is short-term. Many young adults in areas of high Jewish density have high levels of education relative to their incomes and are probably students or just beginning their careers. Among older Jews, the reverse relationship between income and Jewish density results primarily from the limitations of our family income measure. Older Jews in areas of higher Jewish density are more likely to be living with their children than are those in areas of lower Jewish density. This household pattern inflates a measure of overall family, rather than individual, income when households are extended.

Hence, for both age groups, these patterns seem to reflect complex

TABLE 3.3
Perception of Jewish Neighborhood Density by Selected Characteristics

	Most	Half	Few	Almost None	Total Percent
TOTAL	20.2	27.9	32.7	19.2	100.0
Age					
18–29	12.4	32.9	26.3	28.4	100.0
30–39	20.9	21.3	41.5	16.3	100.0
40–59	29.9	24.8	35.0	10.3	100.0
60+	17.4	28.6	33.4	20.6	100.0
Education					
High school	19.5	31.1	28.6	20.8	100.0
Some college	18.6	25.2	37.5	18.6	100.0
College graduate	28.7	21.9	31.7	17.7	100.0
Postgraduate	12.6	33.4	34.1	19.9	100.0
Income					
<$10,000	8.4	32.7	26.6	32.2	100.0
10–20,000	13.0	23.0	39.4	24.7	100.0
20–35,000	25.0	30.4	34.3	10.4	100.0
35,000+	30.3	26.4	37.1	6.2	100.0
Denomination					
Orthodox	20.8	25.4	30.9	23.0	100.0
Conservative	17.5	30.2	37.0	15.3	100.0
Reform	23.0	24.0	33.3	19.7	100.0
Other	21.5	29.3	26.3	22.9	100.0
Synagogue					
Member	28.7	27.2	30.5	13.6	100.0
Nonmember	14.3	28.2	34.3	23.1	100.0

career, household, and income configurations and not simple assimilation tendencies. This conclusion is strongly reinforced when the central age group is examined. For those in the more stable career and household segments of the life cycle (age 40–59), no relationship appears between income and residential concentration.

THE JEWISHNESS OF JEWISH AREAS

How Jewish are the people who live in areas of high and low Jewish density? Are those in areas of low Jewish population density disassociated from Judaism and Jewishness? Do those in areas of high Jewish density see the Jewishness of their neighborhood as an expression of their Jewish values? Is there a desire on the part of Jews in areas of low Jewish density to be isolated from other Jews? These are the key questions of our ensuing analysis. Again, the units of analysis are the census tracts classified by Jewish density (table 3.4).

The data show that few Jews living anywhere attend synagogue services frequently and that synagogue attendance is only weakly related to the density of Jewish areas. The percentage who often attend religious services is higher in areas of medium-high than in areas of high Jewish con-

TABLE 3.4
**Selected Measures of Jewishness by Census Tracts
Classified by Jewish Density**

Selected Measures of Jewishness	Census Tract Jewish Density			
	High	Medium-high	Medium-low	Low
Synagogue Attendance				
% attending often	9	16	9	16
% rarely or never	33	39	41	43
Denominational Identification				
Orthodox	4	7	2	6
Conservative	37	34	37	33
Reform	34	34	37	39
Other	26	26	25	22
	100	100	100	100
Friends				
All/most Jewish	57	65	49	31
Most non-Jewish	4	9	18	23
Percent Who Value Living in Jewish Neighborhood	63	49	38	26
Desire for Jewish Neighbors				
More	15	15	39	44
Less	9	4	2	1
Indices				
% High Jewish Values	46	35	33	36
% High Personal Ritual	25	23	25	21
% High Family Ritual	76	70	73	69
% High Ethnic-Community	29	30	30	31

centration and higher in areas of low Jewish density than in areas of high Jewish density. The proportion who rarely or never attend the synagogue is higher in areas of lower Jewish density than in areas of higher Jewish density. Formal synagogue membership, on the other hand, follows the predicted pattern: areas of higher Jewish density have a larger proportion who are members of synagogues than areas of lower Jewish density, suggesting that membership is associated with some, but not much, attendance at religious services.

Although formal ties are weaker in areas of low Jewish concentration, there are no differences among the areas of different Jewish densities in the degree or type of religious denominational affiliation. The Orthodox are not particularly concentrated in areas of high Jewish density, and no significant differences characterize the nondenominational. Similar patterns characterize the data on Jewish neighborhood perception. The proportion of the nondenominational who perceive their neighborhoods as mostly Jewish is about the same as for the Orthodox, and no differences among the three religious denominations emerge. The same is true when age is controlled.

Jews in areas of low Jewish density are less likely than Jews in areas of high Jewish density to have all or most of their friends Jewish and more likely to have mostly non-Jewish friends. In part, this tendency reflects the availability of Jews in their neighborhoods. In part it reflects how Jews in areas of low Jewish density see living in Jewish neighborhhoods as an expression of being Jewish. Significantly fewer Jews living in areas of low Jewish density define the Jewishness of their neighborhood as part of their being Jewish.

The lower value placed on living in a Jewish neighborhood and the lower percentage of friends who are Jewish among those living in areas of low Jewish density do not appear to reflect a desire to be isolated from other Jews. Fully 44 percent of those in areas of low Jewish density would like to have more Jewish neighbors, and almost none want fewer Jewish neighbors. Those in areas of high or medium-high Jewish density are much more satisfied with the number of Jewish neighbors they have. Hence, these data point unmistakably to the conclusion that Jews in areas of higher Jewish density are relatively satisfied with the Jewish composition of their areas; those who live in areas of lower Jewish concentration are less satisfied with the Jewish composition of their areas and want more Jewish neighbors. Overall, Jews seem to value living in Jewish neighborhoods. Some are able to achieve their desires. Others, for reasons that may be relatively unrelated to their Jewishness per se, live in areas of lower Jewish density than they desire.

If Jews in areas of low Jewish concentration want more Jews in their neighborhoods, why do they live in their current "un-Jewish" neighborhoods? There is no indication from these data that Jews in Jewish neighborhoods are particularly seeking non-Jewish neighbors or that Jews in areas of low Jewish concentration consider their neighborhood selection a reflection of a desire to assimilate. It is not preference but issues of cost and availability, i.e., structural constraints rather than normative preferences.

Perhaps the choice of neighborhood is influenced more by housing availability, costs, schooling, and transportation, lifestyle, and social class than by Jewishness. In turn, those general factors suggest a set of priorities in decision making which places particular Jewish values at lower levels. Nevertheless, it is likely that the ethnic composition of a neighborhood plays a minor role in housing choices for most Jews. It is also clear from the evidence that a desire to assimilate residentially is not characteristic of most of those who live in areas of low Jewish density. Even among those who perceive that their neighborhoods have almost no Jews, two-thirds would like to have more Jews living there. It is clearly inconsistent with the evidence to treat those who perceive that they are living in a neighborhood of almost no Jews as "lost" to Judaism and the Jewish community.

What specific aspects of Jewishness characterize those who live in neighborhoods of different levels of Jewish density? Clearly not synagogue attendance or specific religious denominational affiliation. In general, there are few differences in the Jewishness of Jews living in areas of different Jewish densities. Jews in areas of lower Jewish density seem to express fewer Jewish values, but differences are small. Few observe personal religious rituals in areas of low Jewish density, but neither do many Jews in areas of high Jewish density. Most of their associations with Jewishness tend to be family rituals and ethnic-community activities. It should be emphasized that over three-fourths of those in areas which do not have a high concentration of Jews report that more than half of their friends are Jewish.

Taken together, these data do not portray those who are in areas of low Jewish density as alienated from other Jews, preferring assimilation, or on the edge of ethnic survival. The community defined in geographic terms does not appear to be significantly associated with Jewish continuity. We need to focus elsewhere, beyond neighborhoods, to identify the social ties and networks which link Jews to each other and to their community.

FOUR

Migration and Integration

The Jewish population is unevenly distributed over regions and areas of the United States. Jews have been more concentrated than non-Jews in metropolitan areas and have disproportionately resided in particular regions and states. Despite patterns of dispersal and deconcentration in the last two decades, the distribution of the Jewish population remains distinctive (see Goldscheider 1982; Goldstein 1982).

The major mechanism affecting the distribution pattern of Jews is migration. Our interest focuses on two key aspects of the migration patterns of Jews. First, are Jewish migration patterns different from non-Jewish patterns? How do the migration patterns of Jews relate to their social, demographic, and economic characteristics? Second, does the migration of Jews affect their attachments to family and the Jewish community? Does migration affect their religious behavior and Jewish values? Combined, these questions address at the broadest level the issue of whether the migration patterns of Jews are linked to the cohesiveness of the Jewish community and the assimilation of American Jews.

National migration data for the Jewish population are not available from any official source. Data from the National Jewish Population Survey found that migration levels are not low: only 62 percent of the Jewish population age 20 and over in 1970 were still living in the same city in which they resided in 1965. The rates of mobility are even higher among young Jews: of those 25–39, over half changed their city of residence at least once in the five years 1965–1970, and over 20 percent lived in a different state. Even among the elderly age 65 and over, 30 percent had moved within a five-year period (Goldstein 1979).

Comparisons between the National Jewish Population Study and the total U.S. population suggest that patterns of lifetime migration and migration between 1965 and 1970 were very similar for Jews and non-Jews. However, because of definitional and duration issues, detailed comparisons could not be made between Jews and non-Jews controlling for socioeconomic and regional differences. Hence, it is not clear whether there are differences in migration patterns between Jews and non-Jews. In general, the data suggest that the Jewish population "adheres very closely to the patterns characterizing the American population as a whole" in terms of lifetime and five-year migration (Goldstein 1982).

Looking at national migration patterns can reveal differential rates of movement and some broad patterns of regional redistribution. Analysis at the community level, however, allows a more detailed focus on the differential streams of movement and the impact of these on communal structure. For example, a study of Jewish and non-Jewish out-migration from one community of declining population showed very high absolute rates of Jewish out-migration, higher rates relative to those of other religious and ethnic subgroups. Over 70 percent of the Jewish children of couples interviewed in Rhode Island (1967–69) migrated out of the state, compared to less than half of the Protestant children and about one-third of the children of Catholics. Among Jewish parents with some college education, the proportion of children migrating out of the state was even higher. Even controlling for education level, out-migration was higher among Jews (Kobrin and Goldscheider 1978).

Each community is unique in its particular combination of in- and out-migration. Over time, a community will vary in terms of its attractiveness to migrants and to the local population. As local neighborhoods change, expand, deteriorate, and are renewed, so the population and its composition change. That is no less true for the Jewish population and its residential and migration patterns. Rates based on national data will neutralize the important variation among communities. Although migration rates of particular communities are limited as a basis for generalizing about the national pattern, only a community focus allows for a detailed analysis of the impact of migration on Jewish cohesion.

In the process of redistribution, many Jewish communities have lost populations, and others have gained. Cities, neighborhoods, and regions have been transformed over the last several decades. Unlike Rhode Island, for example, the Boston metropolitan area has been an area of attraction to young persons, particularly because of the large number of colleges and universities and the wide range of new economic opportunities associated with high-technology industries. From a Jewish point of view, Boston is a long-established community, with a rich array of institutions and services. Thus, it allows for an analysis of the relative selectivity of Jews to a community with expanding economic opportunities and the effects of migration on the Jewishness of the in-movers.

The availability of comparable migration information on the non-Jewish population and detailed data linking migration to measures of Jewishness are unique features of the Boston data. Most previous research has not been able to make systematic comparisons between Jews and non-Jews and has not addressed the connections between migration and Jewish continuity except by inference.

Our objective, therefore, is not to describe the migration patterns of Jews in Boston or to focus on the changing neighborhood configurations. Rather, it is to focus on the determinants of Jewish migration to this community, to identify whether and why it is different from non-Jewish migration, and to clarify the implications and consequences of migration for Jewish continuity.

Three measures of migration provide the basis for the ensuing analysis: (1) place of birth, subdivided into those born in the city areas of Boston, in the suburban areas of Boston, or outside the Boston Standard Metropolitan Statistical Area (SMSA), and the foreign-born; (2) duration of residence in the particular city, town, or neighborhood of Boston; and (3) place of residence (city or town) ten years earlier (i.e., in 1965), subdivided into those who were in the same city or town in 1975 as in 1965 (nonmovers) and those who moved categorized by place of residence in 1965 (Boston city, Boston suburbs, and outside the SMSA).

JEWISH MIGRATION: THE OVERALL PATTERN

Data on place of birth, duration of residence, and place of residence ten years earlier provide the basis for constructing a mobility profile of the Jewish community, contrasting it with the non-Jewish community, and isolating the particular features of Jewish migration which require explanation.

Is migration to Boston a characteristic of a small segment of the community, marginal to the stability of the majority of the Jewish population? The evidence shows that only about half of the adult Jews living in Boston in 1975 were born in the Boston Standard Metropolitan Statistical Area (SMSA), equally divided between city and suburban areas (table 4.1). About 12 percent were foreign-born, and 40 percent were in-migrants to Boston from outside the metropolis. Of the U.S.-born Jewish population, 55 percent were born in the Boston SMSA. Forty-five percent migrated from outside.

Consistent with this picture of high turnover are the duration-of-residence data. Only about one out of five residents lived in his or her current community for over twenty years; two out of five residents lived in their current communities for ten or more years. In contrast, 39 percent lived in their communities for less than three years. Thus, over the last decade, 60 percent of the adult Jewish population changed their place of residence.

Residential changes among Jews, as is the case generally, vary in relationship to life cycle stages. One of the most established generalizations in demographic research is the strong relationship between age and migration: young adults move more than older persons, as marriage, jobs, and careers demand movement (Goldscheider 1971). In general, migration rates decline as family and community roots are established in the middle and later stages of the life cycle. Selected movement of older persons occurs as their labor force participation declines and their children move to other communities. For Jews, as for some other immigrant groups, age

TABLE 4.1

Measures of Migration Status by Age and Religion

	Jews					Non-Jews				
	All ages	18–29	30–44	45–59	60+	All ages	18–29	30–44	45–59	60+
Place of Birth										
Boston city	25.6	16.5	27.7	29.1	37.2	24.0	19.3	22.5	26.2	29.5
Boston suburb	23.0	15.2	29.3	39.4	15.1	34.1	38.5	38.0	38.6	20.0
Outside SMSA	39.9	64.5	38.7	20.1	11.8	28.7	35.2	26.8	23.3	27.6
Foreign-born	11.5	3.8	4.3	11.4	35.9	13.2	7.0	12.7	11.9	22.9
	100.0	100.0	100.0	100.0	100.0	100.0	100.0	100.0	100.0	100.0
Duration of Residence										
Less than 3 yrs.	39.0	77.0	29.8	7.8	9.4	25.3	52.2	22.1	11.7	5.5
4–9 years	19.8	12.0	38.5	14.7	19.9	17.5	16.8	29.6	13.9	8.9
10–19 years	20.2	5.8	21.7	45.2	18.5	19.0	9.2	27.3	28.3	14.4
20 + years	21.0	5.2	10.0	32.3	52.3	38.2	21.8	20.9	46.2	71.2
	100.0	100.0	100.0	100.0	100.0	100.0	100.0	100.0	100.0	100.0
Place of Residence 10 Years Earlier										
Movers	59.5	88.7	68.1	22.7	29.2	42.4	68.8	51.3	25.0	14.1
Boston city	8.4	4.3	5.2	9.2	19.6	9.0	8.3	13.1	6.7	7.7
Boston suburb	18.9	19.6	37.9	6.6	9.3	11.0	15.6	14.3	8.9	3.4
Outside SMSA	31.2	64.8	25.0	6.9	0.3	22.4	44.9	23.9	9.4	3.0
Nonmovers	41.5	11.3	31.9	77.3	70.8	57.6	31.2	48.6	75.0	86.0
	100.0	100.0	100.0	100.0	100.0	100.0	100.0	100.0	100.0	100.0

variation in residential mobility also reflects the immigrant status of members of the older generation.

Indeed, there is a consistent and strong relationship between our measures of migration and age: the proportion foreign-born increases with age, from 4 percent among those 18–29 to 36 percent among those age 60 and over; at the same time, the proportion born outside the Boston SMSA decreases, from 65 percent among the young to 12 percent among the older population. Not only are young people much more likely to be born outside Boston, but an increasing number of those born in the metropolitan area were born in suburban neighborhoods. Reflecting changing levels of suburbanization, the ratio of those born in the city to those born in the suburban areas of Boston decreases, from 2.5 among those age 60 and over to 1.1 among the youngest age group.

The effects of life cycle on migration are clearly evident in the duration data. Over three-fourths of the young population have resided in their communities of current residence less than three years, and almost 90 percent have moved at least once in the last decade. The proportion living in their community of current residence increases systematically with age: over half of those age 60 and over have lived in the same neighborhood for over twenty years. While 11 percent of the young have not changed their place of residence over the last decade, 32 percent of the middle-aged cohort were nonmovers, and about 75 percent of those 45 years of age and over did not change residences between 1965 and 1975. Of those who moved in the last decade, most of the young moved from outside the SMSA; most of the older Jews moved from Boston city areas. Thus, the importance of these age differences goes beyond the issue of the greater migration of the young. Among those who move, the young are much more likely to be coming from a different community, without family or communal roots, while older persons who have moved are likely to be moving among neighborhoods within the same community.

A brief migration profile of the youngest generation, therefore, differs sharply from that of the oldest generation. Almost all of the Jews 18–29 years of age were born in the United States, and 65 percent were not born in the Boston metropolitan area. Less than one-fourth have lived in their neighborhoods for more than three years, and fully 89 percent changed neighborhoods during the last decade. In contrast, over one-third of those age 60 and over were born outside the United States; almost 60 percent of the native-born were born in the city areas of Boston. Over half of the older population have lived in their neighborhoods for more than twenty years, and 71 percent have been residentially stable for the last decade.

The overall Jewish migration patterns and the variations by age not only reflect the cohort immigration and life cycle patterns, they also are related to what has been happening in the Boston area over the period. In particular, the data reflect the changing structure and distribution of housing, jobs, and opportunities in the area, the growth of universities and industries attractive to younger people, and the changing ethnic-racial composition of neighborhoods. In their aggregate forms, the patterns of migration are conspicious clues to suburbanization and in-migration, the decline of the foreign-born, and the expansion and dispersal of the Jewish population throughout the metropolis.

These are not startling or surprising conclusions. In their specific form, the migration patterns and distribution of population are unique features of the Boston Jewish community. They should not be expected to characterize declining centers of Jewish population, communities of different sizes and economic conditions, or newly formed communities in other geographic regions. It is not unexpected that younger Jews are more likely to move than older Jews, that educational and professional opportunities in the area attract young individuals and their families, and that as families are formed, greater residential stability ensues. Moreover, these patterns and relationships are not particularly Jewish. Are there any aspects of these migration patterns which are more characteristic of the Jewish population? Are they unique to Jews in Boston, or do they characterize non-Jews in Boston as well? More broadly, have suburbanization, in-migration, and residential changes been more pronounced among Jews than non-Jews?

ARE JEWISH MIGRATION PATTERNS UNIQUE?

A great part of the value of the Boston data, in contrast to the National Jewish Population Study and most if not all of the Jewish community surveys carried out in the 1970s and early 1980s, is in the parallel information obtained from representative samples of non-Jews. The contrasts between migration among Jews and migration among non-Jews sharpen our understanding of whether Jewish migration patterns are unique.

Overall, on every measure, Jews have higher mobility rates than non-Jews, and different mobility patterns. A higher proportion of Jews than non-Jews was born outside the Boston metropolitan area, and a lower proportion was born in the suburban areas of the metropolis. Jews have shorter durations of residence than non-Jews, and a larger number of non-Jews than Jews have resided in their cities and towns for twenty years or more. Over the last decade, more Jews than non-Jews changed residence, although of those who changed their residences, an identical proportion of Jews and non-Jews has migrated to Boston from other SMSAs.

Do these contrasts between Jews and non-Jews characterize all age–life-cycle groups? Examining the migration patterns of Jews and non-Jews by age clarifies what is unique in the migration pattern of young Jews and in the residential mobility of the oldest, long-term residents of Boston. Younger Jews are conspicuous in the degree to which they have migrated to Boston from outside the metropolitan area and are residentially mobile within Boston. While 65 percent of the Jews age 18–29 were born outside the Boston SMSA, this pattern characterized only 35 percent of the non-Jews. The higher proportions of Jewish migrants are reflected in their lower duration of residence: 77 percent of the Jews compared to 52 percent of the non-Jews have lived less than three years in their current neighborhoods. Over 20 percent of the non-Jews in this young age group have lived in their current neighborhoods almost all their lives (i.e., twenty years or more), compared to only 5 percent of the Jews; over 30 percent of the non-Jews have lived at least half their lives (i.e., ten or more years) in their area of residence, compared to 11 percent of the Jews. Thus, many more young Jews have moved in the last decade than non-Jews, with over 2.5 times as many non-Jews as Jews residentially stable. With minor exceptions, this same pattern contrasting Jews and non-Jews characterizes the 30–44 age group. These contrasting patterns suggest that the changing structure of opportunities over the last decades in Boston has attracted disproportionate numbers of Jews in the young adult groups—more so than non-Jews and Jews of other ages. Indeed, comparisons between Jews and non-Jews in the 45–59 age group reveal remarkable similarities. Data on place of birth, duration of residence, and place of residence in 1965 show virtually identical patterns between Jews and non-Jews.

For the older age group, further contrasts between Jews and non-Jews emerge which differentiate them from both the 18–45 and 45–59 age groups. Among those 60 years of age and older, the proportion foreign-born is higher among Jews than non-Jews; while the proportion of those born in the United States who were not born in the Boston SMSA is twice as high among non-Jews as among Jews. These patterns are the reverse of those noted for the 18–45 age groups and reflect differential immigration and settlement patterns. Furthermore, movement within the metropolitan area during the last decade is higher for older Jews than non-Jews; in contrast to non-Jews, most Jews have moved from sections of Boston's city rather than from the suburbs, and very few Jews of this age group have moved in from outside Boston. Thus, not only are older Jews more likely to move than older non-Jews, but the direction of mobility has been different as well—for non-Jews it has been from outside the SMSA and from the suburbs, while for Jews migration has been away from Boston city areas. Hence, contrasts between the migration patterns of younger and older Jews distinguish type as well as rate of movement, more sharply than among non-Jews.

It should be reemphasized that persons moving out of the Boston metropolitan area are not included in this community sample. Young locals who move out (perhaps to be replaced by young Jews from outside the SMSA) and older locals who may be moving south (permanently or for part of the year) were not enumerated, despite their importance. In interpreting the cross-section, we have only the residual of in- and out-flows and the origins of those who move in. Nevertheless, the contrasts between Boston's Jews and non-Jews are striking, even if we are analyzing differential residuals. They suggest that young Jewish adults are less rooted in the Boston community than older Jews and than non-Jews. Even among the movers, young Jews tend to be migrating from outside the community, rather than moving among the various neighborhoods of the community.

Are these conclusions, based on the contrasts between Jews and non-Jews, affected by the heterogeneity of the non-Jewish population? Are young Protestants and Jews more similar in their migration patterns? How much of the migration differences between Jews and specific non-Jewish populations reflects the educational, income, and life cycle differences between groups?

Migration variations by religion and ethnicity within the non-Jewish population are extensive (cf. Kobrin and Goldscheider 1978). We shall only highlight some of the major differences which are relevant in our context. First, the proportion foreign-born is significantly higher among Catholics than among Protestants and Jews. Overall, 17 percent of Boston Catholics are foreign-born, compared to 12 percent of the Jews and 5 percent of the Protestants. However, that is not true at all ages: among those age 60 and over, 29 percent of the Catholics are foreign-born, compared to 9 percent of the Protestants, and 35 percent of the Jews. The larger foreign-born percentage among older Jews reflects the concentration of their immigration patterns in time, compared to the wider spread of Catholic immigrants (Irish, Italian, and, more recently, Hispanic).

The critical comparison in our context is the migration patterns of the native-born. Except for those 18–29, Protestants have a higher rate of inmigration to Boston than Jews. Among native-born Catholics, the proportion born outside the SMSA is about 17 percent for each of the age groups 18–59. For Protestants the proportion is about 50 percent. The percentage for Jews is higher than for Catholics in each age group, but higher than for Protestants only for the 18–29 cohort (65 percent compared to 54 percent).

At each age, Catholic duration of residence is longer than Protestant (44 percent of the Catholics have lived in their current city or town twenty years or more, compared to 38 percent of the Protestants and 21 percent of the Jews). Jewish mobility rates, measured by duration of residence or place of residence in 1965, are higher than those of Catholics and Protestants at each age. Hence, young Jews are much more likely to be moving to Boston from outside the community than Protestants or Catholics.

One important factor in the migration of young adults is education. Previous research on the Jews, as among the total population, has found a general positive relationship between educational attainment and migration (Goldstein 1982). Two interrelated issues are associated with this relationship: one, people move to take advantage of educational opportunities; two, people with higher levels of education are more likely to be responsive to occupational opportunities in different communities. Our questions here are whether the migration-education linkage operates for Jews and whether that linkage is different from that for non-Jews.

The Boston data (table 4.2) show a very clear pattern of higher educational attainment among migrants than among nonmigrants. The relationship is particularly strong among Jews moving to Boston from outside the SMSA and among those with less than three years' duration in the area.

Some of the overall relationship between migration and education reflects the concentration of young adults among migrants. However, when we neutralize the age effects and examine the relationship between migration and education adjusted for age (column 2 of table 4.2), the same strong association remains.

TABLE 4.2
**Measures of Migration Status and Education by Religion:
Unadjusted and Adjusted for Age
(Multiple Classification Analysis)**

	Jews		Non-Jews		Catholics		Protestants	
	AVERAGE EDUCATION							
	Unadj.	Adj. for age	Unadj.	Adj. for age	Unadj.	Adj. for age	Unadj.	Adj. for age
Place of Birth								
Boston city	14.1	14.3	12.2	12.3	11.8	11.9	12.4	12.5
Boston suburb	15.0	14.9	13.0	12.9	12.7	12.5	13.3	13.2
Outside SMSA	16.3	15.9	14.4	14.4	13.0	13.0	14.9	14.9
Foreign-born	13.7	14.9	10.6	10.9	10.1	10.3	10.9	11.1
eta	.35	.21	.42	.38	.37	.32	.43	.42
Duration of Residence								
Less than 3 yrs.	16.3	15.9	14.2	13.9	13.3	12.8	14.3	14.0
4–9 years	15.3	15.1	12.5	12.4	12.2	12.0	12.5	12.5
10–19 years	14.2	14.3	12.2	12.3	11.6	11.7	12.7	12.7
20+ years	13.9	14.8	12.2	12.5	11.7	11.9	13.2	13.4
eta	.33	.20	.29	.22	.23	.15	.23	.20
Place of Residence 10 Years Earlier Movers								
Boston city	12.5	13.0	12.0	12.0	11.8	11.6	12.3	12.4
Boston suburb	16.0	15.6	13.4	13.2	13.3	12.9	13.3	13.2
Outside SMSA	16.7	16.6	14.3	13.9	13.2	12.8	14.0	13.7
Nonmovers	14.0	14.3	12.2	12.4	11.7	11.8	13.0	13.2
eta	.47	.38	.30	.23	.25	.17	.18	.11

In general, this relationship between migration and education characterizes the non-Jewish population. Several features of these patterns are
important in our context. First, differences between Jews and Protestants
are less striking than those between Jews and Catholics. Second, both
Protestants and Catholics have much greater educational variation by migration status than do Jews. There is almost a four-year difference in the
number of school years completed by place of birth among Protestants,
and about a three-year difference among Catholics. Among Jews, educational variation (by place of birth) varies by only one year.

The shorter-duration migrants of all religions have the highest educational levels. While the pattern is relatively similar for Jews and Catholics,
Protestants of both the lowest and highest durations have higher levels of
education. The recent Jewish movers from outside Boston are significantly
higher in educational level than nonmovers. For Protestants and Catholics, the patterns are less clear.

Taken together, these data suggest two important conclusions about the
relationship between migration and education. First, the educational contribution of recent Jewish migrants to the socioeconomic composition of
the Boston Jewish community is substantial. It is greater than the contribution made by recent Protestant and Catholic migrants to the area.[1] Second, while all communities face the issue of integrating young adults into
the ongoing and continuous activities of the older generation, the problems are compounded among Jews. In Boston, young adults are much
more likely to be recent migrants from outside the community—more
than non-Jews and more than older Jews. Unlike other communities in
the United States, which face the issue of the out-migration of younger
Jews, the Boston Jewish community exemplifies the challenge of integrating these recent, highly educated migrants. In particular, when migration
levels are high and migrants are not linked to the community, the process
of moving may threaten Jewish continuity.

MIGRATION AND JEWISH CONTINUITY

Therefore, the significance of migration goes beyond issues of demographic growth, structure, and distribution. Although there are specific
features of Jewish migration which are related to family formation, household structure, and stratification, a key question remains: Does migration
have an effect on Jewish continuity? Do migrants move away from family
and friends toward greater assimilation? Do patterns of internal migration

1. It should be noted that the higher educational level of Jews in the Boston area is not a
simple function of recent migrants from outside the SMSA. Even among the native-born,
whether of Boston urban or suburban areas, the educational level is significantly higher
among Jews than non-Jews. In no category, foreign-born included, are Jews less educated
than Protestants or Catholics (cf. chapter 9).

contribute negatively to Jewish survival? To answer these questions, we shall compare the Jewishness of migrants and nonmigrants within Boston.

Previous research on this issue has been weak and largely inferential. Often, migration patterns are described and the implications for Jewish continuity inferred rather than tested. Some research, based on limited data, has suggested that migration has different implications for various segments of the Jewish population: strengthening the Jewishness of the more religiously committed and weakening that of the more secular (cf. Jarret 1978; Goldstein 1982).

A recent review and analysis of national Jewish migration patterns based on the National Jewish Population Study suggested two types of relationships between migration and Jewish continuity (Goldstein 1982). The first argues that migration means detachment and uprootedness, not only from community but from family, friends, and ethnic networks. Community roots are difficult to establish when mobility rates are high and movement occurs away from Jewish population centers. Hence, migration should be associated with declining levels of Jewishness. As migration rates increase in association with educational and occupational opportunities, they will become an increasingly important threat to Jewish continuity.

An alternative view suggests that migration represents a "new challenge," not a "new threat," to Jewish continuity. Migration may contribute to renewed vitality of the Jewish community as it brings more Jews to areas of lower Jewish concentration, facilitating the development of a wide range of new networks and institutions. Moreover, migration rates tend to be highest at certain points in the life cycle. In those ages where community detachments represent the major threat to continuity, i.e., families with children, Jews, as well as others, tend to be most stable.

These contrasting hypotheses have not been tested systematically either with the National Jewish Population Study data or within one community. We shall examine the net impact of migration on a series of measures of Jewishness. Our analytic objective is to determine the extent to which migration is related to Jewishness net of the effects of age and education. In particular, we already know that age and education are related to migration and are related to Jewishness (cf. chapter 10). We want to examine whether there is a relationship between migration and Jewishness and whether it is particularly associated with the uprooting effects of migration. We shall focus on eight measures of Jewishness, which tap associational ties (friends and neighbors who are Jewish), religious dimensions (denominational identification and synagogue attendance), family and religious rituals, ethnic-community dimensions, and Jewish attitudes and values. (These are described in detail in chapter 10.)

The first issue relating migration to Jewish continuity focuses on the extent to which movement is toward areas of lower Jewish density. We have data on the Jewish density of areas of destination but not of areas of origin. Hence, we can answer only part of the question, i.e., whether migrants tend toward areas of low Jewish concentration. Data in table 4.3 show the proportion of those of various migration statuses who live in areas of high or low Jewish density (see chapter 3). These data show very little overall variation in the proportion in areas of low Jewish density. Indeed, movers in the decade 1965–75 were more likely to be residing in areas of higher Jewish density than were nonmovers. The same characterizes short-term movers, and this pattern is particularly pronounced among the young. About 15 percent of those 18–29 who moved in the decade 1965–75 or who were resident in their neighborhood less than three years lived in areas of high Jewish density, compared to 2–3 percent of those who were nonmovers or who had lived in their neighborhoods for ten or more years. But movers were also more likely to be in areas of low Jewish density. For older ages, the pattern is mixed. In short, there is no evidence that migration necessarily results in greater residential integration in areas of lower Jewish density or that migrants live in areas significantly different from those of comparable nonmigrants. Jews move to areas of high as well as to areas of low Jewish density.

If migration results in the weakening of Jewish ties, we would expect that those born outside Boston, with short residential durations, and who have moved during the last decade would have fewer Jewish friends and lower Jewish values, would not identify denominationally, would attend synagogue infrequently, and would express less-Jewish attitudes and norms. Overall, our analysis does not support those associations. Except for short-term effects on recent movers, the data are not consistent with the view that migration per se uproots and alienates Jews from their Jewishness. The absence of a clear relationship between migration and a wide range of Jewishness measures suggests that the disruption of Jewish networks at origin by internal migration and movement to the new communities has been accompanied by the formation of new networks of Jewishness. With new jobs and homes in new places, the migrant seems to have found new bonds and ties to Jews and the Jewish community. Hence, if these migration patterns are increasing, they should not be viewed with alarm or as further evidence of secularization, alienation, and the disintegration of Jewish cohesiveness.

Let us review some of the more detailed evidence, examining the relationship between types of migration and measures of Jewishness. Data in table 4.4 show that those born outside the Boston SMSA have fewer Jewish friends and more non-Jewish friends than those born in Boston or the foreign-born. The duration-of-residence data clarify this pattern. The proportion with all or mostly Jewish friends is low only among those with very short durations (less than three years in the community). No other systematic pattern by duration emerges. Similarly, the higher proportion of nonmovers than movers who have mostly Jewish friends is largely a func-

TABLE 4.3

Measures of Migration Status by Percent in Census Tracts of High and Low Jewish Density and Age

	All Ages		18–29		30–44		45–59		60+	
	% in high	% in low	% in high	% in low	% in high	% in low	% in high	% in low	% in high	% in low
Place of Birth										
Boston city	11	22	15	19	7	29	9	19	12	20
Boston suburb	7	26	2	27	8	18	6	25	20	43
Outside SMSA	11	26	14	22	2	41	8	30	20	16
Foreign-born	14	25	*	*	*	*	8	10	7	30
Duration of Residence										
Less than 3 yrs.	13	27	16	23	6	36	0	55	3	38
4–9 years	11	20	8	13	8	25	6	14	27	20
10–19 years	9	19	2	6	6	32	13	11	8	30
20+ years	6	29	2	31	4	31	2	35	9	26
Place of Residence in 1965										
Mover										
Boston city	13	30	23	44	4	60	5	13	15	22
Boston suburb	9	24	11	22	6	20	0	43	24	35
Outside SMSA	14	25	16	22	9	35	7	38	*	*
Nonmover	8	24	3	18	6	32	9	21	10	27

Table 4.4

Measures of Migration Status and Selected Measures of Jewishness

	Percent All or Mostly Jewish Friends	Value Living in Jewish Nghbrhood	Percent Nondenomi- national	Percent Never Attend Synagogue
Place of Birth				
Boston city	59.1	44.4	15.7	20.0
Boston suburb	57.5	41.2	28.3	16.8
Outside SMSA	37.9	32.9	27.6	27.7
Foreign-born	61.9	66.1	24.5	24.3
Duration of Residence				
Less than 3 yrs.	31.1	33.3	35.1	31.3
4–9 years	69.7	51.2	19.8	24.8
10–19 years	58.3	35.5	23.5	13.3
20+ years	60.1	50.9	10.1	14.2
Place of Residence in 1965				
Mover	44.4	39.9	30.4	29.6
Boston city	66.6	54.7	14.8	35.6
Boston suburb	53.0	43.0	22.7	18.7
Outside SMSA	33.3	34.0	39.6	34.6
Nonmover	59.1	43.3	16.7	13.9

tion of movers from outside the SMSA. Therefore, overall, the proportion of those who have mostly Jewish friends does not systematically relate to migration status, except for the short-term migrant. To the extent that these cross-sectional data can be viewed as a process of change, we can infer that as short-term migrants from outside the Boston area settle in, they will have characteristics similar to those of the longer-duration residents. Hence, the effects of migration are short-term disassociations from community, with no long-term effects. These findings parallel what has been observed in general studies of migrant adjustment in a wide range of countries (cf. Goldscheider 1983, chapter 7).

These findings vary somewhat within age groups. For example, the proportion of friends who are mostly Jewish is lower among those 18–29 years of age who were born outside the SMSA compared to those born in Boston. This pattern does not, however, characterize the older ages. Similarly, the higher proportion with non-Jewish friends among the short-duration migrants characterizes those age 18–29, but not the 30–44 age group. Hence, no long-term implications can be identified in the relationship between migration status and patterns of Jewish friendship.

Another area of Jewishness relates to values expressed about living in Jewish neighborhoods. Here, too, the foreign-born are most likely to express such a value, and those born outside the SMSA are least likely to prefer Jewish neighborhoods. However, only short-duration migrants have lower preferences, and few differences can be discerned by duration. Nonmovers generally have slightly higher preferences for Jewish neighborhoods than movers, but that largely depends on where the movers are coming from. Movers from the suburbs place the same value on Jewish neighborhoods as nonmovers, while those moving in the last decade from outside the SMSA have the least preference. That, as the duration data show, is only for the short term. Data not presented in tabular form show that these differences do not appear at all among the young.

Do migrants tend to be nonaffiliated denominationally? Again, the answer is mixed. About 28 percent of those born outside the Boston SMSA do not define themselves institutionally as Orthodox, Conservative, or Reform Jews, the same percentage as for those born in the Boston suburbs and only slightly higher than for those who were born abroad. While those born outside the SMSA are more likely to be Reform rather than Conservative, that is hardly an indication of disaffection and unaffiliation. The higher proportion Orthodox among the foreign-born is largely an age-generational pattern, not one associated with the uprootedness of migration.

Those who have lived in their neighborhoods for short periods of time or who have recently migrated from outside the Boston SMSA have a higher proportion nondenominational: 40 percent of those moving from outside the SMSA, compared to 30 percent of all movers and 17 percent of nonmovers. That is, however, for short durations only. Details by age show no systematic patterns between migration status and denominational affiliation. Those with the shortest duration have higher nondenominational affiliation, but only among those age 30 and over; those with the longest duration (twenty or more years) have lower nonaffiliation, with some exceptions, and no systematic patterns.

Synagogue attendance patterns are consistent with this picture. The percentage who never attend a synagogue is highest among those born outside the Boston SMSA. But duration of residence shows a more or less consistent pattern of reduced nonattendance as duration increases. We carried out a multivariate test of the relationship between migration status and synagogue attendance, adjusting for age and education. The results showed no significant relationship between place of birth and synagogue attendance, when age and education were controlled. However, when the findings were adjusted for age and education, there remained a consistent relationship between duration of residence and synagogue attendance: the

TABLE 4.5
Net Effects of Migration Status on Measures of Jewishness:
Adjusted for Age and Education
(Multiple Classification Analysis)

	Jewish Values	Ritual	Family Ritual	Ethnic
Place of Birth				
Boston city	2.69	2.96	1.66	1.38
Boston suburb	2.86	3.21	1.69	1.34
Outside SMSA	2.47	2.39	1.55	1.07
Foreign-born	2.75	2.54	1.57	1.57
Duration of Residence				
Less than 3 yrs.	2.31	2.26	1.46	0.88
4–9 years	2.82	2.97	1.69	1.49
10–19 years	2.64	2.83	1.70	1.32
20+ years	3.01	3.39	1.73	1.76
Place of Residence in 1965				
Mover				
Boston city	2.81	2.32	1.48	0.82
Boston suburb	2.65	3.02	1.71	1.32
Outside SMSA	2.34	2.30	1.47	1.14
Nonmover	2.84	3.04	1.70	1.44

shorter the duration, the more likely Jews were never to attend synagogue services. This pattern changes as duration increases. Hence, recent migrants are much less likely to frequent a synagogue; over time, they seem to increase their attendance. Finally, while nonmovers are more likely than movers to attend synagogue services, they are no more likely than movers from suburban areas, when age and education are controlled.

A final set of indices of Jewishness relates to Jewish values, personal ritual and religious observances, family ritual, and ethnic-community factors. The specific statistics based on these scales have no intrinsic meaning except relative to each other and to averages for the population as a whole. Our objective here is not to examine these indices in detail (cf. chapter 10) but to focus on the relative significance of them by migration status. The evidence presented in table 4.5 is adjusted for age and education.

Three major conclusions can be drawn from these data: (1) There are no significant relationships between family ritual and ethnic-community dimensions and migration status, when age and education are adjusted. (2) Recent movers from outside Boston and those whose duration of residence is less than three years have significantly lower rates of Jewishness as measured by Jewish values and personal religious ritual. These are not simply a reflection of age and education but seem to be the direct consequence of the migration process per se. However, as for other indicators of Jewishness, these patterns tend to be short-term and do not extend beyond the three-year duration. (3) A substantial part of the general relationship between migration status and Jewishness is a function of the age-educational associations with migration. Thus, while there appears to be a relationship between migration and disaffection from the Jewish community, that relationship is mainly because movers are younger and more educated. The net effects of migration per se are weak, except among those with the shortest durations of residence.

Taken together, these data suggest that we need to revise our oversimplified model connecting migration to uprootedness from Jewishness and the Jewish community. At least for one Jewish community of medium size with a large influx of migrants from outside the area and a high rate of internal mobility, the evidence points to but short-term effects of migration on Jewish continuity.

It is likely that migration patterns of Jews in the United States will remain high, particularly among those who are enrolled in universities or are at the beginning of their occupational careers. They may also be high among the retired population who are sufficiently affluent to move to new communities in new places. These migration patterns should not be viewed as a further threat to Jewish continuity. Migrants, after a relatively short period of time, seem to link up with existing Jewish networks of friends and neighbors and with established Jewish communal institutions, religious and ethnic. Often, they seem to develop new networks or extend established ones. These need to be studied directly.

FIVE

Marriage and Family Formation

The analysis of the intermarried, Jews in non-Jewish neighborhoods, and recent migrants focuses attention on the fringes of the community. However, most Jews, as we have shown, are not at the margins. They interact with other Jews in many contexts, but first and foremost in their families. Families are primary sources of cultural transmission and the major link between generations. The economic resources of families facilitate educational attainment and the development of networks—social and economic. As such, the family represents a major connection between the individual and the community and is a core basis of group continuity.

In the past, American Jews had been remarkably successful in maintaining patterns of family stability and cohesion. The family remained central in the lives of Jews, despite social and geographic mobility and general acculturation and integration. The pattern of almost universal marriage and low divorce rates was indeed exceptional, considering the radical social transformation of American Jews in the last century and the changes among non-Jewish families (Goldstein and Goldscheider 1968).

Data from the 1957 Current Population Survey show the very high proportion of Jewish men and women who ever marry: only 5 percent of Jewish men and 8 percent of Jewish women were single (never married) among those age 35–44. These findings have been repeatedly observed in various community studies (see Goldstein 1971; Kobrin, forthcoming). Moreover, divorce rates seem to be lower for Jews than for the total American population (see Goldberg 1968). Recent data pooled from the general social surveys carried out in 1972–1980 by the National Opinion Research Center indicated that Jews were less likely than non-Jews to have been separated or divorced, even after controlling for social class and other factors (Cherlin and Celebuski 1983).

Patterns of high marriage rates and the stability of marriage are consistent with later age at marriage. In general, age at marriage has tended to be higher among Jews than for the total American population (see Goldscheider and Goldstein 1967; Goldstein 1971; Kobrin and Goldscheider 1978; Waxman 1982; Cohen 1982). Marriage cohort data reveal that later age at marriage has characterized Jewish women since at least 1920. Average age at marriage increased from 19 to 23 years up to the World War II cohorts and declined subsequently for cohorts marrying in the 1950s and early 1960s. Delayed age at marriage appears to be related to the educa-

58

tional attainment of Jews, although the fluctuations in the post-World War II period cannot be a simple consequence of education.

In the decade of the 1970s, a variety of indirect indicators suggested that major family changes are unfolding among the younger generation of Jews. Concerns have been expressed over the growing rates of nonmarriage among men and women in their twenties. In particular, changes in the role of women and families in America among the more educated have led to the assumption that delayed marriage may imply nonmarriage. Similarly, increasing divorce rates among the American population as a whole have raised the question about the extent of continuing marital stability among Jews, increasing one-parent families, and a general breakdown of the Jewish family.

The concerns expressed go beyond the issue of marriage and focus on the alienation of the young from their families during the period of time between when children leave home and when they begin their own families. Moreover, if young Jews are marrying late or not at all, concerns may be raised about the adequacy of the low fertility of the married to replace the current generation.

Together, issues of family formation, childbearing, and the residential independence of young adults before they marry have been raised both as demographic concerns and as a basis for erosion of the Jewishness of the younger generation.

Concerns have been expressed more often than systematic research has been carried out. Some evidence has suggested that increasing numbers of young Jewish persons live away from families and that there are increasing divorce rates and some nonmarriage (see Massarik and Chenkin 1973; Cohen 1982). Inferences about the demographic and community implications of these patterns have been made. However, the marriage-family processes have rarely been studied systematically, particularly in relationship to non-Jews; nor have the inferences been examined carefully.

Jews have tended in the past to be in the forefront of major socioeconomic revolutions. American Jews are located in social statuses and geographic locations that are the most responsive to changes in marriage and the family. The high proportion of Jews with college- and graduate-level educations, their disproportionate concentration in major metropolitan centers, and their middle-class backgrounds and values place them in the avant garde of social change. For Jews, changes in family stability and in marriage may imply strains on Jewish social, cultural, and demographic continuity in America. These issues will be examined in this and the next two chapters.

For the most part, the evidence available is limited in time, method, and coverage. The more precisely and in detail we want to explore, the more frustrating the inadequacies of the data available become. Many of our research questions require a careful longitudinal design to identify the dynamics of family formation and change. No such data are available. We can sketch only with broad strokes some of the major patterns. Some of the facts and details are in dispute, but we do know the basic pattern. More controversial are the interpretations of the evidence and, in particular, what the family patterns tell us about the future of the American Jewish community.

In this chapter we focus on the extent and timing of marriage and the rate of marital dissolution. Analytically, we shall explore the major changes in marriage and family formation among Jews and compare them to those among non-Jews. In part, the underlying issue relates to whether the Jewish family is disintegrating, and with it American Jewry in the future. Some have viewed changes in the Jewish family as the major indicators of declining Jewishness. An assessment and analysis of the American Jewish family in the early 1980s asserted that "the Jewish family and Jewishness are inextricably intertwined" and, therefore, that "changes in American Jewish family life also imply changes in Jewish identification" (Cohen 1982, p. 137; cf. Waxman 1982). Similarly, a recent policy statement begins, "Jewish community is Jewish family: The fate of one is the fate of the other" (Bulka 1982). The evidence from the Boston study of 1975 suggests that, contrary to popular reports, the Jewish family continues to be a major source of strength in the community. While there are clear indications of change, there is no systematic evidence of family decline and disintegration. The data suggest that reports of the imminent death of the Jewish family have been greatly exaggerated. (Similar conclusions for the American population as a whole have been reached in Cherlin 1981, p. 74 and passim.)

THE EXTENT OF MARRIAGE

We begin the analysis by examining the marital-status distribution of Jews and non-Jews. (Table 5.1). In the cross-section of the adult Jewish community, 63 percent of the men and 54 percent of the women are married; the rest are mostly single (never married), with about 10 percent formerly married (divorced, separated, or widowed who have not remarried). For the age cohorts 18–59, there are few differences between Jewish men and women in the proportion married; the largest differences appear for those age 60 and over, where 65 percent of the men and 40 percent of the women are married. These differences mainly reflect differences in the proportion widowed among older Jews: 39 percent of the Jewish women 60 years of age and older are widowed, compared to 18 percent of the men. These patterns are related to the longer life expectancy of women and the higher rates of remarriage among widowed men compared to widowed women.

Are these patterns similar to the marital-status distribution patterns of non-Jews? For simplicity, we will examine data on the total non-Jewish sample. Protestants and Catholics differ in some family patterns, with less

TABLE 5.1
Marital Status by Age, Sex, and Religion

	Married	Divorced or Separated	Widowed	Single-Never Married	Total
Jews					
Males	62.8	5.3	3.9	28.0	100.0
18–29	34.5	2.6	0.0	62.9	100.0
30–44	80.7	6.3	2.6	10.4	100.0
45–59	85.4	11.4	1.0	2.1	100.0
60 +	65.0	2.0	18.2	14.7	100.0
Females	53.6	2.8	10.4	33.2	100.0
18–29	34.2	1.8	0.0	64.0	100.0
30–44	86.7	4.8	0.5	8.0	100.0
45–59	81.6	4.2	5.2	9.1	100.0
60 +	40.4	2.0	39.0	18.5	100.0
Non-Jews					
Males	64.8	6.9	2.8	25.3	100.0
18–29	42.1	3.6	0.0	54.3	100.0
30–44	73.6	14.2	0.0	12.3	100.0
45–59	82.1	5.3	2.1	10.5	100.0
60 +	72.2	5.1	12.7	10.1	100.0
Females	48.1	14.6	16.5	20.8	100.0
18–29	39.3	14.0	1.3	45.3	100.0
30–44	63.4	23.7	6.1	6.9	100.0
45–59	62.9	15.5	12.1	9.5	100.0
60 +	31.0	7.0	45.1	16.9	100.0

variation among Catholic ethnics. That is particularly the case for divorce and remarriage. Nevertheless, almost all the patterns distinguishing Jews from non-Jews apply to Jewish-Protestant, as well as Jewish-Catholic, comparisons.

The proportion married among Jewish and non-Jewish men is about the same overall, but higher for non-Jews than Jews age 18–29 and higher for Jews than non-Jews 30–59 years of age. Differences in the youngest cohort reflect the later timing of marriage among Jews; the reversal in the middle ages reflects the higher proportion of Jewish men who marry and their rates of family stability. In general, there is a higher rate of divorce among non-Jews than Jews, which is particularly pronounced in the Jewish-Protestant comparisons.

Jewish women are also more likely to be married than non-Jewish women among those age 30 and over. As among males, the divorce-separation proportion among Jewish women is lower than among non-Jewish women, but the differences between Jewish and non-Jewish women are greater than those between Jewish and non-Jewish men. Almost 15 percent of the non-Jewish women are divorced, compared to 3 percent of the Jewish women, with very large differences for all age groups. Among all women there has been an increase in the proportion divorced from those age 60 and over to those 30–44. Among non-Jewish women the increase is from 7 percent to 24 percent; among Jewish women the increase is from 2 percent to 5 percent.

Jewish women age 18–29 are heavily concentrated in the never-married category, more so than non-Jewish women and to about the same extent as Jewish men. The pattern seems mainly to reflect issues of timing of marriage, since there is a sharp decline from 64 percent to 8 percent in the proportion never married between the ages 18–29 and 30–44. It is not clear, however, whether the women age 30–44 represent the level toward which those age 18–29 will move in the future.

THE STABILITY OF MARRIAGE

The distributions of marital status among Jews and non-Jews are snapshots of marital stability and the timing of marriage. The analysis of these two issues can be expanded. We first examine in greater detail the extent of marital stability by focusing on the marital backgrounds of couples who are currently married (rather than on the current marital status of individuals). These data show the very high proportion of Jewish couples in first marriages: 92–96 percent of those age 18–60 are in their first marriage. Differences between Jews and non-Jews start at around age 30, where consistently more Jews than non-Jews are in first marriages (table 5.2).

Among Jews there is a tendency for husbands to be in remarriages and wives to be in their first marriage, with very few remarried wives of husbands who are in their first marriage. This pattern contrasts with the non-Jewish pattern. Generally, the proportion where both spouses are in a remarriage is lower among Jews than non-Jews. Overall, then, these data support the impression of greater family stability among Jews.

Another way to examine the issue of family stability is to relate the divorced to the ever-married rather than to the total population. This ratio approximates a divorce rate of those eligible (i.e., those who are married). For Jewish men and women, the divorce ratio is about 6 per 100 ever-married. It is significantly lower than among non-Jewish men and women (table 5.3). This difference holds within age cohorts and educational levels.

Is educational attainment correlated positively with higher divorce? Jewish men and women with a postgraduate education have higher divorce rates than those with a college education. That contrasts with a tendency toward an inverse relationship between education and divorce among non-Jews. Again, the important feature of these data is the overwhelming stability of Jewish marriages for all educational levels.

The data on the percentage ever married by education clarify two points: First, high levels of educational attainment among Jews do not result in disproportionate nonmarriage. There may be some delayed marriage, particularly among younger Jewish women who go beyond college, but that does not characterize Jewish men. Indeed, the proportion ever married is positively related to educational levels among Jewish men and negatively related to educational levels among Jewish women. The male pattern is consistent for Jews and non-Jews, while the impact of education on delayed marriage among Jewish women is sharper than for non-Jewish women. The increasing college enrollment of married women indicates the growing acceptability of a combination of marriage and educational attainment (cf. Glick and Norton 1977). There is no evidence from these data of major conflicts between the attainment of higher education and marriage.

A second feature of these data is the very high proportion ever married (of Jews and non-Jews, men and women) of all educational levels in the age 30–44 age cohort. At least in terms of that cohort, high levels of educational attainment did not interfere with an emphasis on almost universal marriages. It should be stressed, however, that these data do not necessarily indicate the trajectory of marriage among the youngest cohort who are currently nonmarried.

TABLE 5.2

Marriage and Remarriage of the Currently Married by Age and Religion

	Both in First Marriage	Wife in First, Husband in Remarriage	Wife in Remarriage, Husband in First	Both in Remarriage	Total %	N
Jews						
All ages	90.6	5.4	0.9	3.0	100.0	1,216
18–29	92.3	7.7	0.0	0.0	100.0	274
30–44	91.8	5.1	1.0	2.1	100.0	390
45–59	95.5	0.6	1.1	2.8	100.0	353
60+	77.8	11.6	1.5	9.0	100.0	198
Non-Jews						
All ages	87.1	4.9	3.8	4.2	100.0	528
18–29	93.2	5.1	1.7	0.0	100.0	118
30–44	88.6	3.8	3.2	4.4	100.0	158
45–59	83.7	6.5	3.3	6.5	100.0	153
60+	82.8	4.0	8.1	5.1	100.0	99

TABLE 5.3
Proportion Married and Divorced by Education, Age, Sex, and Religion

	High School	Some College	College Graduate	Postgraduate	
Percent Ever Married					
Jews					
Males					
18–29	*	28	30	56	
30–44	100	97	84	90	
Females					
18–29	40	37	32	29	
30–44	85	100	98	87	
Non-Jews					
Males					
18–29	49	37	48	53	
30–44	87	93	88	90	
Females					
18–29	73	40	36	50	
30–44	95	100	88	*	

	High School	Some College	College Graduate	Postgraduate	Total
Percent Currently Divorced of the Ever-Married					
Jews					
Males					
18–29	*	0	3	10	6
30–44	0	0	3	14	8
Females					
18–29	*	0	0	3	6
30–44	2	8	3	6	5
Non-Jews					
Males					
18–29	7	13	8	*	8
30–44	21	14	7	*	16
Females					
18–29	35	21	0	0	26
30–44	28	27	14	*	26

THE TIMING OF MARRIAGE

In addition to the question of marital stability are issues associated with the timing of marriage. Are Jews older at marriage than non-Jews? Do Jews marry late, and does that significantly limit the childbearing years? Has the pursuit of higher education seriously affected the timing of Jewish marriages?

All cross-sectional data have serious methodological limitations for an analysis of the timing of marriage. First, the analysis must be limited to those who have married by a cutoff date or age or by focusing only on those who have completed the transition to marriage. Second, explanations of age at marriage usually refer to characteristics of the family of origin or of the couple at the time of marriage, while most of the data refer to characteristics at the time of the survey (cf. Waite and Spitz 1981). We cannot overcome these limitations with the Boston data. Nevertheless, important insights into the timing of Jewish and non-Jewish marriages emerge from our analysis.

The data on age at first marriage refer to all those who are currently married. They include men and women who have ever married, i.e., those in their first marriage as well as the remarried. Excluded are the previously married who had not remarried at the time of the survey (i.e., the currently widowed, divorced, and separated). A similar set of tabular materials of age at first marriage for those currently in their first marriage was also prepared. These showed identical patterns. Illustrative comparisons are presented in table 5.4 for Jews and non-Jews. Ages at first marriage for the ever-married and once-married are so similar that the latter will not be presented in subsequent tables. The data are presented separately for men and women, because of the consistently later age at marriage among men.

The median age of first marriage among Jewish males is 25.2 years; it is three years younger for Jewish women (22.2). There are no differences in age at first marriage of Jewish, Italian, and Irish Catholic males among those in their first marriage. In large part, the overall differences among the ever-married reflect differential remarriage rates of Jews and Catho-

TABLE 5.4

Median Age of First Marriage for the Ever-Married and the Once-Married by Religion, Ethnicity, and Sex

	Ever-Married Males	Once-Married Males	Ever-Married Females	Once-Married Females
Jews	25.2	25.0	22.2	22.2
Total non-Jews	24.0	24.2	21.9	22.0
Blacks	24.8	24.7	23.3	23.0
White Protestants	23.4	23.5	21.7	21.9
Irish Catholics	24.7	25.0	23.0	23.6
Italian Catholics	24.7	24.9	21.4	21.4
Other white Catholics	23.8	24.0	21.8	21.8
Catholics	24.2	24.4	21.8	21.8
Protestants	23.5	23.7	22.1	22.2

Table 5.5
Proportion Marrying at Younger and Older Ages by Religion, Ethnicity, and Sex

	MALES		FEMALES	
	Before age 21	Age 30 and over	Before age 19	Age 25 and over
Jews	14	19	13	21
Non-Jews	21	16	24	22
Blacks	20	26	22	33
White Protestants	22	11	27	21
Irish Catholics	18	24	27	28
Italian Catholics	16	16	21	15
Other white Catholics	26	11	20	19
Catholics	21	17	23	20
Protestants	21	14	24	24

lics. Similarly, there is no overall distinctive age-at-marriage pattern for Jewish women. Their average age at marriage is slightly later than that of the total non-Jewish female population but is identical to that of Protestant women and earlier than that of Irish Catholics and blacks.

Median age at marriage measures the mid-point of the distribution of ages at marriage. An examination of the upper and lower ends of the distribution (table 5.5) shows that smaller numbers of Jews marry at young ages (less than 22 for men and 20 for women) than non-Jews. This finding characterizes both sexes and contrasts with each of the ethnic and religious subpopulations. At the other end of the distribution, Jews are not distinctive. While a high number of Jews marry at later ages (25 and over for women and 30 and over for men), similar proportions characterize other ethnic and religious groups. The wide variation in the proportion marrying at younger ages and older ages within the non-Jewish population contrasts with the Jewish pattern: about two-thirds of the Jews marry within a relatively narrow age range, age 22–29 for men and age 20–25 for women.

These overall patterns are affected by age and cohort variations. For males, the pattern is sharp and clear: among those age 18–29 and 30–39, Jewish males marry later than non-Jews (with but one exception among those age 18–29). For the oldest age group, the Jewish pattern is not different from that for Catholics, particularly Irish and Italians. For Jewish women, distinctively late age at marriage characterizes only the youngest age group (table 5.6).

A further examination of these age-at-marriage patterns by age reveals some built-in biases. For Jewish males, for example, there is a clear downward shift, from an average marriage age of 26 years for those currently 40 years of age and older to 23 years for the younger age group. This downward shift reflects the fact that many of those 18–29 have not yet married. We can calculate age at marriage only for those who marry and are currently married; hence, there is downward bias for the youngest ages. Comparing the two oldest ages reveals much less change. Part of the age-at-marriage difference between Jews and non-Jews in the 18–29 age group, therefore, reflects the differential proportion married. Interestingly, this downward bias is not observable for Jewish women, where there is much greater stability by age.

The data reinforce another point. Comparisons between Jews and non-Jews often assume that non-Jews are a relatively homogeneous group. Such is clearly not the case. A comparison of Jewish and non-Jewish males over age 40 would have confirmed the later age at which Jews first married. A careful, detailed look at Irish and Italian Catholics shows that such a conclusion would have been unwarranted. Similarly, Jewish women age 30–39 marry at later ages than non-Jewish women, but Italian and Irish Catholics marry later than Jews.

Despite some biases created by the age groupings, we can pursue the issues through a comparative examination of marriage cohorts (table 5.7). For those who married 1966–75, Jewish males married the latest of all

TABLE 5.6
**Median Age at First Marriage for the Currently Married
by Religion, Ethnicity, Age, and Sex**

	18–29	30–39	40+
Males			
Jews	23.0	25.8	26.1
Non-Jews	22.1	23.7	25.4
Blacks	22.3	22.5	27.8
White Protestants	21.7	23.3	24.7
Irish Catholics	22.0	24.4	26.5
Italian Catholics	22.2	24.2	26.6
Other white Catholics	22.9	23.3	24.8
Catholics	22.6	24.0	25.5
Protestants	21.8	22.7	25.3
Females			
Jews	22.1	21.9	22.4
Non-Jews	20.8	21.6	22.8
Blacks	19.5	21.3	26.5
White Protestants	20.6	21.7	22.8
Irish Catholics	21.7	23.0	24.1
Italian Catholics	20.0	22.0	21.9
Other white Catholics	21.8	21.3	22.3
Catholics	20.7	21.5	22.4
Protestants	20.6	21.8	23.2

TABLE 5.7
Median Age at First Marriage for the Currently Married by Religion, Ethnicity, Sex, and Marriage Cohorts

Sex and Marriage Cohort	Jews	Non-Jews	Protestants	Catholics	Irish Catholics	Italian Catholics	Other White Catholics
Males							
Before 1949	24.9	24.3	24.6	24.3	24.8	24.0	24.5
1949–59	25.2	24.6	23.7	25.4	25.0	27.3	23.8
1960–65	25.5	23.7	23.8	23.4	*	23.3	24.3
1966–75	25.5	23.3	22.1	23.9	25.0	24.2	23.1
Females							
Before 1949	22.5	22.0	22.6	21.6	22.0	21.6	21.6
1949–59	21.6	21.9	21.7	22.0	22.5	21.8	21.5
1960–65	21.9	21.5	23.8	21.1	*	21.0	21.2
1966–75	22.8	21.8	21.4	22.0	23.5	20.8	22.2

ethnic and religious groups; Jewish women of this cohort married later than non-Jews (22.8 to 21.8) but earlier than Irish Catholic women. The Jewish male pattern characterizes the 1960–65 cohort as well, but not earlier cohorts—particularly when comparing them to all Catholics, or particularly to Irish Catholics. In each cohort, Jewish women marry later than some, and earlier than other, religious or ethnic groups.

Viewing cohorts as indicators of time suggests different patterns for men and women and for Jews and non-Jews. There is general stability over cohorts for Jewish males, particularly since the postwar period. For Jewish women, the pattern appears curvilinear—age at marriage later for the cohorts marrying before 1949 (including the delayed marriages associated with the war) and earlier in the postwar baby boom period up to the mid-1960s; for the most recent cohort, Jewish women marry about one year later than earlier postwar cohorts. That has been noted in other research as well (Goldscheider and Goldstein 1967; DellaPergola 1980).

One conclusion emerges clearly: most Jewish women are not delaying marriage beyond their childbearing period, nor are Jews particularly marrying at later ages compared to other ethnic and religious groups. The timing of marriage among young Jews does not appear exceptional.

TIMING OF MARRIAGE AND
EDUCATIONAL TRADE-OFFS

There are two interrelated patterns that provide a context for understanding differential age at marriage and connect it to marriage and reproduction. The first relates to the educational attainment of Jews. Later age at marriage is often linked to education at college and postgraduate training. The values of marriage and education are so institutionalized within the Jewish community that when both are accepted, the trade-off becomes one of timing. Given the general conflict between continuing education and marriage, the choice often becomes marrying after educational goals have been attained. That results in delayed marriage.

Nevertheless, there is an implicit assumption about the burden of the marriage-education combination. One factor adding to the combined burden is childbearing. Essentially, delayed marriage is one mechanism for postponing early childbearing. Having children early within marriage, when marriage occurs before education is complete, is associated with weaker economic foundations of the marriage, lower cumulative savings, and greater socioeconomic dependency on the families of origin.

The potential education-marriage conflict can be dealt with in a variety of ways: (1) Marry early but delay childbearing within marriage by effective use of efficient contraception while continuing educational advancement. In part, this solution implies continuous parental financial support for a longer period of time, even for married couples. That has evidently been the response of American Jewish women. (2) Marry later, after edu-

TABLE 5.8

**Median Age at First Marriage for the Currently Married
by Education, Income, Sex, and Religion**

	Jews		Non-Jews	
	Females	Males	Females	Males
Education				
High-school graduate	21.6	25.6	21.2	23.6
Some college	21.9	24.5	22.1	23.9
College graduate	22.4	25.8	23.5	24.6
Postgraduate	23.9	24.7	24.0	25.1
*Family Income**				
Low	22.3	24.2	21.4	23.5
Medium	22.5	26.0	22.9	24.8
High	22.2	26.6	24.7	24.9

*Low = less than $20,000; Medium = $20-35,000; High = $35,000 and over.

cational goals have been attained, or forego higher education for earlier marriage. That has been the response of Irish and Italian Catholics in the past, particularly given some normative restrictions on the use of effective means of contraception for early spacing. (3) Another response is foregoing marriage and education, but not childbearing. That has been the response of poor blacks, as indicated by their high rates of out-of-wedlock births and delayed marriage. (4) A final pattern is not to marry at all. This approach has in the past characterized some Catholics and may characterize select segments of the Jewish population.

Clearly the black response has not been acceptable to most whites; the Jewish response had been less acceptable to Catholics. These alternatives suggest important trade-offs between marriage, education, and the timing of childbearing.

An examination of the education–age-at-marriage connection (table 5.8) suggests that, controlling for education, Jewish women do not marry at later ages than non-Jewish women, while Jewish men marry later than non-Jewish men, except at the postgraduate level. Higher levels of education tend to delay marriage for all women and for non-Jewish men. Generally, there is a positive relationship between education and age at marriage, except for Jewish men. It is possible that some other factors, perhaps those associated with careers and independence, affect the timing of marriage for Jewish males beyond the education connection.

Some clue to this pattern may be observed with the relationship between income and age at marriage. Before we examine the evidence, the weakness of the income measure needs to be stressed (see also chapter 8). It is a current indicator, while age at marriage is retrospective; it measures family rather than individual income, and a disproportionate number did not respond to the income question. Most important, we would want to examine income (and other economic resources) of the family of origin at the time of marriage. Nevertheless, it seems reasonable that the available measure will be highly correlated with more appropriate measures. Hence, we can contrast the relationship between income and age at marriage with the relationship between education and age at marriage.

For males, there is a clear positive association between higher income and later marriage. Among Jews with higher incomes, age at first marriage is 26.6 years, compared to 24.2 for low-income males. At each income level, Jewish males marry at later ages than non-Jewish males. That suggests that the education-marriage connection for males is socioeconomic, not simply the conflict between educational attainment and marriage. In contrast, there is no relationship between income and age at marriage among Jewish women, and Jewish women do not marry later than non-Jewish women, except in the low-income group.

The lack of relationship between income and the age at which Jews marry is, therefore, gender-specific. Measurement problems cannot account for the different patterns of Jewish men and women. An examination of the relationship between income and age at marriage among non-Jewish women shows that age at first marriage was 24.7 among high-income, compared to 21.4 among low-income, non-Jewish women. A similar pattern characterized non-Jewish males. Hence, it cannot be argued that the income measure is biased solely for Jewish women.

In sum, therefore, the response of Jewish women to the potential conflict between marriage, education, and childbearing is to marry relatively early for their class-education group and to delay childbearing within marriage. Neither social class nor high education interferes with relatively early marriage and *eventual* childbearing. It may affect the timing of childbearing within marriage and perhaps period, but not cohort fertility. We shall review these issues in our discussion of household composition and reproduction (chapters 6 and 7).

Given the similarities in the timing of marriage of Jews and non-Jews, there is little basis for arguing that Jewish values affect age at marriage. An examination of variation in the timing of marriage among religious denominations shows that Orthodox men marry somewhat later than Conservative or Reform men, but that is eliminated with cohort controls. Reform men marry at younger ages than Conservative men, but that does not characterize the youngest cohort (table 5.9).

The range among women is much smaller, with Reform women marrying at the youngest ages. No conspicuous patterns appear when cohort is controlled. The trends for nondenominational and Reform women are quite similar, but nondenominational men marry significantly later than men who identify as Orthodox, Conservative, or Reform. That is particularly the case among the youngest cohort: the average age at first marriage of those marrying 1966–75 who did not identify denominationally

Table 5.9

Median Age at First Marriage for Currently Married Jews by Religious Denomination, Marriage Cohort, and Sex

	Females	Males
Orthodox	22.3	26.1
Pre–1949	22.6	23.6
1949–59	20.2	*
1960–65	*	*
1966–75	*	*
Conservative	22.8	25.4
Pre–1949	22.9	26.1
1949–59	22.1	24.9
1960–65	21.1	25.9
1966–75	24.0	23.5
Reform	22.0	24.0
Pre–1949	22.6	24.2
1949–59	21.0	22.8
1960–65	22.6	24.2
1966–75	22.4	24.4
Other	22.0	26.9
Pre–1949	19.5	24.3
1949–59	21.8	26.8
1960–65	21.9	22.8
1966–75	22.7	28.5

was 28.5 years, significantly higher than that of Reform (24.4) or Conservative (23.5) men of that cohort.

The reason for this pattern is not clear, and the direction of causality is not obvious. An argument could be made that it is precisely their late age at marriage which leads to their lack of affiliation, rather than the lack of denominational identification which results in their late age at marriage (cf. chapter 7 for a similar argument about family size). To clarify the direction of the causal relationship and to explain why the pattern characterizes only men, a dynamic, longitudinal research design is necessary.

These data on the timing of marriage, combined with the analysis of the marriage and divorce rates, portray the Jews as a family-oriented, relatively cohesive community. The only data suggesting increasing nonmarriage relate to the youngest cohort, where delayed marriage rather than permanent nonmarriage seems to have occurred. Without more recent data for younger cohorts or follow-up longitudinal studies, it is premature to conclude that large numbers of young Jewish men and women will remain unmarried. The marriage patterns of Jews in contemporary America do not appear to reflect particular Jewish or religious values. Structural conditions associated with the number of eligible men and women and the particular education–social-class characteristics of Jews account in large part for variation in marriage patterns among Jews and between Jews and non-Jews.

SIX

Household Structure and Living Arrangements

Marriage and marital stability link Jews to the community through a broad network of family relationships. The family is an important center for ritual activities, often more so than formal institutions, and therefore is a major structure reinforcing ethnic continuity. Jewish communal institutions are organized mainly around married couples and/or their children. Hence, they serve as a further basis for linking couples and their families to other Jews. The evidence pointing to continuing high levels of family formation and stability among Jews implies a strong basis of Jewish cohesion.

In this context, the period between the time that children leave the parental home and their marriage becomes a critical gap in which family and community ties are weaker. If children remain in the parental home until they marry, group ties are more likely to remain strong. If, on the other hand, children become residentially independent before marriage, they may have fewer linkages to the Jewish community.

Similarly, at a later stage of the life cycle, for those who are no longer married (because of the death of the spouse) and have not remarried, a break with family and community may occur. Again, these persons may be incorporated into families (e.g., they may move in with their children to create an extended household), but if they live alone, their ties to the family and perhaps to the community will change and may become weaker. Therefore, issues of group continuity among those who are not married and not living with families focus on the younger and older segments of the adult life cycle.

Living alone or in households that do not contain other family members does not necessarily imply the lack of other forms of family interaction. Nevertheless, issues associated with privacy, independence, and companionship, as well as attitudes and values regarding broader family responsibilities and obligations are related to living arrangements and household structure (Kobrin and Goldscheider 1983). A strong group norm on family cohesion would lead to the expectation of continued family living arrangements among younger and older persons. On the other hand, the value placed on family continuity and ethnic ties may be balanced by an emphasis on the independence of children and of other unmarried adults.

74

Research has documented the increase in one-person households as alternatives to extended household patterns. Indeed, the proportion of the life cycle that persons live with other family members is diminishing as both younger and older people live away from families. Family residence has become less continuous over the life cycle (Kobrin 1976a; Kobrin 1976b).

While there has been little systematic research on ethnic differences in household structure and residential choice, a substantial literature exists on family variations among white ethnics in the United States, showing by inference their different family values and kinship norms. In turn, these family patterns have been linked to social and geographic mobility (e.g., Kobrin and Goldscheider 1978).

A study of southern and eastern Europeans based on 1970 U.S. census data compared the living arrangements of those who declared Greek, Polish, Russian, or Yiddish as the language spoken in the home when they were growing up. The vast majority of them were first- and second-generation Americans. For each age group, Yiddish and Russian-speaking groups had a higher proportion living away from the family than either the U.S. total or other groups. Those who reported Yiddish as their mother tongue were significantly more likely to live away from kin, even when life cycle and income were controlled. One conclusion inferred from this statistic is that ethnic groups have different family values, which are expressed in terms of household living arrangements (Korbin and Goldscheider 1983). Consistent with these patterns are data on attitudes toward independence. Jews tend to express stronger norms of independence for their children when compared to non-Jews (Cherlin and Celebuski 1983).

This chapter focuses on patterns of living arrangements of Jews and non-Jews to analyze the extent of premarital residential independence and the incorporation of older non-married persons into the nuclear household. The relative importance of Jewish values and structural factors will be examined as the determinants of variation between groups and within the life cycle. Finally, we shall address directly the impact of non-family living arrangements on Jewish cohesion.

HOUSEHOLD STRUCTURE OF JEWS: THE BASIC PATTERNS

The basic pattern of living arrangements of Jews may be observed with the data in table 6.1, which are presented separately for men and women and by age to capture the sharp life cycle variation. For example, about 20 percent of Jewish males 18–29 years of age live alone, compared to 4 percent of those age 30–59 and 32 percent of those 60 years of age and older. Among the oldest males, 64 percent live in the classic nuclear household (husband-wife or husband-wife-children), about 5 percent live in quasi-

TABLE 6.1
Household Structure by Age, Sex, and Religion

	Living Alone	Husband-Wife	Husband-Wife-Children	Single Parent and Child(ren)	Individual with Relatives	Individual with Non-relatives
Jews						
Males						
18–29	19.3	20.7	13.1	0.1	8.0	38.3
30–44	4.4	16.3	64.4	3.0	1.1	10.7
45–59	4.0	17.0	68.5	8.9	1.6	0.0
60+	31.7	53.2	10.5	4.6	0.0	0.0
Females						
18–29	21.3	18.5	16.2	1.5	8.0	34.5
30–44	8.0	6.0	80.6	4.4	1.0	0.0
45–59	12.7	36.8	44.0	1.9	4.6	0.0
60+	39.3	37.6	3.6	4.8	13.0	1.6
Non-Jews						
Males						
18–29	15.0	16.4	25.7	4.3	19.3	19.3
30–44	11.2	8.4	65.4	1.9	8.4	4.7
45–59	11.6	25.3	56.8	1.1	4.2	1.1
60+	20.3	57.0	16.5	1.3	5.1	0.0
Females						
18–29	14.0	16.7	22.7	20.7	13.3	12.7
30–44	3.1	6.1	58.0	27.5	2.3	3.1
45–59	19.7	30.8	31.6	12.0	4.3	1.7
60+	56.3	28.2	2.8	7.7	3.5	1.4

nuclear households (as a single parent with children), and the rest live alone. This pattern contrasts with that of the youngest males, where 39 percent live with nonrelatives (mostly students), one-third are in nuclear households, and 19 percent live alone.

A detailed examination of the life cycle sequence for males is revealing. In the youngest adult ages, 92 percent of the males have moved away from their family of orientation. About one-third form new families; most live with nonrelatives or alone. In the 30–44 age group, over 80 percent are in classic nuclear households and 3 percent are in quasi-nuclear households. Almost all males not in nuclear households move away from their relatives, to live either with nonrelatives (11 percent) or alone (4 percent). Between ages 45 and 59, 95 percent of the Jewish males are in nuclear households. As children leave home and spouses die, a smaller number of older males are in nuclear households (69 percent). Those not in nuclear households live alone. In large part, despite major life cycle fluctuations, there is no evidence that Jewish males who are not in nuclear households tend to live with family or kin. The overwhelming impression is of either nucleation or independence for males.

We expect the living arrangements for women to differ from those for men, given the younger ages at which women marry, their lower rates of remarriage, and their higher life expectancy. Jewish women have often been portrayed as being more protected in the family. If so, they should be expected to remain longer in households dominated by family and other relatives. The data, however, show that such is not the case. There are indeed striking parallels between the living arrangements of Jewish women and men. In the youngest adult ages, 90 percent of the Jewish women leave home—one-third to marry, one-third to live with non-relatives, and one-fifth to live alone.

Reflecting high rates of marriage and marital stability, over 90 percent of the Jewish women 30–44 are in nuclear households; the remainder live alone. Only 1 percent live with relatives, a pattern similar to the male pattern. This pattern continues into the next age group, where 83 percent are in nuclear households. That is somewhat lower than for Jewish men, reflecting age differences between men and women in families. About 17 percent of the women age 45–59 are in nonnuclear households. Of these, 73 percent live alone, and the rest live with relatives; for Jewish males the proportions are similar. Thus, while more women than men are in non-nuclear households, the relative proportion of those living alone or in extended households is the same.

In the oldest age group, a significant number of women (24 percent of those in nonnuclear households) live with relatives. This pattern does not characterize Jewish men. In short, among older Jews, women are much more likely than men to extend a household by living with relatives. Most older men and women who are not in nuclear households, however, live alone.

While these data provide interesting contrasts by life cycle and gender, their major value lies in comparison to data for non-Jews. In particular, we want to identify whether there are any particularly Jewish patterns in household structure which point to greater (or lesser) kinship ties.

We start with comparisons between Jews and non-Jews in the youngest ages. More non-Jews than Jews start new families by marrying (46 compared to 34 percent). But the contrasts are even sharper when the timing of childbearing is considered. While 61 percent of Jewish men in nuclear households are in husband- or wife-only households, 61 percent of non-Jewish men in nuclear households have children. These contrasts reflect differentials in the timing of marriage and the tempo of childbearing (see chapters 5 and 7).

Non-Jewish men age 18–29 who do not marry are equally divided between those who live with relatives and nonrelatives (36 percent each) and the remainder (28 percent), who live alone. The proportion of Jews living alone is about the same (30 percent), but significantly more Jewish than non-Jewish men live with nonrelatives. Hence, while 85 percent of the Jewish males who do not live in nuclear households live away from family and relatives, this pattern characterizes only 64 percent of the non-Jews.

Early residential independence coupled with later family formation is therefore a more dominant feature of Jewish than non-Jewish males. That implies a longer period of time between leaving home and starting a family, and an even longer time to have children. To the extent that family formation and various aspects of Jewishness are related, such time gaps take on particular significance.

The major contrast among males age 30–44 is among those not in nuclear households: non-Jews are much more likely than Jews to live with relatives (8.4 percent out of 24.3 percent, or 35 percent of non-Jews not in nuclear households compared to 7 percent of Jews). This trend is less characteristic of the 45–59 age group.

Consistent with their higher proportion married, about three-fourths of the oldest non-Jewish males live in nuclear households, compared to 69 percent of the Jewish males. All the other Jews live alone, while 20 percent of the non-Jewish men not in nuclear households live with relatives. For Jewish adult males, therefore, the choice in living arrangements is between nuclear households or living alone, with very few young or old persons remaining with parents or living with other relatives. In this sense, Jewish values on living with family and kin are less important than values on residential independence among Jewish males.

Does the lack of household extension among Jewish males characterize Jewish women? The answer varies for younger and older Jewish women in comparison to non-Jewish women. For women age 18–29, a slightly higher number of non-Jewish women are in the classic nuclear household (39 compared to 34 percent). But the major contrast is the higher proportion of these who have children—58 percent of non-Jewish households are husband-wife-children, compared to 47 percent of the Jewish households. Thus, the timing of childbearing is later for younger Jewish women, even if age at marriage is not significantly later (cf. chapter 5). Moreover, the quasi-nuclear family (single parent with child[ren]) is significantly more common among non-Jewish women.

What characterizes women who are not in nuclear households? Jewish women (like Jewish men) leave home and their family of orientation in much larger numbers than non-Jewish women. When not getting married and having children, i.e., when not forming new nuclear households, non-Jewish women are almost three times as likely to live with relatives as are Jewish women. Of all women in nonnuclear households, 33 percent of the non-Jews live with relatives, compared to 13 percent of the Jews. This pattern is identical to that for males.

These patterns begin to change and contrast more clearly with the male pattern at the later life cycle stages. For the 45–59 age group, 75 percent of the non-Jewish women and 83 percent of the Jewish women are in nuclear households. Jewish women are more likely to be in intact families (with spouse with or without children) than non-Jews, who are more concentrated in quasi-nuclear households. The major contrast again is among women in nonnuclear households: more Jewish women than non-Jewish women live with relatives (27 percent compared to 17 percent).

This pattern appears more strongly among older Jewish women. Jewish women age 60 and over are more likely than non-Jewish women to be in intact households and in nuclear households, in general. About 61 percent of the non-Jewish women do not live in nuclear households. Of these, only 6 percent (3.5 percent out of 61.2 percent) live with relatives, while 92 percent live alone. Among Jewish women not in nuclear households, 73 percent live alone, and almost one-fourth (13 percent out of 54 percent) live with relatives. In short, there is much more of a family-kinship household pattern among older Jewish women than non-Jewish women. But this extended family pattern does not characterize males or earlier stages of the life cycle. Given the variation by age and sex and the contrasts between Jews and non-Jews, it becomes clear that there is no overarching Jewish value on residential arrangements. Structural features associated with the roles of older women compared to men in the household seem to be more important.

We have compared Jews to all non-Jews within sex and age categories. A further breakdown by religion (comparing Protestants and Catholics) shows similar patterns. There are no important differences between them. Major differences, however, characterize ethnic variation among Catholics. Given the very different family patterns of Italians and Irish (cf. Kobrin and Goldscheider 1978; Greeley 1974; Greeley 1976), the differential patterns of living arrangements are not surprising. To analyze these in detail would take us too far from our main theme. Nevertheless, two points are worth noting. First, Italian Catholics are conspicuous by the very small number who live alone compared to other Catholics and Protestants. Overall, the proportion of Irish Catholics or white Protestants who live alone is identical but is two-and-a-half times higher than the proportion of Italian Catholics. This pattern is particularly true for Italian women. (Thirty percent of Irish women live alone, compared to 9 percent of Italian women.) This pattern also characterizes each of the life cycle stages. Among women age 60 and over, half the Irish women live alone, compared to 23 percent of the Italian women. That Italian family ties are stronger than Irish is a well-known and documented feature in American ethnic studies. The Italian family pattern, in contrast to the Jewish, is characterized by low levels of residential independence.

Secondly, none of these ethnic contrasts modify in any fundamental way the major findings about Jewish–non-Jewish differences. For Jews, in contrast to all others examined, family extension in terms of living arrangements is largely confined to older women. Younger Jews leave home early, starting their own households by marrying or living alone. Jewish males continue this pattern over the life cycle; Jewish women are more likely to be part of an extended household at the older ages.

EDUCATION AND HOUSEHOLD STRUCTURE

How much do the differences in living arrangements of Jews and non-Jews reflect their levels of educational attainment? Does education weaken the bonds between generations by moving younger and older persons away from families? As educational levels increase, can we expect that younger and older persons will increase their residential independence from families? Does residential independence reflect the ability to buy privacy and to afford to live alone?

We start with the education of women (table 6.2). About half the Jewish women are married (and are therefore in nuclear households), irrespective of educational level. Only women with postgraduate educations have a lower proportion in nuclear households (44 percent). The distinguishing feature for Jewish women with only a high-school education is not earlier marriage but earlier childbearing and single parenting (i.e., separation and divorce with children). Over three-fourths of the women with a high-school education who live in nuclear households had children, compared to from one-third to one-half of those with higher educational levels. Hence, the timing of childbearing is affected by educational attainment, not by marriage per se; early childbearing associated with single parenting is characteristic of the less educated. This pattern characterizes Jewish as well as non-Jewish women.

Among women who are not in nuclear households, only the less educated Jewish women live with family among those 18–29. In contrast, college-educated women tend to live alone or with nonrelatives if they are not part of a nuclear household. For the less educated, therefore, the choice is to form a new household by marrying or to live with their family of orientation. For the more educated, the choice is to marry or to move out away from the family. Given these differential choices, it is not surprising that the less educated marry and the more educated move out to live independently.

Compared to non-Jews, however, less-educated Jewish women 18–29 are more likely to live alone and less likely to be in classic or quasi-nuclear households. Non-Jewish women with a high-school level of education who have never married tend to live with family members (i.e., largely with parents). This pattern is less characteristic of Jewish than non-Jewish women at that educational level.

There are few differences between Jewish and non-Jewish women in household structure among higher educational levels of this age group. The major difference relates not to nuclear living arrangements or family extension but to the timing of childbearing, which is delayed longer among Jews than non-Jews.

TABLE 6.2
Household Structure by Age, Education of Women, and Religion

	Living Alone	Husband-Wife	Husband-Wife-Children	Single Parent and Child(ren)	Individual with Relatives	Individual with Non-relatives
Jews						
18–29						
High school	18	12	31	9	19	11
Some college	18	35	19	0	16	12
College graduate	7	33	16	0	1	44
Postgraduate	26	22	22	0	1	29
30–44						
High school	9	7	83	0	1	0
Some college	1	15	81	3	0	0
College graduate	0	24	73	3	1	0
Postgraduate	7	4	86	3	0	0
45–59						
High school	7	33	59	1	1	0
Some college	9	39	48	2	2	0
College graduate	2	13	77	1	7	0
Postgraduate	19	40	40	0	2	0
60 +						
High school	27	52	10	5	6	1
Some college	23	39	4	0	32	2
College graduate	38	54	3	2	4	0
Postgraduate	32	54	4	0	4	7
Non-Jews						
18–29						
High school	1	17	45	29	9	0
Some college	18	26	24	4	16	13
College graduate	21	28	21	3	5	23
Postgraduate	14	43	21	0	0	21
30–44						
High school	2	6	71	20	1	0
Some college	0	7	74	16	2	0
College graduate	4	19	58	8	8	4
45–59						
High school	8	32	46	10	3	1
Some college	23	20	53	0	3	0
College graduate	6	33	61	0	0	0
60 +						
High school	39	42	9	6	3	1
Some college	43	43	4	4	4	4
College graduate	33	42	17	8	0	0

In the middle ages (30–59), most Jewish and non-Jewish women are in nuclear households. The major difference is in the significantly larger proportion of non-Jewish women in quasi-nuclear households (within educational levels). Among those age 45–59, Jewish women who have postgraduate educational levels seem to be disproportionately in non-nuclear households. We cannot compare them to non-Jewish women, since there were too few in our sample. Their proportion relative to Jewish women age 30–44 of this educational category is higher. That suggests a pattern of residential independence among never-married, professionally educated Jewish women of this cohort (19 percent). It appears as a passing stage, perhaps associated with delayed marriage and nonmarriage of the late depression and early war years. (These women were born between 1916 and 1930.)

The majority of older Jewish women are in intact families, with some variation by education. Most of the Jewish women not in nuclear households live alone. But comparisons to non-Jewish women of similar educational levels suggest that more Jewish women live with relatives than non-Jewish women. For example, among high-school-educated non-Jewish women who are not in nuclear households, only 7 percent live with relatives, compared to 18 percent among Jewish women. None of the non-Jewish women who graduated from college live with relatives (all live alone), compared to 10 percent among Jewish women.

In sum, household differences between Jews and non-Jews characterize all educational levels and do not reflect solely educational differences. Most younger Jewish women move away from their parents' homes when they marry, or they live alone or with nonrelatives. That is less true for high-school-educated compared to college-educated Jewish women, but more characteristic of high-school-educated Jewish than non-Jewish women. For older women, the reverse pattern found in general also characterizes each educational level: Jewish women not in nuclear households are more likely than non-Jewish women to live with family.

The household pattern for young Jewish men is similar to that for young Jewish women for each of the educational levels. Three points stand out: (1) Jewish men with a high-school education tend to marry and establish a nuclear household earlier than those with higher levels of education. The alternative living arrangement for the less educated is to stay at home with parents. Hence, early nest leaving among Jews is associated with some college education. (2) The more educated Jewish men tend to establish a nuclear household but delay having children (except for postgraduates, who are somewhat older in this age group). (3) More-educated Jews who do not set up a nuclear household move away from family by living alone or with nonrelatives (table 6.3).

The greater family attachments of less-educated young Jews compared to more-educated Jews characterize comparisons with non-Jews. A larger number of Jews with high-school education (age 18–29) establish a nuclear household than non-Jews, and a larger number remain with their families of orientation if they do not marry.[1] The greater family orientation of the young, less-educated Jewish males does not extend to higher educational levels. For example, among Jews age 18–29 with some college education who have not established a nuclear household, only 9 percent live with relatives, compared to 38 percent among non-Jews.

For the middle ages (30–59), among the small number of those not in nuclear households, more non-Jews than Jews live with relatives. Similarly, for those age 60 and over, Jewish men live either in nuclear households or by themselves. That characterizes each educational level. For non-Jews of this age group, with high-school- or college-graduate-level educations, a significant number (13 percent and 50 percent respectively) live with relatives.

In sum, the pattern of greater independence of Jewish males from families characterizes all educational levels and contrasts with the pattern for non-Jews within educational level.

Our measure of family income is problematic for an analysis of household structure, since we do not know how many persons share the income or how many wage earners are in the household. The large number of nonresponses to this question introduces additional restrictions. In particular, people who live alone have but one income, while people in nuclear or extended households will have reported on the income of larger families. Comparisons between Jews and non-Jews within income levels (rather than internal comparisons by income), however, should have less bias. While the details are not presented in tabular form, two findings are important: (1) The general differences between Jews and non-Jews in living arrangements are not eliminated with income controlled. Household structure variations within income levels continue to characterize Jews and non-Jews. (2) The greater concentration of older Jewish women in extended family households is not simply a function of lower income. It is not because older Jewish women (who are not in nuclear households) cannot afford to live alone. Among those 60 and over in the $20–35,000 income category, for example, a larger proportion of Jews than non-Jews not in nuclear households lives with relatives rather than alone. Incorporating older men may be a greater threat to independence and may involve less contribution by them to the functioning of the household. Older women, however, may be less threatening and can contribute more to household chores. That is particularly the case when labor force participation of younger women is high (see chapter 8).

1. The number of Jewish males with only a high-school education is small and may be selective negatively in a variety of ways. Caution should be used in interpreting these numbers too closely.

TABLE 6.3
Household Structure by Age, Education of Men, and Religion

	Living Alone	Husband-Wife	Husband-Wife-Children	Single Parent and Child(ren)	Individual with Relatives	Individual with Non-relatives
Jews						
18–29						
High school	0	38	38	1	23	0
Some college	18	30	13	0	5	35
College graduate	17	35	7	0	9	33
Postgraduate	12	29	38	0	1	21
30–44						
High school	0	0	100	0	0	0
Some college	0	66	31	0	3	0
College graduate	1	18	67	5	1	9
Postgraduate	5	2	85	0	1	7
45–59						
High school	0	36	64	0	0	0
Some college	0	31	38	31	0	0
College graduate	1	26	70	1	2	0
Postgraduate	8	28	61	2	1	0
60 +						
High school	22	64	10	4	0	0
Some college	8	80	13	0	0	0
College graduate	26	71	3	0	0	0
Postgraduate	4	85	12	0	0	0
Non-Jews						
18–29						
High school	5	19	44	6	19	8
Some college	8	14	35	2	19	23
College graduate	23	36	26	0	5	10
Postgraduate	14	43	25	0	0	18
30–44						
High school	7	7	75	2	7	3
Some college	4	12	77	0	4	4
College graduate	7	3	87	0	0	3
Postgraduate	5	26	68	0	0	0
45–59						
High school	8	39	49	1	4	0
Some college	6	41	47	0	6	0
College graduate	5	24	71	0	0	0
Postgraduate	0	13	80	0	0	7
60 +						
High school	14	72	11	1	2	0
Some college	17	58	25	0	0	0
College graduate	6	69	19	0	6	0

LIVING ARRANGEMENTS AND JEWISHNESS

What factors account for the specific Jewish patterns of living arrangements? Clearly, educational, income, and life cycle factors affect variations in household structure, but differences between Jews and non-Jews cannot be accounted for solely by socioeconomic and demographic characteristics. In general, it is difficult to argue that specific religious values are key factors, since patterns of early nest leaving characterize both sexes, and greater household extension is specific to Jewish women, not men. Data on Jewish family or religious values are not readily available to test this explanation fully. An indirect way to address this question is to examine the household patterns of Orthodox, Conservative, Reform, or nondenominational Jews. If Jewish values emphasize family and kinship relationships (and are shared by those who identify with organized Judaism), we would expect that a higher proportion of more-traditional Jews would be living in families than less-traditional Jews. Certainly, we should expect more of those who identify themselves within religious denominations to live in families than those who are nondenominational.

To examine this issue, we organized the household data to focus on those not living in families (i.e., those who live alone or with nonrelatives). The complement of the figures in each cell is those living in nuclear or extended households (table 6.4). These are presented by age and sex, because of the importance of life cycle, which has already been documented. The data show few consistent patterns among the religious denominations or between them and the nondenominational. Among young males 18–44 years of age, for example, the lowest proportion not living in families characterizes the Reform males, with Conservative and nondenominational Jews about the same. In contrast, the highest proportion living in families characterizes Reform females 18–29, compared to Conservative and nondenominational Jews. Similar patterns characterize those age 45–59: nondenominational males have the highest proportion not living in families, while nondenominational females have the lowest proportion living away from families. Finally, an examination of older Jews suggests that Orthodox males tend to be most likely to be in nonfamilies, and Reform males are least likely. No significant differences characterize older Jewish women by denomination.

While these data show no particular patterns, there is much to be inferred from "negative" findings. First, it is unlikely that the greater incorporation of older Jewish women into extended households and the greater probability of older Jewish men living alone are the consequences of Jewish values in some simple sense. Second, there is no indication that the identification with a particular denomination (or any denomination) is an important factor in the choice of living arrangements among those who are not part of a nuclear household. Finally, the variations by age and sex are powerful indicators of the structural bases of living arrangements. Life cycle factors, the differential roles of men and women, and perhaps more

Table 6.4
Proportion not Living in Families
(i.e., Living Alone or With Nonrelatives)
by Age, Sex, and Religious Denomination

	Males	Females
18–29		
Conservative	69.7	41.0
Reform	53.8	67.8
Other	69.9	53.7
30–44		
Conservative	17.1	12.9
Reform	10.6	7.0
Other	79.0	*
45–59		
Conservative	1.4	14.3
Reform	0.0	15.4
Other	14.5	2.7
60+		
Orthodox	51.9	37.4
Conservative	26.8	36.3
Reform	10.0	32.7

general kinship and family values are the determinants of living arrangements. Religious denominational identification and, by inference, preference for traditional values seem to be of little consequence in this process. Thus, there is little about the preference structure of living arrangements or the inferred familism associated with the greater household extension of Jewish women which is related to religious values.

There is another dimension to the issue of living arrangements which relates directly to Jewish continuity. In the past, the family, and by inference residence in the same household, represented a major source of Jewish socialization. The changing structure of households, in combination with changing neighborhoods and mobility (see chapters 3 and 4), has been viewed as a problem for Jewish continuity. If the long-term transition has been from extended to nuclear households, over the last several decades there has been a further change toward single-person households at both ends of the adult life cycle. Living away from the family has raised concerns about the breakdown of family life and the core of Jewish socialization. We have documented the extent to which early nest leaving and residential independence among the older population characterize the Jewish community. We now investigate directly whether these new family forms have implications for Jewish continuity.

The analytic question is straightforward: Do those who live in family and nonfamily households differ in terms of various dimensions of Jewishness? Given the household variation over the life cycle and the relationship between Jewishness and age (chapter 10), we examine these within age cohorts and separately for men and women (table 6.5). In particular, we address whether nonfamily living arrangements imply greater detachments from the Jewish community.[2]

The evidence does not support unequivocally the argument that living in a family results in a greater attachment to Judaism or to Jewishness. For example, among young males, differences between those in family and those in nonfamily households are small and not statistically significant. A larger percentage of young Jews in families than in nonfamilies tend to have mostly Jewish friends, live in mostly Jewish neighborhoods, and prefer Jewish neighborhoods. On the other hand, those in nonfamilies tend to attend synagogue more regularly and rank higher on family ritual and ethnic-community dimensions. Moreover, even among the young in nonfamily households, 65 percent have mostly Jewish friends, most identify denominationally, and most participate in religious rituals associated with the family. Those data do not describe alienation or rejection of the Jewish community.

Among older males, as well, the patterns are not sharply different for those in families and those not in families. One major difference is the proportion observing rituals that are family-related—94 percent of those in families observe them, compared to 64 percent of those not in families. This tendency may, however, simply reflect the absence of family with which to celebrate religious events, rather than a residential choice which reflects Jewish disaffection. Similar differences characterize older women.

Over 80 percent of the young women' living away from families have mostly Jewish friends, and about the same proportions of those living outside, or within, families live in mostly Jewish neighborhoods, identify denominationally, and observe religious rituals in a family setting. Women in nonfamily households are less likely than those in family households to see living in Jewish neighborhoods as a Jewish value, to attend synagogue regularly, to have specific Jewish values, or to observe personal religious rituals. While some of these patterns also characterize older Jewish women, it is clear that household living arrangements are not consistently related to Jewish discontinuity.

Two major conclusions of these data should be stressed. First, variations in household structure and living arrangements between Jews and non-

2. A detailed discussion of these dimensions will be presented in chapter 10. Briefly, these items refer to the percentage (1) who said that at least half of their friends are Jewish; (2) who said that most of their neighbors were Jewish; (3) who defined living in a Jewish neighborhood as a Jewish value; (4) who attended synagogue services every few months or more; (5) who identified themselves as Orthodox, Conservative, or Reform; and who ranked high on (6) a Jewish values scale, (7) a personal ritual scale, (8) a family ritual scale, and (9) a community-ethnic scale.

TABLE 6.5
Measures of Jewishness by Household Structure, Age, and Sex

	Percent Mostly Jewish Friends	Percent Mostly Jewish Neighbors	Prefer Living in Jewish Neighborhood	Regular Synagogue Attendance	Percent Denominational	High Jewish Values	Personal Ritual	Family Ritual	Ethnic-Community Activities
Males									
18–29									
Family	73.9	43.2	42.2	15.6	69.1	16.4	17.0	63.3	13.6
Nonfamily	64.9	31.9	25.9	18.5	59.1	10.7	10.2	66.3	17.6
60+									
Family	82.6	38.1	52.1	50.3	91.1	67.5	40.8	93.9	51.7
Nonfamily	82.2	32.5	63.3	43.0	92.7	58.2	35.5	63.9	33.2
Females									
18–29									
Family	78.6	51.3	48.8	25.0	61.4	29.0	17.5	67.2	34.4
Nonfamily	82.6	51.7	31.6	10.2	68.5	18.5	3.1	71.3	18.5
45–59									
Family	94.2	55.5	42.9	44.8	81.1	50.5	38.0	90.5	35.0
Nonfamily	96.4	51.8	43.5	43.4	96.4	42.4	40.0	47.0	18.8
60+									
Family	99.3	55.8	65.1	28.8	94.5	75.1	49.6	78.7	58.2
Nonfamily	79.2	47.6	53.0	15.8	75.0	55.4	59.4	59.4	29.7

Jews do not seem to reflect Jewish norms and values. They are primarily the consequence of educational and marriage patterns, life cycle, and gender variation. Structural determinants are the major influences in the living arrangements of Jews; perhaps norms and values underlie these determinants and, as a result, affect living arrangements indirectly.

A second conclusion relates to the concern that changes in living arrangements, particularly the move away from the nuclear family, would have major consequences for Jewish continuity. The evidence presented suggests that such concerns are misplaced. There seems to be no direct relationship between family structural changes and alienation from the Jewish community. Changes in living arrangements which imply greater residential independence from families are not necessarily associated with "loss" to the Jewish community or assimilation. Structural changes in the direction of nonfamily residence are not equivalent to the decline and weakening of the Jewish community.

SEVEN

Reproduction and Fertility Expectations

Over the last several decades, research in the United States has demonstrated that Jews have lower fertility than the American population as a whole. Major fertility surveys, data from official government sources, and national and local Jewish community studies have confirmed this observation consistently for a wide range of fertility and fertility-related measures. Indicators of fertility norms, desires, expectations, actual family size, and annual birth and reproduction rates all point in the same direction: American Jewish couples want, plan, and have small families. Fertility among Jews is low in absolute level as well as relative to the fertility of other religious, ethnic, and racial groups in the United States (see Goldscheider 1982; Goldstein 1981a; DellaPergola 1980).

Reproductive patterns and the size of families are issues central to Jewish continuity in its most basic form. Fertility levels and variations relate to population growth, on the one hand, and Jewish family structure, on the other. Large family size has been associated nostalgically with the distant past, where the size of immigrant families was supposedly large and by inference warm and protective. More recently, small family size has been associated with the demographic decline of American Jews, who, so the argument goes, are not reproducing in sufficient numbers for replacement and are headed for extinction. A systematic examination of what is known about Jewish fertility in the United States does not support either assertion. Jewish fertility in the United States has been low for cohorts marrying over the last fifty or sixty years and lower than that for non-Jews for well over a century. Nor does the recent evidence on Jewish reproductive patterns suggest that American Jews are, or will be, facing a demographic crisis based on low marital fertility.

PREVIOUS FINDINGS: AN OVERVIEW

In contrast to the paucity of data on many aspects of Jewish demography, a wide range of data sources and research studies has been available to analyze in detail Jewish fertility patterns in the United States. Precisely because we know more about Jewish fertility patterns in America, the analytic questions have become more sophisticated and the issues more

90

complex. That, in turn, demands even more systematic and detailed re-search. Fertility fluctuations over the last several decades have been sub-stantial and have been responsive to economic fluctuations, war and post-war social changes, and the revolutions in women's roles and sexual norms. Annual birth rates have varied much more than completed family size. Changes in population composition (for example, in the number of women of reproductive age) and changes in marriage patterns (the propor-tions married and ages at marriage) have important effects on annual birth rates, reproduction, and population replacement, and often on family size as well. Changes in the timing of births and the tempo of childbearing and family formation are also important for an understanding of fertility trends and differentials.

A variety of data sources (including limited census and birth records, major fertility surveys, and Jewish community studies) have provided a reasonably sound basis for the following conclusions:

First, low Jewish fertility is clearly not a new American pattern. As far as can be discerned from the available data by marriage cohort, fluctua-tions around replacement-level fertility characterized Jewish marriage co-horts as early as the mid-1920s. Marriage cohort data in one study (Goldscheider 1966) reveal that the average Jewish family size of those marrying before 1910 was 3.5 children, declining to 2 children for the cohorts marrying between 1925 and 1944. Moreover, the postwar marriage cohorts, as was true for other American couples, experienced an increase in family size to around 2.3 children. The decline and postwar increase are indicated not only by average family size but by specific parity data. Retrospective analysis of cohort patterns and reconstructed period rates from the National Jewish Population Survey confirm these patterns (Del-laPergola 1980). Similar prewar declines and postwar increases have been reported when family size was examined by generation. The increase in family size among third-generation Jews may have been followed by a subsequent turndown, particularly for marriage cohorts of the 1960s and 1970s. That would parallel what has happened in the American population in general. Period data on annual births of Jews between 1967 and 1969 point in that direction. It is, however, unclear whether these period rates will reflect eventual family size or whether changes in the timing and tempo of childbearing have pushed these annual rates to unprecedented low levels (cf. Goldstein 1981a).

It is important to note that an examination of the fertility of married couples may differ from an examination of the fertility of the total Jewish population when there are significant proportions nonmarried or when there are delays in marriage and childbearing. Similarly, cohort patterns (births to women who marry or are born during a particular time period) may differ from a cross-sectional view of annual birth rates. Both perspec-tives are necessary for a full examination of fertility levels. An examination of family size changes among different cohorts of women as they pass through their childbearing cycle is essential for a view of completed family size and the dynamics of family formation. Data of this type have not been available for recent marriage cohorts among Jews. In the 1960s, families of orientation and procreation were small in size: almost all Jewish women who were giving birth during this period were characterized by relatively small families, efficient contraceptive usage, and the planning of the number and spacing of all births. Almost all had grown-up children in small families as well.

During the 1960s and 1970s, some delayed marriage and nonmarriage began to emerge among American Jews (see chapter 5). These marriage and family-formation changes have been accompanied by changes in the timing of childbearing among married women. If the proportion of women married declines significantly and delayed childbearing within marriage takes place, a family size of two to three children will not necessarily imply *annual* population replacement rates. While the long-range trend in Jewish fertility among married couples is toward the two-child family annual birth rates during the 1960s and 1970s may have been distorted by timing and marriage changes. A substantial part of the explanation of very low annual Jewish birth rates in the last decade lies in these combined changes in the timing of family formation and childbearing and in the number of Jewish persons entering the childbearing period.

Community planning, educational enrollments, and the general presence of children in communities are based not on a cohort view of childbearing but on the number of babies born in particular time periods. Delayed childbearing and nonmarriage, combined with the changing numbers of persons reaching the childbearing ages, the general low, replacement-level fertility of Jews, and the ability of Jewish couples to plan total family size and the spacing of all children have resulted in an impressive and conspicuous reduction in the number of Jewish children born in the decade of the 1970s.

Finally, when family size is low and marriage patterns, cohort age structure, and the timing of family formation and childbearing are all changing to push total fertility rates below population replacement, a small minority group cannot sustain losses due to either out-migration or out-marriage. Small population declines become problems when additional sociodemographic processes exaggerate that decline. For Jews in America, rates of intermarriage increased precisely during the period of the 1960s and early 1970s (see chapter 2). Young Jews marrying in this latter period were largely third- or fourth-generation Americans, characterized by lower levels of Jewish commitment. Even minimum net losses through out-marriage combined with these annual patterns of replacement fertility have raised the specter of the declining Jewish American population.

The low absolute and relative levels of Jewish fertility are consistent with the general socioeconomic and residential characteristics of Jews in the United States. The high level of educational attainment among Jews, their concentration in professional and managerial occupations, their higher incomes, and their unique urban-metropolitan distribution have been well documented. These characteristics, individually and in combination, have been generally associated with low fertility. Since fertility levels in general reflect these status and residential categories, the "uniqueness" of Jewish fertility, particularly its overall low level, reflects in large part the unique socioeconomic and ecological characteristics of the Jewish population.

Indeed, it has often been argued that as Jews become more educated and more concentrated in metropolitan areas, and as Jewish women become more career-oriented, working outside the family, fertility levels will further decline. The underlying assumption is that the links between these characteristics and fertility are similar among groups and that Jews are in the forefront of change.

Several pieces of evidence, however, suggest that such an explanation is incomplete. First, Jewish fertility tends to be lower than Protestant and Catholic fertility for those of similar socioeconomic and residential characteristics. A variety of national and local community studies have shown that fertility differences between Jews and non-Jews remain after the socioeconomic and residential variations have been controlled. Second, the socioeconomic and residential characteristics of Jews in the United States have been transformed, while fertility levels have remained low. It is not clear that the relationship between educational attainment and fertility, for example, is the same now as a generation ago or the same for Jews as for non-Jews.

There is no clear consensus among social scientists as to what additional factors need to be considered in studying Jewish fertility. Some have argued that social mobility factors are operating (Rosenthal 1961). Low fertility has been associated with the rise of Jews into the middle class. Indeed, even before attaining middle-class status, it is argued that Jews had a middle-class "mentality" and psychologically shared middle-class values, including small family size. Some have argued that low fertility relates to the changing role and status of Jewish women and their changing self-conceptions (Sklare 1971). Others have attempted to relate low fertility to broader patterns of assimilation and acculturation and have argued for a more comprehensive theory related to the changing nature of Jewish social structure and culture (Goldscheider 1971). This approach places particular emphasis on the changing role of minority group status, discrimination, and insecurity. While not neglecting social characteristics, social mobility, and changing roles and statuses of Jewish women, this view suggests that the uniqueness of Jewish fertility relates to the particular position of Jews in the social structure.

The Boston data allow us to address two key issues: (1) the changing levels of Jewish fertility for recent marriage cohorts and (2) the bases for continued Jewish uniqueness in reproductive behavior. Included in the survey were questions on the number of children ever born and the number of additional children expected. Since these questions were addressed to currently married women 18–45 years of age, the first question was insufficient for analyzing completed family size. The number of additional children expected for those whose childbearing was not complete provides a reasonable basis for estimation. General studies have found that expected fertility measures show very high aggregate prediction for actual fertility. That has been the case particularly for Jews (and socioeconomic groups) who plan and attain their family size desires with extreme accuracy (see Hendershot and Placek 1981; O'Connell and Moore 1977).

In the Boston data, we combined the total number of children ever born with the number of additional children expected, to yield an estimate of the total family size expected. These are the data presented in this chapter. It should be noted that despite the relative accuracy of prediction at the group level, specific focus will be less on the actual level than on the patterns. We shall look first at the differerences between Jews and non-Jews.

FERTILITY PATTERNS AND RELIGIOUS DIFFERENCES

The total expected family size of currently married Jewish women in Boston was 2.2 children (table 7.1 and figure 7.1). This level is sufficient for replacement of the married Jewish population. Whether it relates to all women or compensates for the nonmarried is open to question (cf. Goldscheider 1982; Goldscheider and Zuckerman 1984; see also chapter 5). This level of minimum replacement is consistent with the results of the National Jewish Population Survey and other studies (cf. DellaPergola 1980; Goldstein 1981a).

Almost half of the Jews expect two children as their completed family size, and few expect only one child or none; 30 percent expect three children. Few expect more than three children—94 percent expect fewer than four. How does this pattern compare with that of other groups? Consistent with the previous literature, the expected family size of Jews is lower than that of any other group considered. A detailed look at the data by parity reveals no particular Jewish preference for childless or one-child families and no disproportionate concentration in the two-to-three-child family size. White Protestants, for example, are quite similar to Jews in their concentration in two- or three-child parities. One key parity difference is in the four-or-more-child family. Only 6 percent of the Jews expect to have four or more children, compared to at least 20 percent for white ethnic and religious groups.

The data by marriage cohort and age show identical patterns: a clear-cut decline from older to younger Jewish persons in the number of children expected (tables 7.2 and 7.3). For the cohort of longest duration, average expected family size was 2.8 children; for the shortest-duration cohort

TABLE 7.1
Expected Family Size by Religion and Ethnicity

Total Expected Births	Total Non-Jews	Jews	Blacks	White Protestants	Irish Catholics	Italian Catholics	Other white Catholics
0	5.4	8.0	0.0	2.8	0.0	2.3	12.9
1	6.6	7.2	3.7	2.8	3.3	6.8	3.2
2	41.6	47.8	55.6	45.8	30.0	38.6	41.9
3	23.7	30.6	25.9	29.2	40.0	25.0	14.5
4+	22.5	6.3	14.8	19.5	26.7	27.2	27.4
Total	100.0	100.0	100.0	100.0	100.0	100.0	100.0
Average	2.7	2.2	2.7	2.8	3.2	2.9	2.6
N	257	701	27	72	30	44	62

Note: These and related data on expected births refer to currently married women age 18–45.

(1966–75), the number of children expected by Jewish couples is 1.9 children. The reduction from an average of 3 to 2 children reflects an increase in expectations of no children and of one-child families, as well as a continuous reduction in family-size expectations above 4 children. About one-fourth of the Jewish women married 1966–75 expected 3 or more children, compared to 68 percent of those married 1949–59. The major parity contrasts between those married 1960–65 and 1966–75 are in the significant increase in the recent cohort of childless and one-child families. Differences between Jews and non-Jews in the recent cohort reside in the higher proportion of non-Jews who expect 4 or more children (13 percent, compared to 3 percent among Jews) and the higher proportion of Jewish women who expect no children or only 1 child.

Again, we note that these are "expected" family size data. They may change over the life cycle; they should not be viewed as fixed targets that are imprinted and unalterable. It would not be surprising if, as younger

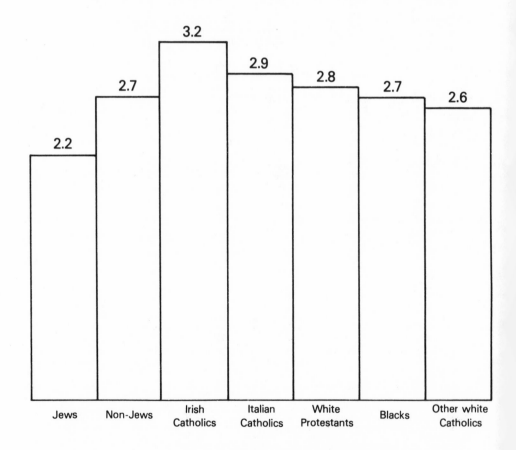

7.1   Expected Family Size by Religion and Ethnicity

TABLE 7.2
Average Expected Family Size by Religion, Ethnicity, and Age

	Total	18–29	30–39	40–45
Jews	2.2	1.9	2.2	2.8
Non-Jews	2.7	2.4	2.9	3.2
Blacks	2.7	2.5	2.6	*
White Protestants	2.8	2.6	2.8	3.4
Irish Catholics	3.2	2.7	3.1	*
Italian Catholics	2.9	2.3	3.4	2.8
Other white Catholics	2.6	2.2	2.8	3.1
Protestants	2.8	2.6	2.8	3.1
Catholics	2.8	2.4	3.2	3.3

TABLE 7.3
**Average Expected Family Size by Marriage Cohort,
Religion, and Ethnicity**

	MARRIAGE COHORT		
	1966–75	1960–65	1949–59
Jews	1.9	2.3	2.8
Non-Jews	2.4	2.9	3.2
Blacks	2.6	2.6	*
White Protestants	2.6	3.1	3.1
Irish Catholics	2.6	4.3[a]	*
Italian Catholics	2.4	3.5	3.2
Other white Catholics	2.3	2.8	3.2
Protestants	2.4	3.2	3.3
Catholics	2.6	2.8	3.1

[a] pre-1960

women have children, their family size expectations are revised upward. Nor would it be surprising if divorce and remarriage were to alter family size expectations.

Several additional comparative features of these data are noteworthy. Not all religious and ethnic groups have experienced downward shifts. For example, the expected family size of blacks does not vary by age or cohort, nor have white Protestants changed between the two oldest cohorts. All whites have shifted family size expectations downward between the two most recently married cohorts. These patterns are consistent with the general literature of the late 1960s and 1970s. As such, it provides support for the overall validity of our measure of expected family size.

Are variations between Jews and non-Jews a function of age and cohort?

The answer is clearly in the negative. For each marriage cohort and age, Jews have smaller family size expectations than non-Jews, Protestants as well as Catholics. The question of diminished differences between Jews and non-Jews is difficult to establish from the data available; there seems to be no basis for concluding that the gap in family size expectations between Jews and non-Jews has narrowed. Looking at marriage cohorts, for example, there was a 14 percent difference between Jews and non-Jews in the oldest cohort. For more recent cohorts, the gap has increased to 26 percent (1.9 compared to 2.4). Some convergence between Jews and Catholics seems to have occurred, largely because of the sharp decline in the mid-1960s in family size expectations among Catholics (cf. Westoff and Jones 1977; Mosher and Hendershot 1984).

SOCIOECONOMIC VARIATION AND FERTILITY CONVERGENCES

These patterns lead to the question whether convergence in fertility for specific socioeconomic groups within religious and ethnic communities has occurred. Concurrently, they raise the question whether distinctive Jewish fertility patterns reflect the socioeconomic characteristics of the Jews. More generally, given the overall pattern of low fertility levels and norms among American Jews, it is instructive to ask whether any subgroups within the American Jewish population have larger family size patterns.

On the basis of the evidence now available, it is reasonable to argue that there are few major differences in the fertility of contemporary American Jews. The American Jewish population has become relatively homogeneous in terms of major socioeconomic characteristics, compared to that of the past (see chapter 8). Moreover, there has been a diffusion of family planning practices and the development of overall American norms of small family size, such that all segments of the Jewish community, with but minor exceptions, have been exposed to and have adopted these norms. Indeed, for the American population as a whole, fertility differentials have converged substantially over the last decade. The traditional variables associated with higher fertility in America—rural residence, poverty, contraceptive ignorance, low education, farm and blue-collar occupations—are virtually nonexistent among Jewish men and women in the childbearing years.

Research available suggests that the traditional inverse relationship between socioeconomic status and fertility characterized only foreign-born, first-generation American Jews. For second- and third-generation Jewish couples, socioeconomic variation in fertility has been unclear, with some indication of a positive relationship, i.e., higher-status Jews had somewhat larger families than lower-status Jews. There is evidence of convergence and greater homogeneity in the fertility patterns of socioeconomic group-

TABLE 7.4
**Average Expected Family Size by Religion,
Cohort, and Education**

	Jews	Non-Jews
All Cohorts	2.2	2.7
High school	2.3	3.0
Some college	2.2	2.7
College graduate	2.1	2.1
Postgraduate	2.5	1.8
1949–59	2.8	3.2
High school	2.6	3.4
Some college	2.9	3.3
College graduate	2.9	*
Postgraduate	3.5	*
1960–65	2.3	2.9
High school	2.1	3.1
Some college	2.5	3.2
College graduate	2.2	*
Postgraduate	2.3	*
1966–75	1.9	2.4
High school	1.7	2.7
Some college	1.6	2.3
College graduate	1.8	2.2
Postgraduate	2.3	*

ings among American-born Jewish couples. The lack of wide social-class distinctions among third-generation Jews may account for the absence of striking fertility differences within the Jewish population (see Goldscheider 1967; Goldstein and Goldscheider 1968; Goldscheider 1982; Goldstein 1973b, 1981a).

The Boston data allow us to address two critical issues: (1) the relative effects of educational attainment on family size expectations and (2) the effects of changes in women's roles on family size. Our focus is first on the wife's educational level and family size expectations for three marriage cohorts (table 7.4). Overall, family size expectations of women with only a high-school level of education are slightly higher than for those with some college education or who are college graduates. But differences are small and not statistically significant. There is an interesting increase from those with a college education to those who have some postgraduate education. The most educated Jewish women have the largest family size expectations (2.5 children).

This pattern is interesting for several reasons. First, it does not characterize non-Jews, Protestant or Catholic. For non-Jews, there is a clear and consistent inverse relationship between educational attainment and fertility expectations. As a consequence of the different patterns for Jews and non-Jews, more-educated Jewish women have *higher* family size expectations than more-educated non-Jewish women. Second, the pattern implies that there is no necessary contradiction among Jewish women between postgraduate education and childbearing. As more Jewish women obtain higher levels of education, family size should not necessarily or automatically decline. If the data are accurate reflections of actual future fertility patterns, more-educated Jewish women will have larger families than previous cohorts. Predictions of demographic erosion for the Jewish community as a result of inadequate reproduction for generational replacement are not consistent with these data for married women.

Do these patterns characterize all marriage cohorts? For Jews, the higher fertility expectations of the more educated describe the 1949–59 and the 1966–75 cohorts. It is particularly important that women who married 1966–75 and had some postgraduate education had the highest family size expectations. Where comparisons are possible, these patterns uniquely describe Jewish couples. For non-Jews, the inverse relationship between education and fertility expectations characterizes each marriage cohort. For example, for the most recent cohort of non-Jewish women, high-school graduates expected 2.7 children, compared to 2.2 children expected among college graduates. For Jews, the parallel is 1.7 children compared to 2.3 children. Hence, fertility differences between Jews and non-Jews are much sharper among the less educated and older cohorts. The apparent convergence between Jews and non-Jews among the most educated and those with shorter marriage durations seems to reflect the different relationships between education and family size expectations— positive for Jews, inverse for non-Jews. That suggests, again by inference, that convergence is the result of changes on the part of Jewish *and* non-Jewish couples, rather than the movement of one toward the pattern of the other.

Given the importance of these conclusions for understanding Jewish fertility and demographic continuity, we pursued the same analysis by age groups instead of cohorts (table 7.5). These results parallel identically the patterns found for marriage cohorts. For the oldest (age 40–45) and youngest (age 18–29) age groups, women with the highest education had higher family size expectations. Of equal imortance are the simultaneous comparisons with non-Jews. Looking at married women age 18–29, Jewish women with postgraduate educations expected 2.2 children, compared to 1.6 for those with some college education. The respective figures for non-Jews are 2.1 children and 2.7 children. Not only do opposite patterns characterize Jews and non-Jews, but, as a result, differences in family size expectations between Jews and non-Jews characterize only lower educational levels.

Other indicators of socioeconomic status do not show a clear rela-

TABLE 7.5
Average Expected Family Size by Religion, Age, and Education

Age and Education	Jews	Non-Jews
18–29		
Total	1.9	2.4
High school	*	2.7
Some college	1.6	2.0
College graduate	2.1	2.1
Postgraduate	2.2	*
30–39		
Total	2.2	2.9
High school	2.3	3.0
Some college	2.5	3.2
College graduate	1.9	1.9
Postgraduate	2.4	*
40–45		
Total	2.8	3.2
High school	2.6	3.2
Some college	2.9	3.6
College graduate	2.6	*
Postgraduate	3.6	*

tionship to family size expectations. An analysis of family size expectations was less clear by husband's occupation or by family income than by education. Neither occupational status nor income is a powerful predictor of expected family size. Their effects are eliminated when marriage cohort and educational attainment are controlled statistically.

LABOR FORCE PARTICIPATION AND EXPECTED FERTILITY

A more important socioeconomic correlate of fertility is labor force participation of women. In general, there tends to be a strong negative correlation between labor force participation and fertility: women who work have fewer children than those who do not work. Partly this pattern relates to the incompatibility of work and family roles and the choices between careers and childbearing-childrearing activities. An unknown part of the relationship reflects selectivity factors: women who do not want children (or cannot have them) tend to work. Whether working patterns determine childbearing or fertility patterns determine participation in the labor force remains unclear. Cross-sectional designs cannot fully resolve this controversy (cf. Waite and Stolzenberg 1976; Kupinsky 1977).

The relationship between labor force participation and fertility is one of the most consistently reported in the literature. Since some have suggested that the role and status of women among Jews are important parts of the explanation of lower Jewish fertility, we can examine empirically whether the work-family role conflict characterizes Jewish women. Moreover, we can determine the extent to which lower Jewish than non-Jewish fertility reflects the different work patterns of Jews. Finally, it is important to recall that the educational and occupational patterns of women generally, and Jewish women particularly, have undergone revolutionary changes over the last decade (cf. chapter 8). The data allow us to examine whether the employment-career shifts for Jewish women are associated with accentuated lower fertility in the recent period. If there is an incompatibility between work and family roles, as more Jewish women enter into the labor force with long-term careers, Jewish fertility may decline further. These issues may be examined with the data on expected family size for women currently working or not.[1]

In contrast to the hypothesized negative correlation, few differences in expected family size appear among Jews (table 7.6). Expected family size is about the same for Jewish women who are currently working or not working, for each marriage cohort. If there is any direction to the data, it is the reverse of that expected: working women have larger family size expectations. There is some basis for arguing that work patterns have more important effects on the timing of childbearing than on family size. That may be the case particularly among those who effectively plan the spacing of children and the size of their families. These data clearly show that working does not interfere with family size goals of Jewish women.

Comparisons with Protestant and Catholic women reinforce the uniqueness of the Jewish pattern. In particular, the hypothesized relationship between working and lower fertility characterizes non-Jews, in general, and Protestants and Catholics, in particular. For each group and within each marriage cohort, non-Jewish women who work have smaller family size expectations than those who are not working. Overall, Jewish women have lower family size expectations than Catholic or Protestant women, controlling for work patterns. Nevertheless, the expected family size differences between Jews and non-Jews are much smaller among working women. The reduced gap between Jews and non-Jews largely reflects the major changes among non-Jewish women between the 1960–65 and 1966–75 cohorts. For Jewish women, the major changes took place between the 1949–59 and later cohorts.

These data suggest, therefore, that for younger Jewish women, labor force participation will not have any major impact on family size. To the extent that we can generalize further, the data imply that there is no conspicuous work-family role conflict for Jewish women. The incompatibility of working and childbearing, however, characterizes both Protestant and

---

1. A similar pattern emerges for women who ever worked compared to those who never worked, so these have not been included.

TABLE 7.6
**Average Expected Family Size by Labor Force
Participation of Women by Marriage Cohort and Religion**

		Marriage Cohorts		
	Total	1949–59	1960–65	1966–75
Jews				
Working	2.4	3.0	2.1	2.2
Not working	2.2	2.8	2.3	2.1
Non-Jews				
Working	2.5	2.9	2.6	2.2
Not working	2.9	3.7	3.1	2.4
Catholics				
Working	2.7	3.0	2.9	2.3
Not working	3.0	3.9	3.5	2.5
Protestants				
Working	2.5	2.8	*	2.4
Not working	3.0	3.6	3.1	2.5

Catholic women. Lower Jewish fertility appears to be a group phenomenon not particularly limited to working women or other subgroups
among Jews. Furthermore, the data suggest that the growing numbers of
young Jewish women who are working in professional and managerial careers have similar family size expectations to those of women who are not
in the labor force. Hence, the data provide no support for the argument
that the work patterns of young, educated, career-oriented Jewish women
pose a threat to Jewish demographic continuity. Some of the difference
between the patterns for Jews and non-Jews may reflect the particular
occupational patterns of Jewish women. The relationship to fertility may
not be whether women work, but the type of work women do (see chapters 8 and 9).

JEWISH VALUES AND FERTILITY

Traditional Judaism has emphasized norms supporting large family size. If
judged by the overall low fertility levels of Jews, these have been largely
ignored in practice. Until recently, there has been no reason to postulate
that religious leaders of the American Jewish community had placed a
high priority on issues of family size. Scattered evidence indicates that
American Jews are not aware of these norms or prohibitions. Nor is there
any clear fertility ideology or theology in Reform or Conservative Judaism
that has been conveyed clearly to those identifying with these denominations.

Research carried out in the late 1960s suggested that the relationship between religiosity (defined in a variety of ways) and Jewish fertility is complex. For the older foreign-born generation, there was a positive relationship—the higher the religiosity, the larger the family size. This pattern did not characterize the younger, American-born generations. Most important, detailed evidence revealed that when socioeconomic status and social-class factors were controlled, family size differences among those identifying with various religious denominations within Judaism narrowed considerably (Goldscheider 1965a). More recent research has confirmed this finding for the specific role of Judaism in fertility behavior and norms but has raised broader questions about Jewish identity and commitments in an ethnic-community context. While the secular nature of religion for modern Jews implies that Judaism as a religion plays a minor role in determining fertility patterns, commitments to the Jewish community and strong Jewish identification may have some influence on childbearing and family roles (Goldscheider 1982; Goldscheider 1978; Cohen and Ritterband 1981; Ritterband and Cohen 1979; Lazerwitz 1973; Cheskis 1980).

The evidence from the 1975 Boston study reinforces some of the conclusions reached by previous research and raises new questions about selected subgroups within the Jewish community. Overall, Orthodox and Conservative Jews have about the same expected family size: higher for both than for Reform and nondenominational Jews (table 7.7). So few Orthodox are in this subset of currently married couples age 18–45 that details by age and cohort cannot be examined. This factor is particularly limiting, since impressionistic evidence suggests that the Orthodox of the younger generation have higher fertility norms and behavior than the non-Orthodox. In part, these traditional Jewish communities have re-

TABLE 7.7

Average Expected Family Size by Religious Denomination, Age, and Marriage Cohort

	Orthodox	Conservative	Reform	Other
Total	2.4	2.5	2.2	2.0
Age				
18–29	*	2.6	1.5	1.7
30–39	*	2.4	2.5	1.5
40–45	*	2.5	2.6	3.5
Marriage Cohort				
1966–75	*	2.6	1.8	1.5
1960–65	2.1[a]	2.4	2.1	3.0[a]
1949–59	*	2.6	2.7	*

[a] pre-1960

jected in a variety of ways the integrationist ideology of the vast majority of American Jews. In their greater emphasis on traditional roles for women and on family and spiritual centrality, and through general resistance to acculturation, large family size values and behavior have been retained and supported. These groups have probably contributed a disproportionate share of children to the American Jewish community. We have rarely documented these patterns systematically.

By empirical necessity, therefore, we focus on Conservative, Reform, and nondenominational Jews. Overall, those identifying themselves as Conservative Jews have higher family size expectations than Reform or nondenominational Jews. The fertility gap between Conservative and Reform is a relatively new one, since it does not characterize either the older ages (30–39 and 40–45) or the 1949–59 marriage cohort. This gap is almost solely a reflection of the sharp declines among those who identify as Reform. While family size expectations are relatively stable across cohorts and age groups among Conservative Jews, younger and more recently married Reform Jews have significantly lower family size expectations. The reduction from the oldest to the youngest age group (or marriage cohort) is about 1 child (from 2.7 to 1.8 children by cohort and from 2.6 to 1.5 by age).

An additional finding relates to family size expectations of the nondenominational Jew. The pattern has been downward and is very low among the recent marriage cohort and younger ages. The below-replacement level of nondenominational Jews is consistent with other data, not presented in tabular form, which show low family size expectations among the least ethnically and ritually committed Jews. The small expected family size among least-committed Jews does not simply reflect socioeconomic differences, since the pattern persists within educational levels.

Are the nondenominational less concerned about the Jewish community, less family-oriented, and less committed to Jewish survival in the demographic sense? Are those at the least-committed end of the Jewish continuum, ethnically and religiously, the least committed to American Jewish demographic survival? Perhaps we have viewed the causal arrows in the wrong direction. Maybe the absence of children is not the *result* of lower Jewish commitments but one of its causes. Perhaps childless couples are more likely to be nondenominational. Turned around, the argument could be that having children reinforces Jewish commitments of all kinds and links couples and families to the organized Jewish community (cf. Sklare and Greenblum 1967; Goldscheider 1973). To unravel the direction of causality from fertility to Jewish commitment, or from Jewish commitment to fertility, requires a longitudinal research design. Jewish commitment and family size expectations change over the life cycle and, therefore, need to be examined within a dynamic research framework. It does not appear that theological or ideological factors are the major source of fertility variations among contemporary Jewish couples.

Whether the weakness of Jewish commitments is the determinant or the consequence of small family size expectations, the analysis of these data points unmistakably to several major conclusions. First, below-replacement fertility expectations are characteristic of a minority within the Jewish population. For the overwhelming number of young, recently married persons, family size expectations are low but not below replacement. To the extent that these expectations are realized behaviorally, American Jewish demographic continuity is not threatened.

A second conclusion is that below-replacement fertility characterizes the least-committed segments of the Jewish community. As such, they are the farthest removed from the influences of the community and are the most difficult to reach effectively. Viewed in another way, the low fertility of the least-Jewishly committed and their nonreplacement generationally have the smallest impact on the structure of the Jewish community and its continuity.

A final point relates to the general homogeneity of the American Jewish community and the lack of wide variations in fertility. Except among the Orthodox, who have been the least studied demographically, there is little systematic fertility variation. Neither high levels of educational attainment nor labor force activities of Jewish women are incompatible with their family size expectations. Indeed, among the most-educated and career-oriented women, no major differences between Jews and non-Jews appear.

Most of the detailed analytic fertility issues require dynamic research designs beyond cross-sectional community studies. In particular, the relationship between educational attainment and childbearing roles for women needs to be explored over time, as does the changing role of minority group status as a factor in Jewish fertility variation. The need to tie fertility to population growth issues has been obvious; the value of relating fertility to family structure and women's roles needs emphasis as well. Having documented that American Jewish fertility is not at a level which will result in the serious quantitative decline suggested by many alarmists, we need to turn our attention to the more challenging analytic issues associated with the determinants and consequences of fertility levels and variations.

EIGHT

Socioeconomic Transformations

Social class and ethnicity are major sources of differentiation and stratification in American society. So powerful is the influence of social class that rarely can we investigate ethnicity without considering elements of socioeconomic status. The intersection of social class and ethnicity provides one fundamental basis for the systematic analysis of American social structure (Glazer and Moynihan 1975; Gordon 1964; Greeley 1974; Kobrin and Goldscheider 1978).

Often class and ethnic factors are viewed as alternative sources of strata formation, where ethnicity is treated as a subcategory of social class. While some conclude that ethnicity is, therefore, epiphenomenal, others argue that ethnicity is based to a greater extent on affective ties than on class and hence is more salient (cf. Bell 1975; Steinberg 1981; and chapter 1).

While the assimilation and integration of American ethnic groups are related to social-class composition and structure, the isolation of specific ethnic elements—structural and cultural—requires a detailed analysis of ethnic stratification. The transformation of ethnic groups generationally is tied in part to socioeconomic changes. Nevertheless, there are areas of ethnic changes and differences which do not solely reflect social-class factors.

One of the major stratification themes tied to ethnicity has been the rapid upward social mobility of many white immigrant groups. The generational shifts in class structure have been viewed as one of the clearest indications of the integration of American ethnics. Changes in educational attainment, occupational achievement, and the fluidity of the class structure have symbolized the "success" of American ethnic groups in the "land of opportunity." Upward mobility has been associated with ethnic assimilation and integration: nonmobility of the lower strata or downward mobility is viewed as a sign of inequality, discrimination, and the persistence of deprivation from generation to generation.

We focus in this chapter on the basic context of Jewish stratification. It includes an analysis of generational transformations at both the individual and the aggregate levels, comparisons with non-Jews to identify the basis of Jewish exceptionalism, and the exploration of educational, labor force, and occupational patterns of Jewish women. The fundamental issues revolve around the changing socioeconomic stratification of the American

Jewish community and the structural implications of these changes for Jewish continuity.

The general descriptive picture of Jewish American stratification is well known and documented. At both the national and local levels, all the evidence points to the higher levels of education attained by Jews compared to non-Jews, the concentration of Jewish men in white-collar occupations, particularly in professional and managerial positions, and the higher incomes of Jews than non-Jews. The very rapid upward mobility of Jews over the generations has been documented through age-cohort inferences and cross-sectional comparisons at different points in time. The changing Jewish social-class structure has resulted in the greater concentration of younger Jews among the college-educated, high white-collar, and upper-middle classes. Jews have, therefore, been in the forefront of socioeconomic changes among white immigrants, men earlier than women, and in sharper contrast to Catholics than to Protestants (see, among others, Goldstein and Goldscheider 1968; Goldstein 1969; Kobrin and Goldscheider 1978; Sklare 1971). The pace of upward mobility and the level of high socioeconomic concentration are, therefore, exceptional features of Jewish Americans.

Patterns of upward social mobility among Jews have also been associated with the expansion of new positions in the high occupational ranks and the decline in lower occupational concentration. These patterns characterize younger Jews, and there is no evidence of occupational convergences among religious, racial, or ethnic American populations. Evidence on the occupational pluralism of ethnic groups in America rejects the "assimilation" arguments of occupational convergence in the changing stratification of American society. Moreover, detailed empirical evidence showing ethnic-religious differences in the factors associated with the attainment of educational levels and occupational prestige has demonstrated the inadequacy of a simple ethnic assimilation-convergence model (Kobrin and Goldscheider 1978).

The high concentration of Jews in certain industries, as workers and owners, has been documented for early periods of twentieth-century America, as has the movement into more-diversified occupations. These shifts away from traditional skilled and unskilled labor into white-collar jobs have been linked to the occupational assimilation of Jews. However, the shift toward new forms of occupational concentration at higher levels has been neglected. Yet there is overwhelming evidence of Jewish occupational and educational exceptionalism in terms of newly established bases for ethnic networks, lifestyles, and community bonds.

The analysis of Jewish stratification in this chapter focuses on the new types of socioeconomic concentration. The Jewish concentration in particular educational levels and occupational statuses means that there is a shared lifestyle and shared work patterns, neighborhood type, and family patterns among Jews. Occupational and educational similarities among group members represent the foundation for powerful associational and contextual ties among ethnics. The increasing homogeneity of Jewish socioeconomic structure and the generational continuity of high occupational and educational status forge structural connections and networks among Jews. Crossing ethnic lines for social interaction may be less necessary or attractive when coethnics are similar in background, education, occupation, and lifestyle. And the reverse is no less accurate: when there are internal diversities within a group, greater disaffection from the group will be evident. Thus, in periods of rapid changes (for example, between immigrants and their children), distances between generations are more pronounced, weakening ties within the group. Greater similarities, however, characterize the younger cohorts of Jews than previous cohorts.

Our focus on the structural underpinnings of Jewish continuity identifies the occupational and educational concentration of Jews and assesses the extent of socioeconomic convergence between Jews and non-Jews. Generational changes in socioeconomic status will be isolated to outline the social mobility patterns of Jews and non-Jews and to clarify differences in the generational transmission of educational and occupational statuses for sons and daughters.

Some of these connections between socioeconomic status and ethnicity have been applied to ethnic groups which are deprived educationally and located in lower occupational strata. Often the basis for an ethnic network argument has been exploitation, discrimination, and conflict in the lower classes. Group members are linked to each other when they are discriminated against and blocked in their mobility out of their social class of origin. We extend that argument to other socioeconomic levels and include issues of competition and generational continuity.

To examine the socioeconomic patterns of Jews in any community is to describe particular patterns unique to specified time periods, as well as the changing fluidity of the social-class structure, competition among groups for resources, and variations and changes in migration patterns to and from the community. Our objective is to minimize the particular descriptions of Boston's occupational and educational structure and to focus on comparisons which elucidate how and why the socioeconomic patterns of Jews have changed and are unique.

OCCUPATIONAL CONCENTRATION

We begin our analysis with an examination of occupational patterns of Jewish males. Data in table 8.1 show the distinctive occupational distributions of Boston's religious and ethnic communities. Overall, there is a very heavy concentration of Jews in high white-collar jobs; 40 percent are in professional occupations, of which 20 percent are physicians; 28 percent are managers, of which 43 percent are self-employed businessmen (for a detailed analysis of self-employment, see chapter 9). Ten percent of Jewish men are workers, mostly skilled; 22 percent are employed in clerical-sales positions, 59 percent of whom are in "outside" saleswork, mainly insurance and real estate.

This descriptive overview raises two analytic questions: (1) Is the occupational structure of Jews particular to them or characteristic of other ethnic-religious groups in Boston? (2) Has the occupational structure of Jews changed over the last several decades in ways different from changes among non-Jews?

To appreciate the exceptional occupational patterns of Jews, we compare them to non-Jews (figure 8.1 and 8.2). The concentration of Jews in professional occupations is double that of non-Jews—over two-and-a-half times higher than that of Catholics and one-and-a-half times higher than that of Protestants. While two-thirds of the Jews are professionals or managers, less than one-third of the Catholics and less than half of the Protes-

Table 8.1

Occupational Distribution of Males by Age and Religion

	TOTAL	18–29	30–39	40–49	50–59	60 +
Jews						
Professionals	40.1	47.1	59.7	40.9	26.2	21.8
Physicians	8.1	13.1	15.8	5.4	1.8	1.3
Managers	27.7	13.8	16.8	47.0	36.1	34.8
Self-employed	11.9	0.5	3.5	15.1	22.2	25.4
Clerical-sales	21.8	26.5	20.6	10.9	19.4	28.4
Outside sales	12.9	8.6	17.9	7.1	15.3	17.4
Workers	10.4	12.7	2.7	1.3	18.2	15.0
TOTAL	100.0	100.0	100.0	100.0	100.0	100.0
Non-Jews						
Professionals	20.1	25.9	23.0	24.3	9.9	14.8
Managers	15.8	8.2	17.0	21.4	21.6	14.8
Clerical-sales	13.9	19.4	9.6	15.5	12.6	10.9
Workers	50.2	46.5	50.4	38.8	55.9	59.5
	100.0	100.0	100.0	100.0	100.0	100.0
Catholics						
Professionals	15.1	20.0	15.6	18.9	4.8	14.6
Managers	16.4	10.0	20.0	18.9	16.7	18.8
Clerical-sales	13.8	20.0	11.1	10.8	16.7	8.3
Workers	54.8	50.0	53.3	51.3	61.9	58.3
White Protestants						
Professionals	27.9	33.3	25.0	33.3	30.0	18.5
Managers	20.7	13.9	43.8	25.0	20.0	14.8
Clerical-sales	12.6	13.9	0.0	16.7	10.0	18.5
Workers	29.7	38.9	31.3	25.0	40.0	48.1

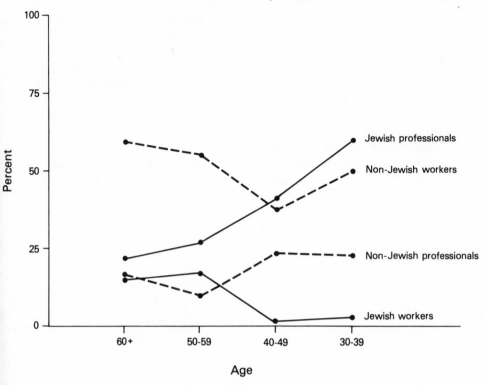

8.1 Percent Professionals and Workers by Age: Jews and Non-Jews

tants are in these occupations. The most conspicuous occupational differences between Jews and non-Jews is the proportion who are workers: half the non-Jews, compared to 10 percent of the Jews. In general, occupational differences between Jews and Protestants are smaller than those between Jews and Catholics.

The level of occupational concentration among Jews is even more pronounced when particular age segments of the community are examined. Age variation reflects a combination of generational and life cycle factors, indicating the results of past mobility and the changing structure of economic opportunity. Since many of the youngest age cohort are still in school or in temporary jobs, we shall focus the analysis on those age 30 and over. While some of those 60 years of age and older are retired, their main occupation when they were in the labor force was obtained.

Viewing the age data as indicators of changes over time reveals very sharp increases in the proportion of professionals among Jews: from 22 percent of those age 60 and over to 60 percent of those 30–39. Within this occupational category, there has been a more dramatic increase in the proportion of Jews who are physicians. For those age 50 and over, about 1– 2 percent of the Jews were physicians; for those age 30–39, 16 percent were physicians. Viewed in another way, while 6–7 percent of the Jewish professionals age 50 and over were physicians, 13 percent of the Jewish professionals age 40–49 were physicians, and fully 26 percent of professionals age 30–39 were physicians. The rate of change increased most sharply for the 1936–45 (postdepression) birth cohort, compared to the 1926–35 cohort. It is too soon to determine from these data what proportion of those age 18–29 will eventually be professionals or physicians. The data indicate that the relative proportion of physicians to total professionals of this age group remains very high (28 percent).

The very sharp increases in professional occupations among the younger cohorts of Jews are a consequence of declines in the proportion of man-

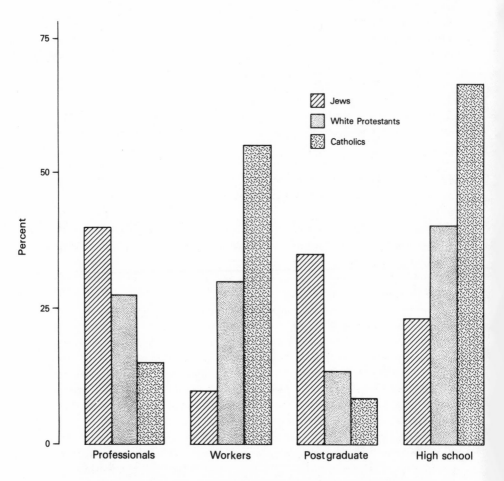

8.2   Percent Professionals, Workers, Postgraduate, and High School: Jews, White Protestants, and Catholics

agers—from 35 percent to 17 percent—and even sharper declines in the proportion of workers—from 15 percent to less than 3 percent. Shifts in clerical-sales have been relatively minor, with no overall change in the proportion in outside sales when those age 60 and over are compared to the 30–39 age group.

One consequence of these occupational shifts is the much greater concentration of younger Jews in a more limited number of occupations and in a very narrow range of occupational statuses. Between 75 and 85 percent of the Jews below age 50 are either professionals or managers, compared to about 60 percent of those over age 50. This concentration has a variety of consequences for the class-economic structure of the Jewish community and for the lifestyle, interaction patterns, and ethnic networks among Jews. Occupational statuses are characterized by common interests and opportunities, sociocultural values, and lifestyles. These shared statuses support and reinforce institutions and networks, family and neighborhood bonds, social class, and political interests.

The salience of these occupational data is reinforced when comparisons to non-Jews are made. For non-Jews generally, there is no sharp or systematic variation by age in the professional, managerial, or clerical-sales occupations. Even among those age 30–39, half of the non-Jews are workers, 23 percent are professionals, 17 percent are managers, and the rest are in clerical-sales work. That, however, is largely a Catholic pattern (and is particularly pronounced among Italian Catholics). Increases among white Protestants in the proportion of managers (from 15 percent to 44 percent) and of professionals may be observed, along with reductions in the proportion of workers and of those in clerical-sales jobs.

The data, therefore, point to growing occupational divergence between Protestants and Catholics. For example, the relative difference between Protestant and Catholic workers over age 60 was 17 percent (58.3 percent for Catholics and 48.1 percent for Protestants); it increased to 41 percent among those age 30–39. The gap between Protestants and Catholics who are professionals also increased from the oldest to the younger cohorts.

The Jewish occupational structure is more concentrated than that of non-Jews in the professional and managerial occupations for all age groups. Has there been convergence or divergence between Jews and non-Jews over time (as measured by age variation)? The data suggest convergence between Jewish and non-Jewish managers but divergences for other occupational categories. For example, the proportion of managers of those age 60 and over was 35 percent among Jews and 15 percent among non-Jews. Among those age 30–39, the managerial proportion was the same for Jews and non-Jews, largely because of the very sharp declines among Jews. While there is some variation between Protestants and Catholics, the basic pattern holds. In contrast, between the ages 60 and over and 30–39, there was an increasing gap between Jewish and non-Jewish professionals (from a difference of 32 percent to 61 percent). The proportion of older Jews who were workers was significantly lower than that of non-Jews, but the changes by age have been even more rapid among Jews, so the gap has widened further.

The growing occupational gap between Jews and non-Jews and their differential occupational concentration suggest that occupational assimilation cannot mean that Jews will become integrated when their occupational patterns are similar to those of non-Jews. That would require substantial Jewish downward occupational mobility and an increased concentration in working-class, blue-collar jobs. For non-Jews to have the same occupational distribution as Jews, very rapid upward occupational mobility would be necessary, with a 60 percent concentration in professional occupations. Even shifts in both populations would have to be substantial for identical distributions to emerge. These alternatives are not a realistic basis for characterizing occupational assimilation. Hence, the assimilation framework hypothesizing converging occupational distributions among Jews and others is empirically incorrect and theoretically limiting.

An alternative argument stresses the emergence of new forms of ethnic stratification. Socioeconomic differences are reinforced generationally and perpetuate themselves through family, educational, occupational, and migration processes. The growing occupational similarity among Jews implies greater similarity in lifestyle, residence, values, schooling, family, and economic and political interests. These patterns mesh together in ways to reinforce Jewish cohesion and distinctiveness. Hence, one key to ethnic cohesion is structural. It places relatively more emphasis on the context of occupational and class similarity for ethnic continuity than on the *search* for ethnic identity or the *desire* for group continuity. The normative and social-psychological factors may be important concomitants and consequences of group cohesion, but the socioeconomic structural underpinnings appear to be one of the major sources of ethnic continuity and of the values which sustain group cohesion.

Viewed dynamically, these arguments suggest that in the past, occupational commonalities at lower socioeconomic levels were clearly one basis for Jewish cohesion. Processes of mobility shifted Jews into new levels of socioeconomic status as new opportunities became available; educational attainment provided alternative avenues for social mobility. As the distance from the immigrant experiences increased, a different occupational concentration emerged at higher socioeconomic levels. Hence, the inferred pattern over time is from low to high socioeconomic status, but with a shift from high levels of occupational concentration to occupational diversity and then *back* to high levels of concentration. The transition *to* occupational homogeneity has rarely been stressed. The assimilation model has focused on the transition *from* occupational homogeneity, emphasizing the role of occupational diversification and mobility in the process of integration. While the emerging Jewish occupational concentration is different from the earlier forms characteristic of first-generation immigrants, the consequences for group cohesion are similar.

EDUCATIONAL ATTAINMENT

One of the immediate determinants of occupational achievement is the level of education attained. For Jews, as well as other ethnic groups, there is a very high correlation between education and occupation. This link remains, even when background variables and current demographic characteristics are statistically controlled. Our objective is to examine the educational levels of Jewish men and women to identify transformations, convergences, and sources of cohesion.

The high levels of and increases in educational attainment have been noted in every study of American Jews. The consequences of education have often been viewed in the context of the liberalization of the educational experience, contacts with non-Jews, and the broad separation of the young from the control of the family and the constraints of ethnic particularism. Hence, as more Jews become college-educated, the greater is their assimilation. This argument misses three important points. First, parents, families, and kin facilitate educational attainment economically, socially, and normatively. Hence, the break with family of orientation is not so drastic. Second, there are ethnic clusters which develop among students. While the options to increase contact with non-Jews are available, institutions and organizations also facilitate interaction among Jews. Finally, most Jews have college experience, and substantial numbers graduate from college. These commonalities develop new peer- and age-connected bonds that are ethnically related. When generational differences in educational attainment are wide, education may be viewed as a further source of generational conflict. However, American Jews are characterized by a large proportion of two-generation college-educated families—men and women. As such, education per se can no longer be viewed as a threat to generational or ethnic continuity.

Data on the structure of education, changes among Jewish men and women, and the links between education and other structural and ethnic continuities support these arguments (table 8.2). The educational patterns of Jews are consistent with their occupational patterns and help clarify some of the distinctiveness of the Jewish occupational structure. Overall, one-third of the Jewish men have had postgraduate educations, and 62 percent have at least graduated from college. The respective figures for non-Jews are 10 percent and 25 percent, with much lower levels of education for Catholics. Indeed, overall differences between Jews and Protestants reflect the very high proportion of Jews who have postgraduate education (34 percent compared to 13 percent), while 27 percent of both Jewish and Protestant males are college graduates. Moreover, the Protestant pattern tends to be more bimodal than the Jewish, with a heavier concentration in the high-school category: 40 percent of the Protestants and 23 percent of the Jews. Overall, 42 percent of the non-Jewish males have at least some college education, compared to 77 percent of the Jewish males (see figure 8.2.).

The educational variation by age is considerable. For all groups there has been a decrease in the proportion of males who had only a high-school education and a concomitant increase in the college-educated. The rate of change among Jews in these processes has been much more rapid. While 64 percent of the Jews age 60 and over had a high-school education or less, this pattern characterized only 7 percent of the youngest cohort. Viewed

TABLE 8.2

Educational Distribution of Males by Age, Religion, and Ethnicity

	High School	Some College	College Graduate	Post-graduate	Total %
Jews					
Total	23.0	15.0	27.4	34.5	100.0
18–29	7.4	25.2	25.4	41.9	100.0
30–44	8.9	7.6	36.8	46.8	100.0
45–59	32.6	13.5	27.6	26.3	100.0
60+	64.0	10.5	14.1	11.4	100.0
Non-Jews					
Total	58.2	16.0	15.8	10.0	100.0
18–29	40.2	26.1	19.6	14.1	100.0
30–44	60.1	13.8	16.0	10.1	100.0
45–59	68.3	10.2	12.6	9.0	100.0
60+	72.1	9.8	13.1	4.9	100.0
Catholics					
Total	66.4	16.0	9.8	7.8	100.0
18–29	43.9	25.8	15.2	15.2	100.0
60+	84.0	6.0	4.0	6.0	100.0
White Protestants					
Total	40.1	18.8	26.8	13.4	100.0
18–29	25.0	30.6	27.8	16.7	100.0
60+	55.5	11.1	25.9	7.4	100.0
Irish Catholics					
Total	68.4	10.5	8.8	12.3	100.0
18–29	50.0	25.0	16.7	8.3	100.0
60+	88.9	5.6	0.0	5.6	100.0
Italian Catholics					
Total	68.4	15.8	9.2	6.6	100.0
18–29	47.6	23.8	14.3	14.3	100.0
60+	85.7	0.0	7.1	7.1	100.0

in another way, 92 percent of the young Jewish males go on to college, compared to 36 percent of the oldest generation. The most conspicuous break in college attendance among Jewish males was among the generation growing up in the 1930s and 1940s, entering college in the educational boom of the late 1950s and 1960s. The increase in college attendance was concomitant with an increase in postgraduate education—from 11 percent of those age 60 and over to 46 percent of those 30-44 years of age. Many of the youngest males are still in school, so figures for them are incomplete.

While the declines in high-school education and increases in college and postgraduate education characterize non-Jews, Protestants, and Catholics, the pace has been slower than for Jews (figure 8.3). The educational differences between Jews and non-Jews have diverged. Hence, the inequalities between groups are greater among the younger cohorts than among the older cohorts. While the educational levels of Jews of each age group are significantly higher than of non-Jews as a whole, white Protestants of the oldest cohort had somewhat higher levels of educational attainment than Jews of age 60 and over. While immigrant Jews had background educational advantages over other immigrants, they were not educationally advantaged relative to white Protestants. However, the pattern shifted dramatically for those born between 1916 and 1930 (mostly second-generation) who advanced rapidly beyond high school to college.

Moreover, the shifts have been more thorough, as well as more rapid, for Jews. The initial thrust out of lower levels of education created educational heterogeneity for the 45–59 age cohort. About one-third of them remained at the high-school-educated level, while one-fourth graduated from college and an additional one-fourth went on to postgraduate education. By the 1960s and through the 1970s, the shift continued such that almost all Jewish males go to college, and indeed, most graduate. The bimodal educational pattern characteristic of second-generation Jews has yielded to the greater homogeneity of the third and fourth generations. The growing educational similarity of younger Jews contrasts with the continuing bimodality of both Protestant and Catholic males. Hence, educational differences between Jews and non-Jews have widened, while differences among Jews have narrowed. Educational convergences between Protestants and Catholics have occurred as both have experienced educational polarization within. These patterns parallel the occupational shifts described earlier and, indeed, are statistically highly correlated with them. These different processes of convergence among Jews and divergences between Jews and non-Jews, along with shifts in the levels of educational attainments, may be referred to as socioeconomic transformation. That implies more than change, since the entire population shifts, rapidly and thoroughly. Our argument is that such transformation implies less conflict and competition within the Jewish group than has often been suggested. Since educational changes have transformed the Jewish population, they have also resulted in a firmer foundation for the development of networks, relationships, and bonds to kin and community institutions, lifestyles, and interests. They also suggest that generational and age gaps have been reduced as educational differences over time have converged for everyone.

The data on family income are consistent with the educational and occupational concentration of Jews (table 8.3). Average family income is significantly higher for Jews than non-Jews, for each age group and when compared to Protestants as well as Catholics. However, family income data are particularly problematic, since family and individual incomes are equivalent only for those living with no other wage earner and cannot be compared directly with incomes of those living with other earners.

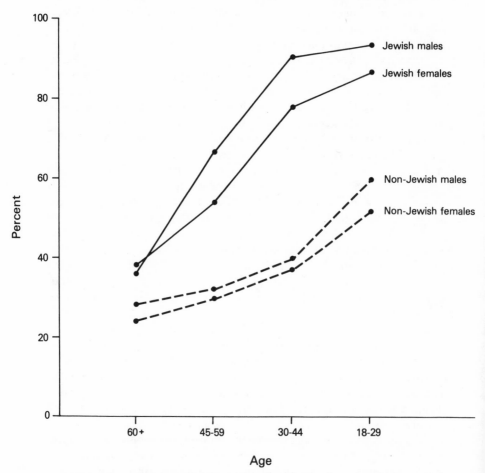

8.3   Percent with at Least Some College Education by Age and Sex: Jews and Non-Jews

TABLE 8.3
Average Family Income by Age and Religion
(in Thousands)

	Jews	Non-Jews	Catholics	Protestants
TOTAL	20.3	13.6	13.0	14.4
18–29	13.5	12.2	13.0	11.6
30–44	30.3	15.3	14.7	14.6
45–59	28.3	17.1	14.7	20.3
60+	13.2	10.0	8.8	12.4

Hence, the effects of life cycle and household composition cannot be disentangled when the income of the 18–29 age group is compared to that of the 30–44 age group. At the other end of the age span, many of those age 60 and over are retired or living in nonfamilies. Hence, family income data are distorted.

GENERATIONAL INHERITANCE

The overall patterns of increases in education and occupational status are consistent with the general features culled from the literature. Nevertheless, one assumption underlying the age cohort and generational model is that the population is closed to migration. We can infer changes from cross-sectional data on older and younger age segments as long as there is a reasonable basis for assuming that the patterns for the older ages are roughly equivalent to those characteristic of the fathers of the younger cohort. In these data, the evidence available suggests that such an assumption is violated. The Boston community has attracted a large number of well-educated professionals in recent years, including a disproportionate number of Jews (see chapter 4). How much does selective in-migration affect the results of the generational changes inferred from age data? Is occupational and educational variation by age, which we have analyzed in terms of change, a reflection of the in-migration of more-educated young people?

To clarify more directly issues of generational changes in socioeconomic status, we compare the occupational patterns of sons with those of their fathers. The question in the survey addressed the work fathers did in their "main job" and was limited to reports by sons below age 36. Some of the sons are not at their occupational peak; hence comparisons are conservative estimates of the upward mobility of sons. These data compensate for the biases introduced by inferring change from age data, when migration is a factor. The data relate to individual-level, rather than aggregate, changes.

TABLE 8.4
Intergenerational Occupational Outflows by Religion:
Males Age 18–36

Occupation of Sons	Occupation of Fathers			
	Professionals	Managers	Clerical-sales	Workers
Jews	*Outflows*			
Professionals	76	52	10	63
Managers	7	15	30	2
Clerical-sales	13	22	55	19
Workers	4	11	15	17
Total %	100	100	100	100
Non-Jews				
Professionals	70	27	27	14
Managers	5	15	18	12
Clerical-sales	15	23	27	6
Workers	10	35	27	68
Total %	100	100	100	100

What are the patterns of occupational inheritance among Jews? The data in table 8.4 have been organized to show the occupational outflows from fathers to sons. Over three-fourths of the fathers who were professionals had sons who were professionals, and a majority of managers had sons who were professionals. The retention of professional status and the movement up from managerial jobs are clearly evident from these data. Among Jewish fathers in real estate and insurance (most are in the clerical-sales category), there is a clear pattern of generational inheritance: most fathers who are in clerical-sales jobs have sons in that occupational status. Most of their sons who are not in the same occupational status as their fathers were upwardly mobile. Among the working classes, however, there is no general pattern of occupational inheritance, and an unusually high number of sons are professionals. Fully 63 percent of Jewish workers have sons who are professionals, higher than the proportion from fathers who are managers or clerical-salesmen. These data suggest that working-class Jewish fathers transfer to their sons educational opportunity rather than job continuity. In turn, the educational opportunity results in very high levels of upward occupational mobility. Fathers who are managers and who are in insurance or real-estate occupations are much more likely to transfer jobs and parallel occupational statuses to sons. These jobs involve networks, connections, and clientele which are more valuable and easily transferable relative to workers. Since workers have less to transfer directly in terms of jobs or contacts, access and opportunity are indirectly transferred through education. In turn, these are reflected in the higher proportion of workers whose sons are professional than among any other group except fathers who are professionals (figure 8.4).[1]

The very strong retention of, and movement into, professional occupations clearly documents the profound upward mobility of Jews and the generational retention of high socioeconomic status. The specification of the effects of occupational origins on occupational inheritance among Jews clarifies one part of the dynamics. Comparisons to non-Jewish generational outflows deepens our understanding of Jewish exceptionalism in the process of occupational inheritance, as well as in the level of occupational achievement.

The outflow patterns of Jewish and non-Jewish professionals are quite similar. Most fathers, Jewish and non-Jewish, who are in professional jobs have sons in the same occupational status. Differences between Jews and non-Jews begin to emerge among fathers who are managers. Most Jewish managers have sons who are professionals (52 percent), compared to about one-fourth of the non-Jewish managers. Downward mobility of the sons of

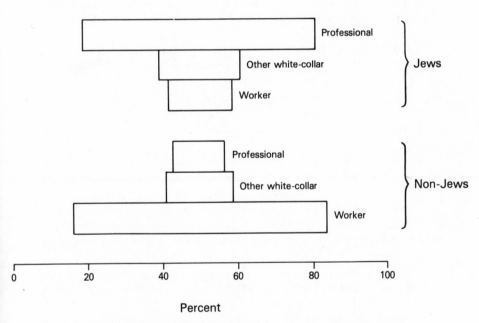

8.4   Occupational Distribution of Workers' Sons: Jews and Non-Jews
       Based on Table 8-4.

1. The very high level of upward mobility of sons from working-class fathers may be linked to the low fertility characteristic of these fathers. That is particularly the case, since the mechanism operates through education. It is therefore not the middle-class "mentality" of the Jewish working class but the desire for upward mobility of their children that resulted in low fertility (see chapter 7).

non-Jewish managers is evident, with over one-third in working-class jobs, three times the Jewish rate. Hence, generational occupational differences between Jewish and non-Jewish managers are not in the direct inheritance of occupational status: Jewish and non-Jewish managers have the same proportion of sons who are managers. Rather, it is the occupational patterns of sons who do not "inherit" managerial positions: Jewish sons of managers become professionals; non-Jewish sons move down in the occupational hierarchy.

Jews in clerical-sales jobs are more likely to transfer their occupational statuses to their sons than non-Jews. Partly this tendency reflects the nature of the jobs in this category, which for Jews are real estate and insurance. These may be highly transferable, since they involve contacts and networks. As a result, Jews in this category have higher generational inheritance than non-Jews and than Jews in managerial positions. It appears to be more difficult to transfer managerial positions to sons. This situation is probably related to the concentration of Jews in this category in self-employed businesses. To transfer these to sons means either retirement of fathers or the placement of sons in nonmanagerial positions. Hence, inheritance of managerial positions is less likely to occur for both Jews and non-Jews.

Very striking differences between Jews and non-Jews characterize workers. Almost two-thirds of the Jewish workers have sons who are professionals, while two-thirds of the non-Jewish workers have sons who are also workers. Workers can transfer neither contacts nor family businesses. They can transfer to sons either similar occupational statuses as their own (as do most non-Jews) or education and, in turn, professional jobs (as do Jews).

Another view of these data focuses on recruitment processes, i.e., what percentage of sons in particular occupational statuses have fathers in that status? These patterns, not shown in tabular form, indicate much greater generational stability in recruitment of high socioeconomic status among Jews than non-Jews. For example, 86 percent of Jewish professionals have fathers who are either professionals or managers, compared to 68 percent of the non-Jews. Over half the Jewish managers have fathers who are managers or professionals, compared to less than 40 percent of the non-Jews. At lower occupational levels, the reverse pattern emerges. Over 70 percent of the non-Jewish workers had fathers who were workers, compared to 15 percent of the Jews. Thus, generational continuity and homogeneity in occupational status are clearly emerging among young Jews, as are growing gaps between the occupational structure of Jews and non-Jews.

Assuming that these generational transfers continue for the next generation, there will be very few Jews in working-class occupations. Indeed, among the younger generation, there are already very few in the working class. A two-tiered occupational system has emerged among Jews, dominated by professionals and managers. The continuation of high rates of inheritance among non-Jewish workers insures that occupational gaps and inequalities between Jews and non-Jews will remain and become more exaggerated. These generational data show clearly the crystallization of occupational differences between Jews and non-Jews.

Part of these generational differences and the very high mobility of sons from working-class fathers reflect the selective in-migration to Boston of the more successful sons of Jewish workers. Obviously, the less successful sons of working-class fathers are more likely to remain in the communities of origin and would not appear in a community sample. Hence, some part of these patterns may be distorted by the educational selectivity and rapid rate of Jewish in-migration (see chapter 4). Nevertheless, the pattern of upward mobility out of the working classes is not solely a product of selective in-migration. Less than 3 percent of Jews age 30–39 are working-class, compared to 15 percent of those age 60 and over. The decline in the working class reflects either the out-migration of sons of working-class Bostonians or their upward mobility. While no data are available on out-migration, it seems likely that most of the sons of the working-class Jews born in Boston have been upwardly mobile.

We examined the distribution of education by age and noted the concentration of Jews in higher levels of education, and we inferred change from the age variation. Generational distributions of fathers and sons reinforce these conclusions (table 8.5). Jews age 18–36 are overwhelmingly college-bound and -educated. Fully 96 percent of these young Jews have at least some college education, compared to 50 percent of the Catholics and 70 percent of the Protestants. The generational shifts among Jews and their very high level of educational attainment are consistent with the occupational patterns. The important additional fact that emerges clearly is the very high educational level of *both* generations—sons and fathers: 30 percent of the Jewish fathers have postgraduate education, compared to 10 percent of the Protestants and 4 percent of the Catholics; 62 percent of the Jewish fathers had at least some college education, compared to one-fourth of the Catholics and half of the Protestants.

The value of the generational data on education goes beyond confirmation of the higher levels, greater educational mobility, and greater generational continuity of Jews than non-Jews. The analysis of individual educational outflows allows us to identify the dynamics of generational transfers of education. As with occupation, there is a very high transmission of high educational levels. Among fathers who graduated from college, 84 percent of their sons have already graduated from college; 54 percent of the fathers with a postgraduate education had sons with a postgraduate education.[2]

The more interesting pattern is not generational continuity at high educational levels but the outflows from less educated fathers. The data show significantly higher rates of upward educational mobility from the lowest

2. This estimate is conservative, since the sons' age group is 18–36, with a significant percentage still in college.

Table 8.5
Intergenerational Educational Outflows by Religion:
Males Age 18–36

Education of Sons	Education of Fathers					
	Less than high school	High-school graduate	Some college	College graduate	Post-graduate	
Jews	11	27	19	15	29	100
Less than high school	0	4	0	0	0	1
High-school graduate	12	1	0	9	4	4
Some college	4	11	44	7	31	22
College graduate	35	18	44	49	13	28
Postgraduate	49	66	12	35	53	45
Total %	100	100	100	100	100	100
Catholics	46	28	10	13	4	100
Less than high school	36	5	5[a]	*	*	19
High-school graduate	24	50	26	*	*	32
Some college	15	25	21	*	*	19
College graduate	15	5	16	*	*	13
Postgraduate	9	15	32	*	*	17
Total %	100	100	100	*	*	100
White Protestants	24	27	12	27	10	100
Less than high school	20	0	5[a]	*	*	7
High-school graduate	40	36	5	*	*	22
Some college	10	46	20	*	*	24
College graduate	20	9	40	*	*	27
Postgraduate	10	9	30	*	*	19
Total %	100	100	100	*	*	100

[a] Some College and Above (fathers)

than from the middle educational levels. This finding parallels the occupational outflows from workers relative to middle-status occupations. The evidence suggests that Jewish workers with low levels of education provide their sons with opportunities for the highest levels of professional education, since they cannot transfer their occupations. Middle-status businessmen and salesworkers are likely to provide a college rather than a professional education for their sons, since many can transfer their middle-status jobs.

Again, it should be emphasized that these are particularly Jewish patterns. Among Catholics and Protestants, the generational inheritance of low levels of education is much higher than among Jews. The proportion of fathers with a high-school-level education whose sons have a high-school-level education (or less) is 55 percent for Catholics, 36 percent for Protestants, and 5 percent for Jews.[3]

We again note that the age range 18–36 is somewhat confusing, since many of those at the younger end of the age group are still enrolled in college. An analysis controlling for age shows little change in our conclusions comparing Jews and non-Jews. The detailed data for Jews are presented in table 8.6, for ages 30–36, where most will have completed their education. Fully 85 percent of the fathers with a high-school education had sons who were college graduates, compared to 62 percent of fathers with some college education. Viewed in terms of recruitment, 43 percent of Jews with a postgraduate education had fathers with a high-school education, compared to only 5 percent from fathers with some college education. Hence, the data confirm the higher educational attainment of sons from less-educated fathers than from fathers with intermediate levels of education.

SOCIOECONOMIC TRANSFORMATION OF JEWISH WOMEN

There have been few studies which have focused on the socioeconomic patterns of ethnic women in general, and Jewish women in particular.

TABLE 8.6

Intergenerational Educational Outflows and Inflows: Jewish Males Age 30–36

Education of Sons	Education of Fathers				
	High school	Some college	College graduate		
High school	13.5	0.0	10.7		
Some college	2.7	38.3	0.0		
College graduate	83.7	61.6	89.3		
Total %	100.0	100.0	100.0		
N =	74	60	75		
Education of Sons				Total %	N
Non-college graduate	27.9	53.5	18.6	100.0	43
College graduate	27.4	54.9	17.7	100.0	58
Postgraduate	42.7	4.6	52.7	100.0	108

3. The educational level of these fathers is considerably higher than the level of those age 60 and over in the sample and suggests some migratory selectivity by education. Assuming that fathers would be twenty-five to thirty years older than their children, their educational level should be comparable to that of the age group 43–48 to 61–66 (given that these are fathers of those age 18–36). Indeed, their educational level is reasonably close to the level of those age 45–59, with a lower level of college and higher education and a higher level of high-school education. Hence, the distortions by selective in-migration are not as severe as our initial concerns.

Most research has treated the male head of the household as the source of the family's socioeconomic status. Some descriptive studies of Jewish communities have shown the lower labor force participation of Jewish than non-Jewish women. This trend was attributed to the longer period of time Jewish women remain in school, the high proportion of foreign-born Jewish women who did not work, and the higher socioeconomic status of the Jewish population, requiring fewer Jewish women to enter the labor force to supplement family income (see Goldstein and Goldscheider 1968, pp. 73–77).

It is unclear whether these patterns of the early 1960s have persisted for the mid-1970s. Nor is it clear what would characterize the life cycle patterns of women's labor force participation when the proportion foreign-born is low, when educational levels have increased, and when career patterns for women have become more widespread.

Moreover, there are analytic issues associated with the socioeconomic patterns of women which have rarely been addressed systematically. In particular, three themes will be explored: (1) What are the labor force patterns of Jewish women, and how do they link to marriage, and to non-familial roles? In particular, are these links specific to Jewish women, or do they characterize non-Jews as well? (2) What are the occupational patterns of Jewish women? Are they more concentrated in particular jobs compared to men and compared to non-Jewish women? Do patterns of educational concentration characterize Jewish women as they do Jewish men? (3) What are the generational socioeconomic transfers from fathers to daughters? Do these transfers vary between Jewish and non-Jewish women? Are the educational and occupational inheritance patterns of Jewish daughters and sons similar? Do gender differences in educational and occupational continuity vary by ethnicity?

The participation of women in the labor force has a very clear relationship to patterns of education, marriage, and childbearing. Age variations in the percentage of women working reflect life cycle changes in school attendance, the timing of marriage and childbearing, retirement, and socioeconomic status. Overall, about half of the Jewish women over age 18 are working (table 8.7). That is not a distinctively Jewish level of participation. The key variation among ethnic-religious groups relates to life cycle. For Jewish women, there is a high initial entry into the work force (64 percent), but detailed data show much variation within the 18–29 ages, depending on schooling, marriage, and childbearing patterns. There is a sharp drop among the 30–39 age group, greater than for any other group, and a sharper recovery, as children are older and in school. Fully 72 percent of the women age 40–49 are in the labor force, more than in any ethnic or religious subpopulation. From a peak toward the end of the 40–49-year-old age group, there is an earlier and steeper decline among Jews, falling to 23 percent among those 60 years of age and older. These life cycle patterns fit in with Jewish patterns of longer schooling, delayed childbearing, concentrated childbearing within a short period of time,

TABLE 8.7
Percentage of Women in the Labor Force by Religion and Ethnicity

	Jews	Non-Jews	Catholics	White Protestants	Irish Catholics	Italian Catholics	Other Catholics
18–29	64	56	49	72	50	55	58
30–39	42	48	54	50	50	46	50
40–49	72	55	50	60	56	50	39
50–59	47	64	63	50	67	71	57
60+	23	20	24	10	14	42	27
Total	51	47	46	43	42	54	45

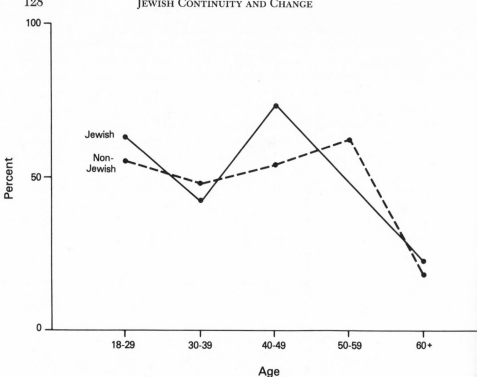

8.5　Percent of Jewish and Non-Jewish Women in the Labor Force by Age

fewer children, higher socioeconomic status, and, hence, earlier withdrawal from the labor force as husbands retire (figure 8.5).

This life cycle labor force pattern is distinctive only to the extent that educational levels, family formation and dissolution, and socioeconomic status of Jewish women are distinctive. There is no indication of particular Jewish family values or normative issues which need to be invoked to account for this pattern. Whether these life cycle variations will characterize younger Jewish women as they age cannot be determined from these data. There are some indications that levels of participation of Jewish women will increase as many more of the younger women have careers and are in rewarding jobs. More systematic research will have to be carried out to follow these changes.

More detailed data on the occupational distribution of working Jewish women (table 8.8) show that over one-third of the Jewish women (currently working or who have had a job) are professionals. Of these, 67 percent are in three particular jobs: teachers, social workers, and medical-health fields, mostly nursing. About one-third are in clerical work, and another 9 percent are saleswomen; 13 percent are managers, and 7 percent are skilled and unskilled workers. Non-Jewish women have lower proportions who are professionals and managers than Jews, and a significantly higher proportion of workers—33 percent compared to 7 percent. Subdividing non-Jewish women into Catholics and Protestants widens the differences between Jewish and Catholic women and narrows the differences between Jewish and Protestant women. Indeed, the latter comparison suggests that the distinctive work pattern for Jewish women is largely in the very small number who are workers. The Catholic-Jewish difference extends as well to ethnic variations within the Catholic population, with Irish women more concentrated in professional jobs than Italians but with a large subgroup of workers.

Reflecting changes associated with educational and employment opportunities, there has been a very sharp increase in the proportion professional among Jewish women, from 18 percent among women age 60 and

TABLE 8.8
Occupational Distribution of Women by Age and Religion

	18–29	30–39	40–49	50–59	60 +	Total
Jews						
Professionals	52	48	22	24	18	36
Teachers	22	16	12	10	8	15
Social workers	2	6	1	2	1	3
Other medical	10	6	1	2	4	6
Managers	10	9	25	16	10	13
Clerical	26	37	32	43	48	35
Sales	3	1	17	15	17	9
Workers	11	3	4	3	8	7
Total %	100	100	100	100	100	100
Non-Jews						
Professionals	25	23	16	17	17	20
Managers	4	3	10	9	6	6
Clerical	39	35	28	30	28	33
Sales	6	11	7	13	7	8
Workers	26	28	38	31	42	33
Total %	100	100	100	100	100	100
Catholics						
Professionals	19	28	18	9	6	16
Clerical-sales	51	39	28	59	32	42
Workers	30	33	44	24	58	37
White Protestants						
Professionals	34	33	21	41	32	32
Clerical-sales	47	33	29	35	39	39
Workers	16	25	43	12	23	22

over to 52 percent among women age 18–29. This increase parallels the decrease of clerical-saleswork among Jewish women—from 65 percent to 29 percent. Among Jewish women of all ages, the proportion of professionals in the teacher-social worker-nurse category fluctuates at around 60 percent, with no major pattern by age. Nor are there any age patterns for managers or workers.

The age pattern of occupation for non-Jewish women is significantly different from that for Jewish women. There is an increase in the proportion who are professional among non-Jewish women, but it is not sharp or monotonic by age. Most of the increase reflects changes among Catholic women, from 6 percent of those age 60 and over to 28 percent of those age 30–39. As a result, the relative difference in the proportion of Protestant and Catholic women who are professionals has declined, from 81 percent among those age 60 and over to 15 percent among those age 30–39. The convergence between Protestant and Catholic women in the proportion professional does not characterize Jewish-non-Jewish differences. The proportion of older Jewish women who had professional jobs was similar to the non-Jewish level but significantly lower than that for Protestants (18 percent compared to 32 percent). Among younger Jewish women (age 30–39), the gap between Jews and non-Jews has increased: while 48 percent of the Jewish women were professionals, one-third of the Protestant women and 28 percent of the Catholic women were professionals. Occupational convergences among non-Jews occurred at the same time as divergences between Jews and non-Jews.

It is interesting to note the timing of this divergence, particularly between Jewish and Protestant women. The proportion professional among Protestant women was significantly higher than for Jewish women for the two oldest cohorts. Jewish women born between 1926 and 1935 (i.e., age 40–49 in 1975) caught up to the Protestant women, with 22 percent of both groups in professional occupations. These were largely second-generation Jewish women born and raised in the United States, exposed to the opportunities for education and professional careers. Jewish women born a decade later (1936–1945) surpassed the Protestant women in the proportion professional (48 percent to 33 percent) and continued to do so for the post-World War II baby boom cohort (1946–1957). Thus, the second generation of Jewish women attained the same percentage in professional jobs as Protestants; the third and subsequent generations of Jewish women surpassed the proportion of professionals among Protestants.

As with Jewish women, there are no age patterns for non-Jewish managers. In contrast to Jewish women, non-Jewish women have experienced no clear changes in the proportion engaged in clerical-sales work. The proportion who are workers is low among Jewish women of all ages, fluctuating around 3–4 percent for those age 30–60. In contrast, there has been a decline in non-Jewish skilled and unskilled workers from the 1926–35 birth cohort to the postwar birth cohort. The Catholic decline overall has been sharper than that for Protestants (from 58 percent to 30 percent for those age 60 and over to those age 18–29). The proportion of Protestant and Catholic women who are workers remains significantly higher than that of Jews.

Data on the education of Jewish women facilitate comparisons addressed to three analytic issues: (1) educational variation by age to focus on change; (2) educational differences between Jews and non-Jews to analyze exceptionalism; and (3) educational differences between women and men to investigate differential gender effects of Jews and non-Jews (table 8.9).

Overall, Jewish women have very high levels of education. Almost one-fifth of adult women have postgraduate educations; almost half have graduated from college. The level is significantly higher than for non-Jewish women, higher than for non-Jewish men, but not quite as high as for Jewish men.

Variation by age reveals very sharp declines in the proportion of Jewish women with only a high-school education, from 62 percent among the oldest age cohort to 13 percent among the youngest age cohort. Fully 87

TABLE 8.9
Educational Distribution of Women by Age and Religion

	High School	Some College	College Graduate	Post-graduate	Total %
Jews					
Total	32.8	19.2	28.6	19.4	100.0
18–29	13.1	20.9	36.0	30.0	100.0
30–44	22.5	23.7	30.5	23.3	100.0
45–59	46.1	16.6	26.4	10.9	100.0
60+	62.3	14.5	15.1	8.1	100.0
Non-Jews					
Total	64.1	19.2	11.8	4.9	100.0
18–29	48.3	26.3	18.7	6.7	100.0
30–44	62.5	20.7	12.5	4.3	100.0
45–59	70.3	15.6	9.4	4.7	100.0
60+	76.5	14.3	6.1	3.1	100.0
Catholics					
Total	70.1	20.4	6.3	3.3	100.0
18–29	54.8	32.1	9.5	3.6	100.0
60+	85.4	12.0	2.7	0.0	100.0
Protestants					
Total	42.4	28.1	21.2	8.2	100.0
18–29	23.0	35.9	33.3	7.7	100.0
60+	60.0	24.0	8.0	8.0	100.0

percent of the Jewish women age 18–29 have gone on to college. The increase in the proportion of Jewish women going beyond college into graduate school is no less impressive. While 8 percent of the Jewish women age 60 and over had some graduate school education, almost one-third of the women 18–29 have already had some postgraduate education. That is a minimum estimate, since many of those in the lower age range will go on to graduate school.

The decrease in high-school education and increase in college education also characterize non-Jewish women, but the pace of change has not been as sharp as for Jewish women. The increase in postgraduate education, for example, is from 3 percent to 7 percent among non-Jewish women and from 8 percent to 30 percent among Jewish women. While the rate of increase in completing college is about the same for Jewish and non-Jewish women, the level continues to be over two-and-a-half times higher among Jewish women (66 percent, compared to 25 percent among women age 30–44).

There are significant differences between Catholic and Protestant women in educational levels, and it is somewhat distorting to focus on non-Jews as if they were a homogeneous category. Protestant women, for example, have much higher levels of education and have experienced much sharper increases in the proportion graduating from college than Catholics. Nevertheless, in no case do our findings comparing Jews to non-Jews change when the comparisons are between Protestant and Jewish women. Similarly, ethnic differences in educational levels among Catholics may be observed, particularly the higher Irish than Italian levels. But Protestant women have higher levels of education than Irish Catholic women.

The differential pace of change and level of educational attainment of Jewish and non-Jewish women have resulted in the widening of educational gaps for the youngest cohort. As with men, there have been growing divergences between Jewish and non-Jewish women, as the educational transformation of Jews moves to university-level education for all Jewish women.

Comparing the educational levels of men and women by age suggests that for Jews, the decade of the 1960s ended the gender gap in the proportion who continued their education beyond high school. By the 1970s, the proportion of Jewish men and women who completed college was about the same (66 percent). It is too soon to know whether the postgraduate gap between Jewish men and women (42 percent of the men and 30 percent of the women age 18–29) will close during the 1980s. The educational gap for non-Jews remains, with some indication of the reduction of the sex difference in the proportion going beyond high school.

What socioeconomic characteristics do Jewish fathers transfer to their daughters? Are these similar among all ethnic and religious groups? Do Jewish fathers transfer socioeconomic status to daughters differently than to sons? These are complex questions, which data on occupational out-flows from fathers to daughters help clarify (table 8.10).

The inheritance of professional status is high between Jewish fathers and daughters: 81 percent of Jewish fathers who are professionals have daughters who are professionals. That is about the same level as for Jewish sons, and it is significantly higher than the level among non-Jews. Oc-cupational inheritance between father and daughter is also high for Jewish managers, higher than for non-Jews and almost as high as for Jewish sons.

TABLE 8.10
Intergenerational Occupational Outflows and Inflows
(Fathers to Daughters) by Religion

	Occupation of Fathers			
	Professionals	Managers	Clerical-sales	Workers
		Outflows		
Daughters				
Jews				
Professionals	81	47	56	46
Managers	2	14	15	0
Clerical-sales	6	35	30	28
Workers	10	4	0	26
	100	100	100	100
Non-Jews				
Professionals	43	33	57	21
Managers	4	3	7	0
Clerical-sales	35	48	14	48
Workers	17	15	21	30
	100	100	100	100

		Inflows			
					Total %
Jews					
Professionals	34	30	26	10	100
Managers	6	52	42	0	100
Clerical-sales	6	50	31	14	100
Workers	34	20	0	46	100
Non-Jews					
Professionals	23	26	19	33	100
Managers	*	*	*	*	*
Clerical-sales	14	28	3	55	100
Workers	13	16	9	62	100

Hence, daughters of Jewish managers are more likely to become professionals or managers than non-Jewish daughters, and almost as likely as Jewish sons.

The daughters of Jewish and non-Jewish clerical-salesmen are similar in the proportion professional, but Jewish daughters are more likely than non-Jews to be managers and unlikely to be workers. This pattern for both Jewish and non-Jewish daughters is clearly gender-related. While sons of Jewish clerical-salesmen are likely to inherit their father's occupational status, daughters are much more likely than sons to move up and become professionals.

Jewish daughters of workers are more likely than non-Jewish daughters to become professionals, with about the same proportion retaining worker status. This pattern again appears to be gender-related. Among Jewish sons of workers, there is a much higher mobility into the professions than among Jewish daughters or non-Jewish sons. Non-Jewish daughters, however, are clearly distinct from non-Jewish sons in the lower levels of inheritance of worker status.

The socioeconomic transformation reflected in these data suggests rapid social mobility of Jewish men and women, high levels of educational and occupational attainment, and generational continuities in high socioeconomic status. Moreover, social-class differences between Jews and non-Jews have crystallized. There is every indication of continuing Jewish socioeconomic exceptionalism. There is also a basis for arguing that class and ethnic interests among Jews overlap and have become more imbedded in the Jewish social structure. If for no other cultural or structural reason, the commonality of class and status among Jews would result in social bonds, economic networks, and common lifestyles and interests. When other structural and cultural factors are added, the socioeconomic pattern reinforces and cements the bases of Jewish cohesion.

NINE

Self-Employment and Jewish Continuity

Imprinted in American popular culture is the image of the immigrant Jews striving to "make it" in America. Part of the imagery relates to the desire to be independent—from family and country of origin, as well as from the control of non-Jews, though it is doubtful whether in reality Jews fully disassociated themselves from kinship ties or their communities of origin. Here we shall focus on a small corner of that reality—occupational independence. Specifically, we shall analyze some evidence on patterns of Jewish self-employment.

In our context, self-employment implies two interrelated facets of Jewish continuity. First, self-employment means direct control over one's own job. Indirectly, it implies greater reliance on family for resources and connections, as well as power over resources to be distributed to others, and, where appropriate, to coethnics. Moreover, to the extent that Jews are more likely to be working for themselves, they may be more likely to form networks and contacts with others in similar positions, i.e., other Jews. The basic issue focuses on the identification of social and economic structures wherein Jews interact in large part with other Jews.

This perspective moves us beyond the oversimplified explanations of Jewish self-employment patterns. It has been argued that the Jewish propensity for self-employment is related to the fear of non-Jewish control over the jobs Jews have. This concern relates to potential anti-Semitism and the desire to be independent. Over time, so the argument goes, there developed a Jewish value which emphasized autonomous or independent occupations. These values stem from, and are continuous with, the pattern of occupational concentration and segregation characteristic of their eastern European origins. However, the transformation of Jewish socioeconomic conditions over the last century, the radical differences between the status of Jews in America and in Europe, and the general economic and social differences between European and American societies make such interpretations of direct continuity superficial. Our emphasis on the structural features of Jewish continuity also calls into question attempts at uncovering universal Jewish values.

We assume, therefore, that the sources of self-employment primarily reflect the economic and social contexts Jews confront in America and the

socioeconomic (educational and occupational) backgrounds their grand-
fathers and fathers brought with them to America. Our question is not on
the past but on the present: What are the current patterns and recent
changes in self-employment, and what significance do they have for Jewish continuity?

Previous studies of ethnic variation in self-employment have been based
on limited data. While inconsistent self-employment differences between
Protestants and Catholics have been reported in the literature (cf. Lenski
1961; Goldstein 1969; Goldscheider and Kobrin 1980), for Jews the evidence has been consistent, although never analyzed in detail. Lenski
notes for his combined sample of Detroit in the 1950s that Jews had significantly higher rates of self-employment than non-Jews. He concludes:

> In short, it appears that even in the bureaucratized modern metropolis there
> are real and significant differences among the major socio-religious groups in
> the degree to which they value occupational independence and autonomy,
> with the Jews ranking first, White Protestants second, and Catholics third.

While the findings of higher self-employment levels among Jews are clear,
Lenski's conclusions about the Jewish value placed on occupational independence are inferential.

National data based on the Current Population Survey of 1957 confirm
the findings for Jews. For example, 37 percent of Jewish professionals
were self-employed, compared to about 15 percent of Roman Catholics
and white Protestants. Self-employment was even higher for managers,
but the same patterns emerge: 69 percent of Jewish managers were self-
employed, compared to about 50 percent of the non-Jews. These differences remain when years of schooling and urban residence are controlled (Goldstein 1969, tables 6 and 7). Hence, differences between Jews
and non-Jews in the level of self-employment do not appear to be limited
to a particular community, nor can they be simply attributed to the different levels of education and urban concentration characteristic of Jews,
Protestants, and Catholics.

More recently, a detailed analysis of self-employment for religious and
ethnic groups focused on Rhode Island data collected in the late 1960s
(Goldscheider and Kobrin 1980; cf. Kobrin and Goldscheider 1978). There
were only 65 Jews in the Rhode Island survey, and detailed analysis was
limited. Nevertheless, some insights into variations in self-employment
across communities may be gained by comparing the Boston and Rhode
Island data. Since the question asked was identical, the timing of the
studies was close, and the ethnic compositions of Rhode Island and the
Boston metropolitan area are similar, these comparisons are analytically
valuable.

The Boston data allow us to examine several key issues associated with
self-employment patterns. First, differences in self-employment between

Jews and non-Jews can be explored, and patterns of convergence among religious groups can be examined. In particular, we shall focus on the direction and intensity of change in self-employment for Jews and other ethnics. In addition, we shall examine what changes in self-employment occur for contemporary Jews as occupational and educational levels change. Once these relationships are analyzed, we then can clarify whether self-employment patterns are solely a reflection of educational, occupational, and other background differences between Jews and non-Jews.

Information on self-employment was collected on all male respondents and husbands of female respondents. The question was whether the man worked for himself or for someone else. A question on whether the father of the respondent worked for himself when the respondent was growing up was also included. This question, however, was asked only of those below age 40. Data on the self-employment patterns of Jewish women were also collected. No previous research on ethnic differences in self-employment patterns of women has been carried out.

JEWISH–NON-JEWISH SELF-EMPLOYMENT

The basic pattern of higher levels of self-employment among Jews may be observed in table 9.1. Over one-third of the Jewish males who are working are self-employed, three times the level of non-Jews. This pattern characterizes all the detailed racial, religious, and ethnic groups.

The absolute level of Jewish self-employment is lower than in Rhode Island, where one half the Jews were self-employed. In part, this difference reflects the age-generational compositional differences between the Jewish communities of Boston and Rhode Island—the latter are significantly older, with a higher percentage foreign-born. However, the particular demographic differences between these Jewish communities are

TABLE 9.1

Proportion Self-Employed by Age, Religion, and Ethnicity: Males

	Total	18–29	30–39	40–49	50–59	60 +
Jews	36.6	16.3	43.2	32.9	54.7	46.3
Non-Jews	11.2	6.2	10.1	18.5	12.3	11.9
Blacks	6.4	4.5	8.3	*	*	*
White Protestants	14.5	5.9	17.6	8.3	25.0	18.5
Irish Catholics	7.0	16.7	7.7	*	*	*
Italian Catholics	14.5	0.0	14.3	38.5	21.4	7.1
Other white Catholics	11.7	6.7	16.7	17.6	5.3	18.8
Protestants	13.2	6.7	23.5	5.6	18.2	18.5
Catholics	11.1	6.2	10.9	20.5	11.6	10.0

not the entire explanation. A detailed examination of self-employment among non-Jews shows that self-employment of Protestants and Catholics (Irish and Italians) in Rhode Island is also higher than in Boston. This finding forces us to search for explanations of self-employment differences beyond the specific features of the Jewish communities. These include the different occupational markets and economies of the two areas, their opportunity structures, and, in turn, the nature of in- and out-migration patterns and their socioeconomic selectivity.

The Boston data further indicate, as did the Rhode Island study, that the most conspicuous ethnic, racial, and religious differences in self-employment are between Jews and non-Jews. The lower rates of Irish Catholic self-employment and the higher rates among Italian Catholics are consistent in both studies.

Patterns of in- and out-migration are of critical importance in understanding differences between Boston and Rhode Island. Many of the Jews in Rhode Island are selective stayers, who may be more likely to enter into family businesses. Fully 70 percent of the children of Rhode Island Jews move out of the state (Kobrin and Goldscheider 1978, pp. 220–24). That is clearly not the pattern of Jews in Boston, where there are high rates of in-migration (see chapter 4). These patterns also characterize the non-Jews of these areas, although not to the same extent as Jews. In Rhode Island, the Italians remain in much larger numbers than the Irish, and a much larger proportion of Italians is involved in ethnic community networks, including self-employment. These migration patterns have direct implications for self-employment in the community. The generational networks of Jewish self-employment are weaker in Boston than in Rhode Island, although stronger than among non-Jews. Jews who remain in Rhode Island are more likely to connect up with family and kin networks, which involve working for oneself.

These comparisons between communities and between Jews and non-Jews point clearly to the importance of the broader demographic and economic structures of communities as key determinants of self-employment. Neither universal values of occupational independence nor uniform patterns across communities characterize American Jews. At the same time, we should not lose sight of the similarities. Despite demographic and economic differences between Boston and Rhode Island, self-employment patterns are remarkably similar.

Changes in self-employment may be inferred from age variation. These data show that without exception, Jews of all age cohorts have significantly higher self-employment levels than non-Jews. This pattern characterizes, with but one minor exception, every comparison between Jews and other racial, ethnic, and religious subgroups. However, there is no clear direction of change in self-employment from these age data. Over 40 percent of Jews age 30–39 are self-employed, a higher percentage than for those age 40–49 but lower than for those age 50–59. Similar fluctuations characterize non-Jews. Among those 18–29 years of age, there is a sharp drop-off of self-employment levels. That appears to reflect a life cycle effect, the beginnings of careers, and the selective employment of those in this age range. In particular, many of the males age 18–29 remain in school and have not permanently entered the labor force.

Among those age 30–39, there appears to be no convergence in self-employment levels between Jews and non-Jews relative to previous age cohorts. Ethnic-religious differences in self-employment in Boston remain strong. A similar conclusion emerged from the Rhode Island data. Clearly there is no basis from these two data sets for concluding that ethnic differences are converging toward some uniform undifferentiated level. These differences hold despite changes over time and variations in levels between communities.

While the age data suggest that Jewish–non-Jewish differences in self-employment have not disappeared, the issue of generational change can be addressed more directly. The Boston data collected information on the self-employment of fathers. Aggregate- and individual-level change can be identified by comparing the self-employment distributions of fathers and sons. It should be clear that we do not have an unbiased sample of fathers' self-employment (cf. chapters 8 and 10). Differential migration, mortality, and fertility of fathers and differential survivorship and migration of sons affect the representativeness of data on fathers derived from the sample (cf. Blau and Duncan 1967; Matras 1975; Kobrin and Goldscheider 1978). However, given the powerful effects of selective in-migration, age comparisons may not reveal changes in self-employment. Hence, the direct generational patterns take on particular significance.

These comparisons show that 63 percent of the Jewish fathers were self-employed, compared to 26 percent of the sons, a relative decline of 59 percent (table 9.2). For non-Jews, the decline is from 32 percent to 9 percent, a relative decrease of 72 percent. Thus, despite the lower level of self-employment among non-Jews, the rate of generational decline is sharper. Since the decline in self-employment by generation is higher for non-Jews, differences in self-employment between Jews and non-Jews have widened. The differences are not small, as Jewish sons have levels of self-employment almost three times as high as those of non-Jewish sons. Neither age cohort variations nor generational changes in self-employment indicate convergence of Jewish–non-Jewish differences, despite a trend toward declining levels of self-employment.

A summary of these generational flows in self-employment at the individual level focuses on the proportion of fathers and sons who were both self-employed, were both working for others, or had changed generationally (table 9.3). These data show that 14 percent of Jewish fathers and sons were both self-employed, compared to less than 2 percent of non-Jews. This level is significantly lower in Boston than in Rhode Island, where the percentage of self-employment of Jewish fathers and sons is

TABLE 9.2
Generational Self-Employment by Age and Religion: Males

	Jews			Non Jews
	Son's Age			
	18–29	30–39	18–39	18–39
Father self-employed	69.6	49.4	62.8	32.2
Son self-employed	15.6	42.6	22.8	5.1
Son employed by other	84.4	57.4	77.2	94.9
Father employed by other	30.4	50.6	37.2	67.8
Son self-employed	19.1	44.4	30.6	11.0
Son employed by other	80.9	55.6	69.4	89.0
Son self-employed	16.7	43.5	25.7	9.1
Father self-employed	65.2	48.4	55.6	18.2
Father employed by other	34.8	51.6	44.4	81.8
Son employed by other	83.3	56.5	74.3	90.9
Father self-employed	70.5	50.2	65.2	33.6
Father employed by other	29.5	49.8	34.8	66.4

TABLE 9.3
Self-Employment of Fathers and Sons by Age and Religion

Father	Son	Jews		Total[a]	Total
		18–29	30–39	Jews	Non-Jews
Self	Self	10.9	21.0	13.9	1.7
Self	Other	58.8	28.3	46.1	30.6
Other	Self	5.8	22.5	11.9	7.4
Other	Other	24.6	28.2	28.2	60.3
		100.0	100.0	100.0	100.0

[a] Includes a small number of cases 40–49.

very high (43 percent). However, the percentage for non-Jews is also higher. The ratio of Jews and non-Jews who are self-employed in two generations is exactly the same in both studies (7 to 1). Again, while the pattern is identical, the level varies.

At the other end of the continuum, the proportion of two generations working for others is twice as common for non-Jews as for Jews. The flow from self-employment to working for others characterizes 46 percent of the Jews, and the ratio of that pattern to the flow from fathers working for others to self-employed sons is about the same for Jews and non-Jews.

The low proportion of two-generational Jewish self-employment reflects, in part, the small percentage self-employed among Jews 18–29. The proportion of two-generational self-employment is much higher for those age 30–39, where the effects of being enrolled in school are reduced. Life cycle factors distort and accentuate the downward generational decline in Jewish self-employment.

The shift toward an individual rather than an aggregate level of analysis allows us to examine the dynamics associated with the attainment and maintenance of self-employment (table 9.2). The self-employment of Jewish sons does not follow directly from the self-employment of their fathers. While 23 percent of fathers who were self-employed had sons who were self-employed, 31 percent of fathers who were not self-employed had sons who were self-employed. The same pattern characterizes non-Jews. There is, therefore, no greater probability of being self-employed if the father was self-employed than if the father worked for others. In this sense, self-employment is not inherited generationally. This finding further suggests that contemporary patterns of Jewish self-employment involve new types of jobs in a transformed economy. Self-employment patterns parallel the data on occupational concentration, where we argued that contemporary occupational concentration among Jews is both similar to and different from previous patterns. Transformation with continuity characterizes this aspect of Jewish social structure as well (see chapter 8).

The data on the lack of direct effects of self-employment origins on current self-employment in Boston differ significantly from the finding of the Rhode Island data, where direct generational continuity in self-employment clearly characterized the Jewish community. A major factor in this difference is the out-migration patterns from Rhode Island, resulting in a greater continuity in self-employment among those who remain. The higher in-migration rates of Jews to Boston (and their lower rates of generational self-employment) contribute to the different findings in the two communities. Since migration is a community characteristic (rather than a specific ethnic or religious trait), the patterns characterize Jews as well as non-Jews. Nevertheless, the major finding is that Jewish sons have higher self-employment than non-Jewish sons, irrespective of the self-employment patterns of fathers.

These conclusions are reinforced when we examine these data from a somewhat different angle. We ask: What are the self-employment origins of sons who are self-employed? The bottom half of table 9.2 shows these recruitment patterns. Over 55 percent of all Jewish sons who are currently self-employed had fathers who were self-employed when the sons were growing up. However, an even higher percentage of those currently working for others had fathers who were self-employed. The lack of direct self-employment recruitment characterizes non-Jews as well and is not restricted to a particular life cycle segment.

Given the relative unimportance of fathers' self-employment for the self-employment of sons, we can explore whether the self-employment of

TABLE 9.4
**Proportion Self-Employed by Father's Education,
Age, and Religion: Males**

Father's Education	Total 18–39	18–29	30–39
	JEWS		
Less than high school	27.9	31.5	*
High school	25.1	11.3	42.0
Some college	50.7	34.8	67.8
College graduate	16.1	10.3	31.6
Postgraduate	16.2	11.5	28.0
	NON-JEWS		
Father's Education			
Less than high school	9.3	5.7	15.8
High school	14.0	10.0	23.1
Some college	22.2	23.1	*
College graduate	3.8	4.8	*

sons derives from the educational attainments of fathers. The data to answer this question are in table 9.4. Among Jews, the lowest levels of self-
employment characterize those whose fathers graduated from college and
did postgraduate work. It is these fathers who have the lowest probability
of transferring directly to their sons their specific occupational self-employment. The highest level of sons' self-employment is among those
whose fathers had some college education. Fully half of Jewish sons whose
father had some college education were self-employed, about twice as
many as sons whose fathers had higher or lower educational levels. This
pattern characterizes both age groups and is particularly pronounced
among those age 30–39, where 68 percent are self-employed. The sons of
fathers with lower educational levels are less likely to be self-employed
than those whose fathers had some college education. That is consistent
with the generational patterns of occupational and educational inheritance
(see chapter 8).

The influence of educational attainment of fathers on sons' self-employment is similar for Jews and non-Jews. The highest self-employment
among non-Jewish sons is from fathers with some college education, and
the lowest is from fathers who were college graduates. However, the
effects of fathers' educations on the self-employment of sons are less pronounced among non-Jews than among Jews.

While current self-employment patterns of Jews and non-Jews are related to the educational attainments of fathers in similar ways, self-employment differences between Jews and non-Jews cannot be accounted for by their different educational origins. The higher self-employment levels of Jews are not mainly a reflection of the particular educational levels of Jewish fathers. For example, comparing the self-employment levels of those whose fathers were college graduates shows that the level is four times higher for Jews than non-Jews. Similarly, over 90 percent of the non-Jews whose fathers had low education worked for others, compared to about 70 percent of the Jews.

EXPLAINING SELF-EMPLOYMENT

The explanation of self-employment differences between Jews and non-Jews does not reside in the educational or self-employment patterns of their fathers. How do we account for the exceptional Jewish concentration in self-employment? There are few theoretical guidelines for formulating specific explanations. From the more general sociological literature, we can deduce two alternative arguments (cf. Goldscheider and Kobrin 1980). One theme suggests that ethnic differences generally are transitional and spurious. To the extent that self-employment patterns differ for Jews and non-Jews, the source of variation should be explored in the social-class concentration of these groups. Since the socioeconomic characteristics of Jews are very different from those of non-Jews, it seems reasonable to hypothesize that such variation may account for self-employment differences. This argument parallels the "characteristics" hypothesis which has been postulated for the explanation of the unique patterns of Jewish fertility (see Goldscheider 1971; and chapter 7).

An alternative argument can be made that ethnicity is a continuing feature of American communities and cannot be reduced solely to socioeconomic characteristics. Specifically, self-employment differences between Jews and non-Jews are not the result of the particular educational and occupational concentration of Jews. Rather, other factors may be operating: Jewish community ties and networks reinforce the particular concentration of Jews in self-employment. This structural argument will be referred to as the "ethnicity" hypothesis.

There is a third possibility, which posits a specific Jewish value on occupational independence. This value is continuous with the European experience of Jewish vulnerability and the particular status of Jews in the European stratification system. The continuity of this value in America reflects the continuing concerns about anti-Semitism and Jewish dependence on non-Jewish control over jobs. This "self-protection" hypothesis cannot be tested directly with the data available. Variations in self-employment over time among communities as well as within the Jewish population raise questions about the centrality of the self-protection, Jewish-value, hypothesis.

The characteristic and ethnicity hypotheses may be partially evaluated

TABLE 9.5

Proportion Self-Employed by Education, Religion, and Ethnicity: Males

	Less Than High School	High School	Some College	College Graduate	Post-graduate
Jews	39.2	37.0	32.7	45.2	31.1
Blacks	7.1	6.7	10.0	*	*
White Protestants	6.3	17.2	14.3	16.7	20.0
Irish Catholics	5.6	14.3	*	*	*
Italian Catholics	14.3	4.2	33.3	*	*
Other white Catholics	16.1	15.2	0.0	*	*
Protestants	8.0	11.4	18.2	15.2	20.0
Catholics	12.2	11.3	13.2	8.3	5.3

by examining Jewish–non-Jewish differences in self-employment, controlling for education, occupation, and related characteristics. If the socio-economic-characteristics hypothesis is correct, then we would expect no differences in self-employment between Jews and non-Jews to remain when the effects of socioeconomic status are controlled. On the other hand, if differences in self-employment remain within socioeconomic categories, then the argument that specific ethnic factors are operating is strengthened. We cannot test whether the remaining differences are structural or cultural. That would require a different research design, with specific questions addressed directly to this issue.

Here we examine variation in self-employment levels among Jews by educational level not of fathers but of sons (table 9.5). In this generation, college graduates have the highest levels of self-employment (45 percent) and postgraduates (mainly professionals) the lowest (31 percent). While there is no clear pattern relating education to self-employment among Protestants and Catholics, it clearly is different from the Jewish pattern. Nor do differences in self-employment levels between Jews and non-Jews reflect their differential educational levels. Self-employment differences between Jews and non-Jews are most clear, and the gap is greatest, among the less educated. Among those with less than a high-school education, self-employment among Jews is three to four times higher than among non-Jews.

To examine whether these educational differences are related to life cycle factors, we compared Jews and non-Jews within educational levels by age. In no case are self-employment levels between Jews and non-Jews similar for any educational level-age group (table 9.6).

The same conclusion emerges when self-employment is related to occupation, although the differences are often reduced (table 9.7). Half the Jewish managers are self-employed, compared to about 30 percent of the non-Jewish managers; 35 percent of the Jewish professionals are self-employed, compared to about 20 percent of the non-Jewish professionals. Even more striking patterns appear for those in clerical-sales: 36 percent of the Jews are self-employed, compared to less than 5 percent of the non-Jews. The proportion of Jewish workers who are self-employed is over two-and-a-half times that of non-Jews. These patterns hold within age groups as well.

Since the occupational concentration of Jews is so skewed, particularly by age, more-detailed comparisons for specific occupations are difficult. Two interesting findings are revealing: First, fully 30 percent of the Jewish

TABLE 9.6

Proportion Self-Employed by Education, Age, and Religion: Males

	High School	Some College	College Graduate	Postgraduate
		JEWS		
18–29	*	22.2	33.0	1.9
30–39	*	57.3	44.2	44.6
40–49	27.8	62.5	31.8	29.3
50–59	46.8	34.9	81.7	51.5
60+	42.8	30.7	52.5	70.2
		NON-JEWS		
18–29	9.3	3.8	4.2	5.9
30–39	15.9	*	11.1	*
40–49	13.5	*	18.2	*
50–59	7.0	30.8	*	*
60+	10.9	*	*	*

TABLE 9.7

Proportion Self-Employed by Occupation, Religion, and Ethnicity: Males

	Professionals	Managers	Clerical-Sales	Workers
Jews	34.5	48.8	36.0	19.0
White Protestants	25.8	26.1	0.0	9.4
Irish Catholics	16.7		0.0	4.5
Italian Catholics	42.1		5.0	6.3
Other white Catholics	21.4	28.6	10.0	4.9
Protestants	26.5	20.8	3.4	7.5
Catholics	14.3	36.8	5.3	4.9

physicians are self-employed, almost twice as many as non-Jewish physicians. Second, the general category clerical-sales can be subdivided to locate the specific occupational sources of Jewish self-employment. The high rate relative to non-Jews reflects the very heavy concentration of Jewish men in outside saleswork (largely real estate and insurance—see chapter 8) and the relationship between that and self-employment. Fully half of the Jewish men in outside saleswork work for themselves. Nevertheless, examining other clerical-sales jobs, about 15 percent of the Jews are self-employed, still three times the non-Jewish rate.

In sum, there is no evidence to support the socioeconomic-characteristics explanation of Jewish self-employment. It remains unclear what specific structural and cultural factors are operating. Multivariate analysis examining several religious and ethnic variables shows no relationship to Jewish self-employment when education, occupation, and age factors are controlled. A regression analysis combining the socioeconomic origin variables (father's education, occupation, and self-employment) and current educational, occupational, and demographic characteristics shows few effects on current self-employment. By inference, therefore, other factors associated with the ethnic networks must be operating to influence self-employment (cf. the conclusions in Goldscheider and Kobrin 1980).

THE SELF-EMPLOYMENT OF JEWISH WOMEN

The analysis of Jewish self-employment patterns has focused on men. No previous research has examined the particular features of self-employment among Jewish women. The extent to which women work for themselves has two important implications. First, the disruption of family roles may be less among self-employed women than among women working for others. Self-employed women may have much more flexible work schedules and may be more able to regulate their participation in the labor force over the life cycle. Second, self-employment may link women to family, friends, and coethnics much as it does for men. Hence, it may be argued that family-work role incompatibilities and work-ethnic interactions are significantly different among women who are self-employed compared to those who work for others.

We address several elementary questions with the Boston data. First, we ask whether self-employment patterns of Jewish women are exceptional relative to those of non-Jewish women. As with men, Jewish women have higher rates of self-employment than non-Jewish women of each age cohort (table 9.8). Of all Jewish women who ever worked, 9.3 percent were self-employed; almost 15 percent of the Jewish women currently working are self-employed. The respective proportions for non-Jewish women were 4.1 percent and 6.8 percent. The differences between the levels of self-employment for women currently working and those who have ever worked imply that more-sporadic workers are less likely to be self-employed. To the extent that a higher number of Jewish women are self-employed than non-Jewish women, their work patterns may be less sporadic. Those not currently working are much less likely to have ever been self-employed. The largest difference between Jewish and non-Jewish women is among the 40–49 age cohort, where the proportion of Jewish women self-employed is 28 percent, compared to less than 9 percent for non-Jewish women. It is this age cohort which is characterized by the highest level of labor force participation (see chapter 8).

A second question relates to the impact of education and occupation on these patterns. The data show a higher concentration in self-employment among those Jewish women who completed high school compared to those with more (or less) education. For each educational level, Jewish women have higher levels of self-employment than non-Jewish women. The largest self-employment difference between Jews and non-Jews is for women who graduated from high school. Self-employment variation by education is much greater among Jewish than among non-Jewish women. In large part, differences between the self-employment of Jewish and non-Jewish women are independent of life cycle effects and dependent on educational level (see table 9.9).

An analysis of the impact of occupation on the self-employment of women shows higher levels of self-employment among Jewish women

TABLE 9.8

Proportion Self-Employed of Those Who Ever Worked by Age, Education, and Occupation: Jewish and Non-Jewish Women

	Jews	Non-Jews
All Ages	9.3	4.1
18–29	2.9	0.5
30–39	4.8	3.9
40–49	27.9	8.7
50–59	15.5	8.5
60+	6.2	2.8
Education		
Less than high school	2.9	2.1
High-school graduate	14.3	5.1
Some college	5.2	3.9
College graduate	8.8	5.3
Postgraduate	9.6	5.1
Occupation		
Professionals	6.3	1.9
Managers	41.7	38.6
Clerical-sales	2.2	1.3
Workers	11.8	3.1

TABLE 9.9
**Proportion Self-Employed by Education, Age, and
Religion: Ever-Employed Women**

Age	Less Than High School	High-School Graduate	Some College	Post-graduate
Jews				
18–29	*	2.3	5.1	2.4
30–39	*	0.0	0.0	7.8
40–49	*	47.4	8.6	16.1
50–59	*	4.8	2.6	35.7
60+	4.1	4.8	9.9	8.6
Non-Jews				
18–29	*	0.0	1.8	0.0
30–39	*	1.6	5.9	6.9
40–49	*	12.0	11.1	7.7
50–59	*	10.7	0.0	18.8
60+	1.6	3.0	3.7	4.8

within broad occupational categories. There is clearly an enormous range: from 42 percent of the managers to 2 percent of the clerical-sales workers. The same characterizes non-Jews. Only small differences in the level of self-employment separate Jewish and non-Jewish managers (42 percent–39 percent) and Jewish and non-Jewish women in clerical-sales (2.2 percent–1.3 percent). Hence, the pattern of Jewish exceptionalism in self-employment is bimodal—among professionals and workers.

We can extend the analysis in two directions. First we can examine occupations in greater detail. These show very high levels of variability, as might be expected. Teachers and social workers—Jews and non-Jews—have very low proportions self-employed; medical and related professionals have higher levels (about 12 percent). The key, therefore, to understanding the self-employment patterns of Jewish women is to focus on their occupational concentration. Unlike the consistently high levels of self-employment among the detailed occupational categories of men, the variance is much greater among women.

Another extension of our analysis focuses on the relationship between education and female self-employment within age cohorts. The general higher level of self-employment of Jewish women holds for twelve out of the sixteen age-educational comparisons. Adding in occupational controls, however, again reduces the self-employment differences between Jewish and non-Jewish women. The high level of self-employment among high-school graduates age 40–49 (47 percent are self-employed) is concentrated in managerial positions. Jewish women are much more likely to have access to those positions—through families and kin networks—than are non-

Jews. Similarly, 36 percent of the Jewish women age 50–59 with high levels of education are self-employed. That is twice the level among non-Jews and is heavily concentrated in the professions.

Hence, in contrast to the patterns of Jewish men, the unique patterns of self-employment of Jewish women reflect occupational-educational-cohort factors. Nevertheless, an examination of the most educated, professional women, and the managers of family businesses suggests continuing differences for the employment pattern of Jewish compared to non-Jewish women. To the extent that self-employment is less disruptive of childbearing, childrearing, and family life, there would be less conflict between working and family roles among Jewish women (cf. chapter 7). Clearly, there is no reason to argue that the self-employment patterns of Jewish women result in a particular disadvantage for Jewish continuity. To the contrary; the self-employment of women, in conjunction with the patterns noted for males, reinforces kin and community networks.

SELF-EMPLOYMENT, SOCIAL CLASS, AND ETHNICITY

One concomitant of the development of modern industrial society is the reduced level of self-employment. In the United States, the level of self-employment among males has fallen by over 55 percent (1940–70), from over one-fourth to one-ninth of the labor force (Goldscheider and Kobrin 1980). Working for oneself has become a marginal phenomenon. The scale of enterprise has increased, large chains have replaced small business, and the occupational-economic structure has been transformed away from working for oneself. Yet, there is some evidence that self-employment patterns remain an important dimension of the stratification system (Robinson and Kelley 1979; Wright and Perrone 1977; Kluegel 1978). Control over resources may increase for managers and employers as the economy changes. Access to jobs, the segmentation of labor markets, occupational concentration, and differential opportunity structure are connected with self-employment and with ethnic stratification. Neither job authority nor class position can be predicted using measures of socioeconomic status (cf. Robinson and Kelley 1979; Goldscheider and Kobrin 1980). Previous research has concluded that, on both theoretical and empirical grounds, there is need to separate status (the occupational achievement model) from class factors (authority and control over the means of production). If we conceptualize self-employment as one aspect of the class rather than the status system, we expect variables affecting self-employment to be different from those associated with occupation. Our argument is that ethnic groups provide differential access to self-employment opportunities and are, therefore, the key to understanding the class system.

We cannot test directly whether self-employment is a class or status dimension or what the particular networks are that link self-employment to ethnicity. A detailed multivariate model reveals that the factors affecting the stratification system associated with occupational, educational, and income levels are not predictors of self-employment. By inference, we suggest that ethnic networks are important considerations both in determining self-employment and in understanding its consequences.

While ethnic groups vary in occupational, educational, and demographic characteristics, self-employment variation is not accounted for by these differences. The cohort and generational data suggest that levels of Jewish self-employment are not static but vary with broader social and economic opportunities. Community variations reflect demographic compositional issues, migratory selectivity, and economic structural factors. It is not likely that community variation and changes over time in self-employment reflect variation and change in norms and values about self-employment.

The ethnic factor in self-employment involves specific networks maintained by ethnic subcommunities. These networks facilitate the process of ethnic variation and change in self-employment. They are also reinforced by self-employment patterns. The higher levels of self-employment characteristic of Jews may represent one mechanism by which contacts and interactions within the Jewish community are maintained and reinforced. Whether self-employment differences between Jews and the others primarily reflect basic structural or cultural differences cannot be determined with the evidence available. The choice to work in a particular job, for oneself or for others, is complex, and constrained by the structure of opportunity, career goals, and values of autonomy and independence. Whatever the specific mix of determinants of self-employment, these patterns have repercussions and implications for community networks and interactions. Self-employment for many Jews reinforces ties and bonds that are powerful forces for ethnic continuity. As with occupational and educational concentration, high levels of self-employment have characterized Jewish men and women for at least two generations. These patterns are part of existing networks across generations and establish continuing bonds within the Jewish community.

TEN

Secularization, Generational Continuity, and the Ethnic Alternative

Socioeconomic transformations, and changes in family structure, residential concentration, and mobility patterns have resulted in new forms of Jewish community networks and associational ties. As an ethnic group, the community has changed its character. As a group sharing a religious tradition and culture, we ask: What changes have occurred in the religion of modern American Jews? How has secularization affected Jewish continuity? Have new forms of Jewish expression emerged to serve as anchors for cohesion among America's Jews? We focus on two themes: (1) the patterns of secularization in Jewish religious behavior and identification and (2) the emergence of alternative forms of Jewish expression. The overriding concern is with the ways in which Jewish cohesion and continuity are manifest in the community.

Previous research has documented extensively the decline of religious behavior, ritual observances, and traditional Orthodox identification among American Jews. The transformation of the more religiously oriented immigrant generation to the secularized second and third generation has been one of the master themes in the sociology of Jews in the United States. In turn, these changes have been associated with broader processes of assimilation and acculturation (see Goldstein and Goldscheider 1968; Sklare 1971; Himmelfarb 1982; Cohen 1983). Some of the fundamental patterns are well known. There is, however, less consensus in the interpretation of the evidence and the inferred connections to assimilation.

The most widespread interpretation of these patterns of generational change in the various dimensions of religiosity derives from the secularization-modernization framework. The argument is that changes in religious behavior and attitudes are part of the assimilation process. As Jews become more American and more modernized in America, they shed their religious particularism. They become less religious in their behavior, view religion as less central in their lives, and mold their religious observances to fit in with the dominant American culture. What remains, therefore, of traditional Judaism are forms of religious expression which do not conflict with the Americanization of the Jews. Family rituals predominate; dietary regulations are observed less frequently; Chanukah and Seder celebrations fit well with children and family-centeredness and parallel Christmas and Easter; Sabbath observances and regular synagogue attendance are more difficult to sustain, since they compete with leisure and occupational activities. In sum, one argument is that Judaism declines with modernization. The residual observances reflect acculturation and imitation of dominant American forms. Alternative activities, such as participation in Jewish communal organizations, are viewed as poor substitutes for traditional religious institutions and behavior. Indeed, these are often included under the rubric "civil religion" (see articles by Leibman and Elazar in Sklare 1982). In this context, therefore, changes in religious identification and behavior are interpreted as the weakening of the religious sources of Jewish continuity. Religious leaders and institutions are the most likely to equate the decline of Judaism with the demise of the Jewish community.

There is another view which understands the processes of secularization as part of the broader transformation of Jews in modern society (cf. Goldscheider and Zuckerman 1984). In this perspective, the decline in the centrality of religion must be seen in the context of the emergence of new forms of Jewish expression. Before one can equate the decline of traditional forms with the loss of community, it is important to examine whether alternative ways to express Jewishness emerge. In the past, religion and Jewishness were inseparable. Changes in Judaism were indeed threatening to Jewish continuity and cohesion. However, in the process of expansion of community size and institutions, and the integration of Jews in the social, economic, political, and cultural patterns of the broader society, opportunities for new forms of expressing Jewishness have developed as alternative ways to reinforce Jewish cohesion, even as links between religion and Jewishness have weakened.

These new forms provide a wide range of options for expressing Jewishness among those at different points in their life cycle. For some, religion remains central; for most, Jewishness is a combination of family, communal, religious, and ethnic forms of Jewish expression. At times, Jewishness revolves around educational experiences; for families with children, the expression of Jewishness is usually in synagogue-related and children-oriented celebrations. For almost all, it is the combination of family, friends, community activities, organizations, and reading about and visiting Israel. Many ways have developed to express Jewishness, and some have become more important than others at different points in the life cycle, in different places, and with different exposures to Jewishness.

In this perspective, the examination of changes in one set of Jewish expressions must be balanced by an investigation of other Jewish expressions. Hence, a decline in ritual observance, synagogue attendance, or Jewish organizational participation must be viewed in the context of the

total array of Jewish-related activities and associations. It is the balance of
the range of expressions which allows for the evaluation of Jewish continuity. Thus, connections between secularization (in the sense of changing forms of religious expression and declines in ritual observances) and
broader Jewish continuity (including a wide range of Jewish-related attitudes, values, and activities which are not necessarily religiously oriented) need to be studied directly rather than by inference.

Two methodological considerations emerge from this view. First, since
the ways in which Jews express their Jewishness vary over the life cycle,
we cannot use life cycle variation as the major indicator of generational
decline. Variation in Jewishness over the life cycle may imply the different
ways young singles, married couples, and older people relate to Judaism
and Jewishness. Inferences from cross-sectional age variation about the
"decline" in a particular dimension of Jewishness need to be made with
caution. Disentangling life-cycle from generational effects is very complex
using cross-sectional data. Longitudinal studies are needed to fully investigate these patterns as they unfold. In their absence, retrospective longitudinal designs (i.e., asking about past behavior and earlier generations)
are appropriate.

A second methodological issue relates to the emergence of new forms of
Jewish expression. While we can identify the decline of traditional forms
of Judaism, we have no clear way of examining the development of new
expressions of communal activities. For example, we have identified in the
Boston study, as in previous research, declining Orthodox identification
and observances of dietary regulations of Kashrut. But the changing concerns about Israel, Jewish communal activities, and other forms of Jewish
expression which are new on the American scene cannot be measured
against the past, where they did not exist. As a result, the tendency is to
focus on those items which are traditionally associated with Jewishness.
We shall attempt to move beyond that focus to include some different
dimensions. Nevertheless, much more research needs to be carried out
on these alternative forms of Jewish expression which are not continuous
with the past but may have a major impact on Jewish continuity in the
future (cf. Himmelfarb 1982).

SECULARIZATION AND THE DECLINE OF RITUAL OBSERVANCES

One implication of the secularization-modernization thesis is that there
have been shifts in the denominational identification of American Jews.
The linear model of assimilation predicts the change from Orthodox identification among first-generation Jewish immigrants to Conservative and
Reform Judaism among their children and grandchildren. If followed to its
logical conclusion, the fourth generation, growing up in the 1960s and
1970s, should be heavily concentrated among the nondenominational.

Nonaffiliation with one of the three major denominations within Judaism is interpreted as the final step toward total assimilation.

There are three ways to document and analyze these changes in religious denomination: (1) comparisons of the two cross-sections 1965 and 1975; (2) changes inferred from age variation in religious denominational identification; and (3) changing denominational affiliation by generation from retrospective longitudinal data. Each has methodological limitations; together they present a consistent pattern.

In 1965, the Boston community was characterized by a larger proportion of Orthodox and Conservative Jews and a smaller proportion of Reform and nonaffiliated Jews than in 1975. During this decade, the proportion Orthodox declined from 14 percent to 5 percent, while the proportion nonaffiliated increased from 14 percent to 25 percent. The age data in 1965 showed a drop in Orthodoxy and an increase in the nondenominational (see Axelrod, Fowler, and Gurin 1967; Fowler 1977; cf. Himmelfarb 1982 for a literature review; Cohen 1983). Some of the changes relate to the changing composition of the community, its demographic structure, migration patterns, and marriage formation patterns, as well as the continual secularization and change of the population. By 1975, most of those age 20–29 in 1965 will be married; some will have moved out of the community, others will have moved in, and those remaining will have been exposed to a wide range of personal, community, and Jewish changes. These cannot be easily disentangled. Comparing, for example, those age 21–29 in 1965 with those age 30–39 in 1975 shows that the proportion with no denominational affiliation was about the same (22 percent), while the proportion Orthodox declined from 6 percent to 3 percent and the proportion Conservative declined from 43 to 35 percent. The proportion Reform increased from 26 percent to 39 percent. Although the net expected pattern appears, it is difficult to understand what actually happened, and thus predict with any confidence future trends from cross-sectional comparisons over time at the aggregate level. Such an analysis cannot adequately deal with whether these changes reflect life cycle effects, the differential impact of selective migration streams into and out of the community, the changing attractiveness of Reform Judaism, or hundreds of events and alterations in individuals or communities during this decade.[1] We therefore focus our attention on the most recent study for a detailed analysis.

The data from the 1975 survey show that one-fourth of the adult Jewish population did not identify with any of the three major denominations within Judaism, only 5 percent identified as Orthodox, and the rest were about equally distributed between Conservative and Reform (table 10.1).

1. The changing level of Jewish organizational membership, including synagogue membership, between 1965 and 1975 seems to reflect demographic and compositional changes in the community (cf. Fowler 1977).

TABLE 10.1

Denominational Identification, Synagogue Attendance and Membership, and the Observance of Religious Rituals by Age

	Total	18–29	30–39	40–59	60+
Denominational Identification					
Orthodox	4.9	0.2	2.7	3.3	17.2
Conservative	34.7	24.4	34.9	38.4	47.3
Reform	36.0	38.2	39.0	40.3	23.9
Other	24.5	37.2	23.3	18.0	11.6
Synagogue Attendance					
Sometimes	30.8	17.0	36.1	45.9	32.9
Seldom	46.2	52.2	42.6	40.9	43.9
Never	23.0	30.8	21.3	13.2	23.2
Synagogue Membership	37.0	13.7	41.3	59.9	47.7
Religious Rituals					
None	18.8	30.0	19.0	11.6	7.3
Some	43.5	51.1	42.1	38.5	36.3
Many	37.7	18.9	38.9	49.9	56.4

It is difficult to argue assimilation and disintegration when three-fourths of the adult Jews identify denominationally. Similarly, while synagogue attendance is not high for most Jews, only 23 percent never attend. Turned around, over three-fourths attend synagogue services sometime during the year, mainly high holidays and some festivals or family-social occasions. Furthermore, fully 80 percent observe at least some personal religious rituals—keeping kosher, reciting prayers, lighting Sabbath candles, fasting on Yom Kippur, affixing a *Mezzuzah* on the door, or observing dietary rules on Passover.[2] Indeed, in cross-section, the Boston Jewish community exhibits a high level of religious commitment. The only serious indication of low levels of religiosity is the extent of membership in synagogues and temples: only 37 percent of the adult Jewish population are synagogue or temple members. Twice as many Jews identify denominationally as join synagogues. Nevertheless, formal membership is a reflection much more of life cycle and communal attachments than of re-

2. A factor analysis disclosed that a single scale emerges from the combination of the six items: (1) keeping Kosher at home; (2) reciting a daily prayer or worshipping at home or at a synagogue; (3) lighting Sabbath candles; (4) putting a Mezzuzah on the door; (5) fasting on Yom Kippur; and (6) observing dietary rules on Passover. These were each given equal weight in one overall index of religious ritual observances.

ligiosity per se. There is no basis for arguing that nonmembership indicates the lack of commitment to Jewish continuity.

The issue of changing religious vitality is of course a question of change relative to the actual past, not necessarily to an ideal. In this regard, the data by age show clear patterns of decline in Orthodox identification, some decline in Conservative identification, general stability in the proportion identifying as Reform among those 18–60 years of age, and a monotonic increase in the proportion nondenominational. The data for the youngest cohort are difficult to interpret, since there is a life cycle effect on religious-denominational identification. The level of identification increases with marriage and childbearing. Hence, it is reasonable to expect an increase in denominational identification as those age 18–29 marry. A general estimate of the level of nondenominational identification among the young would be around 25 percent, i.e., the level of those age 30–39. That is the same proportion characteristic of those age 21–29 in the 1965 study. We are thus tempted to see this level as a reasonable estimate for this cohort, suggesting that even among the young, between two-thirds and three-fourths are identified with a specific religious denomination within Judaism. The same set of assumptions would characterize synagogue attendance and membership and the observance of religious rituals.

If we take the cohort age 30–39 as the level of religiosity of young Jewish families, we can infer that only about 20–25 percent are religiously secular, i.e., do not identify denominationally, never attend the synagogue, and observe no personal religious rituals. An even larger number (perhaps the majority) are not members of religious institutions.

Overall, therefore, these data show some systematic variation, largely over time and partly over the life cycle, in Jewish religiosity. They also show patterns of continuity and vitality in Jewish religious identification and behavior.

Another aspect of the secularization theme focuses on the education-religiosity connection. Again the simple argument is that higher levels of educational attainment result in lower levels of religiosity. This connection is based on the assumed process of liberalization associated with education, exposure to ideas which challenge traditional beliefs, and the role of college and university education in changing family attachments and particularistic attitudes and behavior. The data in table 10.2 only partially support these connections. There is a systematic inverse relationship between educational attainment and the nonobservance of religious rituals and synagogue membership. However, there are no significant differences in the proportions nondenominational among those with high-school, some college, and completed college educations. Differences between those with the highest level of education and others reflect age factors, since when it is controlled, no systematic differences emerge. The same is true for the relationship between educational attainment and synagogue attendance. In short, life cycle and generational factors affect these measures of religiosity more than educational attainment. Moreover, it is clear from these data that higher levels of educational attainment are not an important threat to Jewish religious continuity. (Similar findings have been reported in national and other local studies. Cf. the review by Himmelfarb 1982.)

GENERATIONAL DENOMINATIONAL ROOTS AND CHANGES

These cross-sectional data focus on aggregate changes inferred from age variation. Most previous research has used that or a generational model to highlight changes over time in religiosity (Cohen 1983). Another way to examine these changes is to compare the denominational identification of respondents directly with that of their parents. In the Boston study, a question was included on the religious denomination of the respondent's parents. This question measures a subjective dimension imputed by the respondent. It should not be taken as an unbiased distributional measure of the denominational affiliation of the parental generation. A series of methodological limitations makes this assessment of parental denominational affiliation problematic.[3] There are differences between the denominational affiliation attributed by children to parents and the self-identification of parents. Children may ascribe more-traditional affiliation to parents, particularly in periods of rapid change. Moreover, denominational affiliation is not an ascribed characteristic, constant throughout the life

TABLE 10.2

Proportion Low Jewishness on Selected Measures by Education

	High School	Some College	College Graduate	Post-graduate
Percent				
Nondenominational	20.2	19.0	22.7	33.0
Never attending synagogue	22.8	20.0	23.0	24.3
Nonmember of synagogue	57.6	57.8	60.5	73.6
Nonobservance of rituals	11.7	18.2	21.8	21.9
Low Jewish values	12.2	16.5	27.9	26.4
Nonobservance of family rituals	8.9	12.0	6.7	12.6
No community-ethnic association	44.7	47.0	41.0	36.5
Mostly non-Jewish friends	19.0	15.4	12.4	11.6

3. Differential fertility, mortality, and migration have effects on survivorship. These limitations apply as well to our discussion of generational changes in socioeconomic and demographic processes.

TABLE 10.3

Comparison between Religious Denominational Self-Identification and Imputed Identification, Selected Ages

	Orthodox	Conservative	Reform	Total Percentage
Religious denominational identification[a] of those currently age 40–59	4.0	46.8	49.1	100.0
Parental denominational identification imputed by children age 18–29	3.5	49.5	47.0	100.0
Religious denominational identification[a] of those currently age 60+	19.5	53.5	27.0	100.0
Parental denominational identification imputed by children age 30–39	26.1	46.8	27.2	100.0

[a] Eliminating the proportion who currently are nondenominational.

cycle. Hence, it is reasonable to assume that changes in denominational affiliation characterized parents over their life cycle, and perhaps the religious denomination attributed by children to parents varies over the children's life cycle. Taken together, we assume that there is some error in treating attributed identification as equivalent to self-identification. Nevertheless, the uniqueness of these data for an assessment of generational change and the denominational roots of current religious identification at the individual level, argue strongly for the analysis of these data.

Furthermore, comparing the denominational distribution attributed to parents by children age 18–29 and 30–39 to the distribution of the self-identification of those currently age 40–59 and 60 and over reveals striking parallels (table 10.3). Eliminating the nondenominational, the data show almost identical distributions of those currently age 40–59 with the parents of those 18–29 and of those currently age 60 and over with the parents of those age 30–39. Including the nondenominational makes the comparison less similar but still a reasonable approximation.[4]

What are the denominational roots of those who currently identify themselves as Orthodox, Conservative, Reform, or other? For the total sample in 1975, 25 percent identified their parents as Reform, and the remainder were equally divided between Orthodox and Conservative.

4. The distributions of those age 40–59 and 18–29, including the nondenominational, are in table 10.1.

There were so few who identified their parents as nondenominational (or "other") that we did not have enough cases for analysis. Perhaps the children of parents who were nondenominational disproportionately migrate out of Boston or no longer identify as Jews; or, perhaps, those who identified as "others" were childless. We do not have sufficient evidence to confirm any of these explanations. On the basis of the nondenominational of the current generation, neither their Jewishness nor their fertility or migration patterns provide much support for those arguments. The low proportion nondenominational imputed by children to their parents probably reflects nothing more than the tendency to place parents (and others) into convenient categories. If these parents had been asked directly, a larger proportion would probably have responded "other." Indeed, 12 percent of those age 60 and over in the sample did not identify with one of the three major religious divisions within Judaism.

Generational changes away from Orthodox affiliation are striking when examined by current denominational identification (table 10.4). Of those who are currently Orthodox, almost all described their parents as Orthodox. In contrast, less than half of those who are Conservative describe their parents as Conservative; the same characterizes the Reform Jews. What are the denominational origins of Conservative and Reform Jews?

TABLE 10.4
Generational Denominational Identification by Sex: Inflows

Children	Parents				
	Orthodox	Conservative	Reform	Total %	N
TOTAL	37.3	37.5	25.2	100.0	1818
Orthodox	97.0	1.0	2.0	100.0	98
Conservative	50.0	46.6	3.4	100.0	673
Reform	25.0	28.6	46.3	100.0	688
Other	20.7	47.2	32.1	100.0	358
Male					
TOTAL	39.6	37.5	22.8	100.0	840
Orthodox	95.8	2.1	2.1	100.0	47
Conservative	51.2	47.4	1.4	100.0	281
Reform	30.9	28.5	40.6	100.0	308
Other	23.7	45.9	30.4	100.0	203
Female					
TOTAL	35.3	37.4	27.3	100.0	978
Orthodox	98.0	0.0	2.0	100.0	51
Conservative	49.1	46.1	4.8	100.0	392
Reform	20.3	28.7	51.0	100.0	380
Other	16.9	48.8	34.3	100.0	156

TABLE 10.5

Generational Denominational Identification by Sex: Outflows

	Male	Female	Total
Orthodox parent (N)	333	345	678
Orthodox child	13.7	14.4	14.1
Conservative child	43.3	55.7	49.6
Reform child	28.6	22.3	25.4
Other child	14.4	7.6	11.0
Conservative parent (N)	315	366	681
Orthodox child	0.3	0.0	0.1
Conservative child	42.3	49.4	46.1
Reform child	27.9	29.8	28.9
Other child	29.5	20.8	24.8
Reform parent (N)	192	267	459
Orthodox child	0.5	0.4	0.4
Conservative child	2.1	7.1	5.0
Reform child	65.3	72.5	69.5
Other child	32.1	20.0	25.1

Most of the Conservative Jews are from Orthodox families; Reform Jews are equally divided between parents who are Orthodox and Conservative. There is a clear general tendency intergenerationally to move from Orthodox to Conservative or Reform, and from Conservative to Reform.

The denominational sources of the nondenominationally identified are complex. They do not overwhelmingly come from Reform parents. Indeed, more identify their parents as Conservative than Reform, and a substantial number define their parents as Orthodox (21 percent). The nondenominational are, therefore, not mainly the children of Reform parents, although they disproportionately identify their parents as Conservative and Reform compared to the total population.

Viewed from the perspective of generational outflows, these data suggest that most Orthodox parents have children who are either Conservative or Reform (table 10.5). The low levels of generational inheritance of Orthodox identification (only 14 percent of the parents who are Orthodox have children who are Orthodox) imply major declines over time in this traditional category. In contrast, there is a much higher level of generational inheritance among Reform and Conservative Jews. Fully 70 percent of the parents who are Reform have children who are Reform, and 46 percent of the Conservative parents have children who identify as Conservative Jews. The outflow generationally is therefore clearly away from Orthodoxy; most of the Orthodox (and most of the Conservative) Jews have shifted to Conservative identification. There is the same outflow to nondenominational identification from Conservative and Reform parents:

about one-fourth of Conservative and Reform parents have children who do not identify with one of the three religious denominations within Judaism.

Thus, the Orthodox have shifted generationally much more to Conservative than to Reform, and few have become nondenominational. The children of Conservative Jews who are not also Conservative tend to be equally divided between Reform and nondenominational. In contrast, Reform parents are more likely to have children who are nondenominational than children who are Conservative or Orthodox and are most likely to have children who identify themselves as Reform Jews.

In general, these patterns characterize males and females. Denominational continuity is weaker among males than females: the proportion of women who are two-generational Orthodox, Conservative, or Reform is higher in each case than that of men. Similarly, the number who shift generationally from one of the three denominations to nondenominational is higher among males than females. For example, about 20 percent of Conservative and Reform parents had daughters who do not identify denominationally; about 30 percent had sons who did not identify denominationally.

More important, there is a much higher level of generational continuity in denominational identification among the youngest cohort. Most young Conservative Jews identify their parents as Conservative Jews (86 percent); most young Reform Jews have parents whom they identify as Reform Jews (71 percent). Those who do not identify denominationally are about equally from Conservative and Reform families. One implication of this generational continuity parallels our argument about education, occupation, fertility, and family processes: there is a growing homogeneity among younger Jews, which forges bonds of continuity and interaction between generations and among age peers. The data for younger cohorts suggest little generational conflict in religious identification. Even the backgrounds of those who are nondenominational (i.e., equally from Conservative and Reform families) do not split them away from their age peers who have similar religious backgrounds.[5]

These patterns of generational continuity are characteristic of the youngest cohorts and are relatively new. In the past, generational differences in denominational identification were much greater. For example, only 20 percent of Conservative Jews 60 years of age and older identified their parents as Conservative Jews; this proportion increases to 32 percent among those age 40–59, 56 percent among those age 30–39, and

5. We have not focused on the complex issues of Jewish education in this study (cf. Bock 1976; Himmelfarb 1982; Cohen 1983). It should be noted in this context that the level of Jewish education is high in the Jewish community of Boston and has remained high in both the 1965 and 1975 studies. Indeed, most Jews receive some Jewish education, and there has been a slight increase among young adults (cf. Fowler 1977). This pattern should also be viewed in the context of generational continuities.

86 percent among the youngest cohort. There is a similar pattern among Reform Jews: from 21 percent among those 40–59 years of age to 71 percent among the youngest cohort.

An examination of the changing denominational roots of nondenominational Jews reveals an increasing equal distribution between Conservative and Reform parents. In the older generation, almost all of those who are nondenominational identified their parents as Orthodox. For the next age group (40–59), there was a greater balance toward Orthodox and Conservative parental roots. Comparing the two youngest cohorts reveals clearly the shift toward a more equal division between Conservative and Reform parents away from mostly Conservative parents.

Most of those who are Orthodox identify their parents as Orthodox. Data on the Orthodoxy of the younger generation are not complete because of the small number included. Generational continuity among those who are currently Orthodox is significant precisely because of the major shifts generationally away from Orthodoxy. While there have been major outflows from Orthodox to non-Orthodox denominations, those who are currently Orthodox are almost exclusively from Orthodox families. There is no evidence from these data of inflows to Orthodoxy from the non-Orthodox.

The critical variable in the continuity of denominational identification between generations is age. That is expected, given the age variation we noted earlier in the cross-section and the patterns of denominational changes in the aggregate from Orthodox to Conservative and Reform. The patterns are striking: of those who are currently 60 years of age and over, three-fourths describe their parents as Orthodox, 15 percent as Conservative, and 9 percent as Reform (table 10.6). These attributed denominations decline among the younger cohorts: 56 percent of those age 40–59 identified their parents as Orthodox, compared to 26 percent among those 30–39 years of age and less than 4 percent among those age 18–29. Concomitantly, the proportion Conservative and Reform increases monotonically with age: from 15 percent to 50 percent Conservative parents among those age 60 and over to the youngest cohort; from 9 percent to 47 percent Reform parents for the same age comparisons. These same conclusions emerge from the outflow data by age and are not presented here in tabular form.

Denominational changes between generations do not vary systematically by education. The general transformation of religious identification is not specific to an educational level. Nor are the recruitment or inheritance patterns more pronounced among the more- or less-educated. As socioeconomic patterns have been transformed, so has denominational identification between generations.

In an attempt to capture in summary form the details of these patterns, we calculated the proportions who had the same religious denomination as the one they attributed to their parents, i.e., two-generational Orthodox, Conservative, and Reform. We subdivided the remainder into those who generationally moved "up" (from nondenominational, Reform or Conservative to Orthodox, from nondenominational or Reform to Conservative, and from nondenominational to Reform) and those who moved "down" (from Orthodox, Conservative, or Reform to none, from Orthodox or Conservative to Reform, from Conservative to Reform). We do not want to convey any judgment in this classification except a direction away from, or toward, traditional Jewish religious identification. (We use *traditional* in its social-normative, not Halachic, sense.)

There is a built-in bias, however, in that so few are reported by their children as nondenominational in the parental generation, and therefore, those who are currently nondenominational must be placed in the "down" category. In this way, each generation feels it moves "down" by comparing its reality with remembered ideals. Nevertheless, this situation is at least in part a reflection of reality and cannot be totally dismissed.

Overall, the data show that 40 percent of the adult Jews have the same

TABLE 10.6
Generational Denominational Identification by Age: Inflows

| | Parents | | | | |
Children	Orthodox	Conservative	Reform	Total Percent	N
18–29	3.5	49.5	47.0	100.0	624
Orthodox	*	*	*	*	*
Conservative	4.9	86.4	8.6	100.0	162
Reform	3.8	25.0	71.2	100.0	264
Other	1.5	52.2	46.3	100.0	197
30–39	26.1	46.8	27.2	100.0	291
Orthodox	*	*	*	*	*
Conservative	41.0	55.5	3.5	100.0	113
Reform	13.0	33.7	53.3	100.0	110
Other	11.8	60.7	27.5	100.0	59
40–59	55.8	33.4	10.8	100.0	509
Orthodox	89.2	5.4	5.4	100.0	19
Conservative	66.1	32.4	1.4	100.0	207
Reform	45.3	34.0	20.7	100.0	215
Other	48.5	42.3	9.2	100.0	69
60+	76.7	14.8	8.6	100.0	366
Orthodox	98.5	0.0	1.5	100.0	67
Conservative	78.7	20.1	1.2	100.0	174
Reform	51.0	19.5	29.5	100.0	92
Other	93.9	3.0	3.0	100.0	33

TABLE 10.7

Generational Denominational Identification: Summary Patterns

	Percent same	Percent "up"	Percent "down"	Total percent	N
TOTAL	40.0	1.5	58.5	100.0	1,818
Sex					
Male	36.2	0.7	63.1	100.0	840
Female	43.4	2.0	54.6	100.0	978
Age					
18–29	52.7	2.2	45.1	100.0	624
30–39	44.6	1.4	54.0	100.0	291
40–59	25.3	1.0	73.7	100.0	509
60+	35.1	0.8	64.9	100.0	366
Income					
$10,000	47.8	3.2	49.0	100.0	474
10–20,000	45.7	0.3	54.0	100.0	368
20–35,000	45.0	1.3	53.7	100.0	315
35,000+	26.9	0.4	72.7	100.0	270
Education					
High school	32.3	0.4	67.3	100.0	477
Some college	37.8	1.8	60.4	100.0	338
College graduate	43.1	2.9	54.0	100.0	511
Postgraduate	46.3	0.6	53.1	100.0	483

denominational identification as their parents (table 10.7). Almost none moved "up" religiously, and 59 percent moved away generationally from more traditional religious identification. (When the nondenominational are eliminated, there is a 50 percent continuity level between generations.) The age patterns are most revealing. Over time, there has been a substantial *increase* in the extent of generational continuity in denominational affiliation. Three-fourths of those age 40–59 had a different denominational identification from that of their parents, and almost all moved away from tradition. Among the youngest cohort, the number who identify with the same denomination as their parents exceeds 50 percent; excluding those who are not yet identified, the proportion generationally similar of the three denominations among the young is 77 percent. Hence, at the same time that there are clear indications of secularization away from religious tradition, there are powerful signs of increasing generational continuity. There are also some indications, although slight, of an increase in the proportion who have moved "up," from less than 1 percent among the oldest cohort to over 2 percent among the young. The change from a pattern of 75 percent downward mobility away from religious traditional identification among the older generation to 77 percent of the younger generation who have the same religious denomination as their parents (if they identify denominationally) is nothing less than a radical transformation. We postulate that this increasing level of generational continuity in religious denominational identification has become an additional source of Jewish cohesion. It is reinforced by other forms of generational continuity, including socioeconomic status and family patterns. Taken together, these social processes are powerful sources of American Jewish continuity in the 1980s.

We note in addition that stability generationally is somewhat higher for women than for men, as is the proportion who move "up." Of greater importance is the higher proportions generationally similar among the more educated. The positive relationship between generational denominational continuity and educational attainment partly reflects age patterns but operates even within age groups. This pattern supports the general findings that generational continuity is high among the younger cohorts and the most educated. These are the future of the American Jewish community.

ALTERNATIVE SOURCES OF JEWISH COHESION

Religiosity is only one of the ways in which Jews express their Jewishness. In the past, Judaism and Jewishness were intertwined, so that any change in religious expression represented a threat to Jewish continuity. That is no longer the case among contemporary Jewish communities (Goldscheider and Zuckerman 1984). Our focus here is on tapping the Boston study for clues about some of these alternative sources of Jewish cohesion which are not religious forms in the narrow sense. We shall focus on Jewish values, family observances, ethnic-community associations, and Jewish friends. These measures of cohesion indicate contexts of interaction, sources of particularistic values, and anchors of ethnic identity. As such, they complement the religious dimension of Jewish cohesion.

A series of questions was included about Jewish values and the meaning of being Jewish. A statistical analysis selected four elements that combined to yield one overall factor. These included the following values: (1) It is important for every Jewish child to be given a serious continuing Jewish education; (2) It is important to observe traditional Jewish religious practices; (3) I feel proud of being a Jew when I hear or read about accomplishments of Jews; (4) The existence of Israel is essential for the continuation of American Jewish life.

A high proportion of Jews expressed most of these values (table 10.8). About 60 percent agreed with at least three out of four of these items. The critical issue is, of course, some indication of change. The age data show

Table 10.8
Selected Measures of Jewishness by Age (Percent)

	Total	18–29	30–39	40–59	60+
Jewish Values					
Low	21.6	30.5	26.0	17.3	7.3
High	58.6	45.9	48.9	63.9	74.7
Family Observances	71.2	68.2	64.2	75.6	75.8
Ethnic-Community Associations					
None	42.0	53.0	38.9	39.6	27.7
Many	30.2	21.3	27.1	31.6	46.3
Proportion Jewish Friends					
Most	49.7	32.4	46.7	62.8	68.9
Few or none	14.8	24.5	13.6	3.7	12.1

some increase in the proportion scoring low and a decrease in the proportion scoring high. Still, 70 percent of those age 18–29 had medium to high scores on this scale.

An equally impressive level of Jewishness emerges from an examination of the celebration of Jewish holidays with family.[6] Over 70 percent of the adult Jewish community participate in religious holiday celebrations with family. There is some indication of decline, from 76 percent among the two oldest cohorts to about 65 percent among the youngest cohort. Nevertheless, the overwhelming impression is that most adult Jews, young and old, connect up with other family members for Jewish-family-related celebrations. In turn, these celebrations have become major sources of group cohesion and anchors of Jewish continuity.

A third set of items which also emerged out of a factor analysis relates to ethnic-community issues. These included: (1) attending lectures or classes of Jewish interest: (2) visiting Israel; and (3) reading newspapers or magazines of Jewish content. Again the pattern is similar: some indications of decline in identifying Jewishly through Israel and direct involvement with the community, but nevertheless an impressive level of some type of community identification.

A final item is the extent to which Jews interact with Jews and non-Jews. The question was: "About how many of your friends are Jewish—all, most, about half, or are most of your friends not Jewish?" Fully 85 percent of the respondents said that at least half of their friends were Jewish, and

6. This index combines two questions which were isolated in a factor analysis as a single dimension of family observances: (1) taking part in a Passover Seder; (2) getting together with relatives to celebrate any Jewish holidays in the past year.

50 percent said that most or all of their friends were Jewish. There is a decline in the proportions who say most of their friends are Jewish, and an increase in the proportion with few or no Jewish friends, with decreasing age. Nevertheless, three-fourths of those age 18-29 and 85 percent of those age 30–39 indicated that at least half of their friends were Jewish. (See figure 10.1, where these patterns are compared to the changing observance of Jewish ritual.) For the older age cohorts, there is a more exclusive pattern of ethnic friendship, where about two thirds had mostly

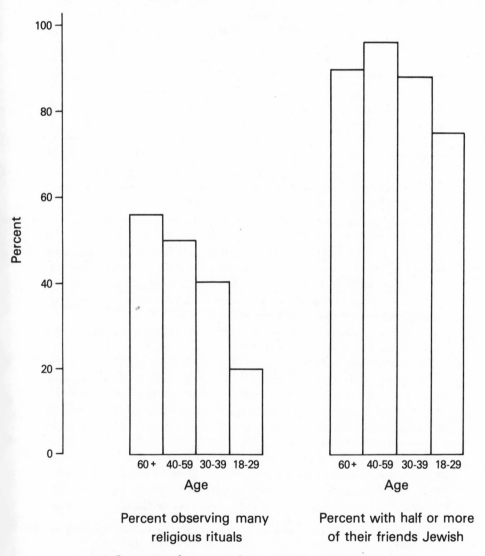

Percent observing many religious rituals

Percent with half or more of their friends Jewish

10.1 A Comparison between Religious Rituals and Jewish Friends by Age

Jewish friends. The pattern among the younger cohorts seems to be a greater balance between Jewish and non-Jewish friends. It is inconsistent to argue on the basis of this evidence that younger Jews do not have important networks of friendship which tie them to other Jews. These networks may be less linked to the organized Jewish community, to formal Jewish organization, or to religious institutions. However, they are tied to new forms of Jewish continuity, and have important relationships to economic, residential, lifestyle, and related values.

How are these ethnic-community aspects of Jewishness related to education? The expression of traditional Jewish values is clearly linked inversely to education—the higher the education, the lower the proportion expressing Jewish values[7] (table 10.2). These patterns characterize the youngest cohort but reverse among those age 30–39. In that cohort, only 22 percent of the most educated express low Jewish values, compared to 36 percent among the college-educated. For family ritual observance and ethnic-community associations, the patterns by education either are unclear or show that the most educated have the greater links to Jewishness. For example, the more educated rank higher on the community-ethnic dimension than the less educated, and these findings are accentuated within age controls. Detailed data not shown reveal that over three-fourths of the most educated ranked medium to high on this dimension, compared to 40 percent of the college-educated.

A similar pattern may be observed with the proportion with mostly non-Jewish friends. Those with postgraduate educations have the *lowest* proportion who said most of their friends are not Jewish. These patterns are even clearer by age. While one-fourth to one-fifth of the college-educated age 18–29 had mostly non-Jewish friends, only 13 percent of the postgraduates had mostly non-Jewish friends. Similarly, for the 30–39 cohort, 38 percent of those with some college education had mostly non-Jewish friends, compared to 11 percent of the college graduates and less than five percent of the postgraduates.

These ethnic-associational patterns by education are consistent with the earlier data on religiosity. Educational attainment is not the source of Jewish secularization, nor does it lead to alienation and disaffection from the community. The data support the argument that new Jewish networks have emerged which are based less on traditional modes of behavior and institutional associations. They are based on lifestyle and jobs, education, residence, and family; they are reinforced by religious observances which have become family–community-based. While religion has lost its centrality and dominance in the modern, secular American community, it continues to play a supportive role in linking educational, family, eco-

7. These are presented in reverse form in the table as the proportion expressing low Jewish values, to be consistent with other data in the table.

nomic, and lifestyle issues to broader communal, ethnic (Israel), and Jewish continuity issues.

JEWISH CONTINUITY OF THE NONDENOMINATIONAL

The nondenominational represent about 25 percent of the adult Jewish population and are more concentrated among the younger age cohorts. Are they "lost" to the Jewish community? Does religious nondenominationalism imply the absence of alternative ways of expressing Jewishness?

The evidence suggests that significant segments of the religiously non-affiliated are linked to Jewishness in a variety of ways. The overwhelming majority of the nondenominational are not synagogue members, and those that are belong to Reform temples. The proportions who are members and who attend religious services are significantly lower among those who do not identify themselves with a religious denomination than among those who are denominationally identified. Nevertheless, almost half of those who are nondenominational attend religious services sometime during the year. Those who do not identify denominationally also are less likely to express traditional Jewish values and will observe fewer religious rituals. Nevertheless, again, fully three-fourths of the nondenominational participate in religious family celebrations, and half are involved with some ethnic-community activities. Only 25 percent of the nondenominational have mostly non-Jewish friends—a slightly higher proportion than among Reform Jews. This tendency is more characteristic of younger Jews age 18–29, where one-third have mostly non-Jewish friends. Nevertheless, for the cohort age 30–39, the percentage of nondenominational drops off very rapidly, and the proportion of those who have mostly non-Jewish friends is lower than among Reform Jews of that age cohort.

In short, the patterns are relatively clear and consistent: most Jews have a wide range of ties to Jewishness. The overwhelming majority have some connections to Judaism and religious institutions. Those whose religious links are weakest have alternative ties to Jewish friends, family, and communal-ethnic activities. While the young tend to have weaker links to religious and social dimensions of Jewishness, they exhibit strong family ties, friendship patterns, and ethnic-Jewish attachments. It is of significance that these ties are not only generationally but life-cycle related. That suggests that the Jewishness of the young is not an ascribed characteristic, nor is it constant over time. They will change as marriages occur and families are formed, as new households are established and new communities are settled, and will continue to change as new educational, occupational, and residential networks emerge.

ELEVEN

Social Change and Jewish Continuity: The Future of the American Jewish Community

The general issue of ethnic continuity in pluralistic societies may be subdivided into two questions: One, what are the distinctive features of ethnic communities, and how have they changed over time? Two, how do these patterns relate to ethnic continuity and cohesion? The Jewish community in America exemplifies the tensions between distinctiveness and assimilation, between social change and ethnic continuity.

What are the bases of Jewish cohesion? In becoming American and modern, have Jews become less Jewish? Are the sources of cohesion weakening and leading to total assimilation? In the absence of discrimination, external threats, economic exploitation, and residential exclusion, can ethnic-religious groups survive in modern societies?

We examine Jews in the context of their community. When we search for sources of continuity and cohesion, our focus is on social processes. In particular, we investigate patterns of marriage and family formation, residence and mobility, social class, lifestyle, occupation, education, socio-economic status, religious and ethnic communal affiliation, identification, and behavior. Themes of family, stratification, population, and ethnicity allow us to answer questions of quantitative and qualitative survival of the Jewish community. While we need to separate these dimensions of social life so as to analyze them in detail, we need as well to see their interrelationships. There are critical links between family and stratification, between social class and migration, between jobs, residence, education, family, and ethnicity. Analysis requires synthesis of the various dimensions of social life and community organization so that the whole pattern may be observed and understood.

Investigating the nature of Jewish cohesion requires empirical evidence. We have examined data for the Jewish community of Boston to analyze the sources of Jewish cohesion and test some of the implications of social change for Jewish continuity. Data were available to explore new themes and to research in greater depth issues emerging from previous studies.

We and others have been constrained by cross-sectional data in studying the dynamics of change. We are limited, as are others, because we focus on one community. The absence of longitudinal data and national comparisons and the unavailability of systematic data to compare communities of different types force us to be tentative in our conclusions. We are particularly concerned about the absence of data on younger cohorts growing up in the late 1970s and early 1980s.

There are, of course, no perfect data sets. We need to build upon what we know imperfectly to evaluate the present and estimate the future. However limited the evidence, the data facilitate the systematic examination of the core themes of social life. In the process, new questions are raised and new relationships are uncovered. Other research will need to verify the findings presented here, qualify them, and generalize them to other communities and different times.

A particular advantage of the Boston data for the study of social change and continuity is the inclusion of non-Jews for comparisons. The question of Jewish exceptionalism has almost been asked in the context of assimilation in America. When we have asked "Are Jews different from non-Jews?" the answers often have been inferential and have focused on whether the differences reflect the lack of integration of Jews or discrimination against them. If Jews have particular family or educational characteristics, for example, that usually is interpreted as reflecting specific Jewish values. Often, growing similarities between Jews and non-Jews in particular traits or characteristics are analyzed in terms of ethnic convergences or assimilation.

The data we present on Jewish exceptionalism reveal some convergences over time between Jews and other groups but indicate continued distinctiveness and important divergences as well. The question of Jewish exceptionalism needs to be answered in the context of how the differences help shape Jewish distinctiveness as a community. A detailed examination of family, marriage, childbearing, social class, residence, occupation, and education among Jews and non-Jews leads to the unmistakable conclusion that Jews are different. Their distinctiveness as a community is further reinforced by religious and ethnic forms of cohesiveness. Some of the differences between Jews and others reflect background characteristics; yet some of the differences remain unexplained. Moreover, the social processes resulting in the distinctive characteristics and behavior of Jews have differed from those of non-Jews. Jewish exceptionalism means more than the absence of assimilation. The distinctive features of American Jewish life imply bonds and linkages among Jews which form the multiple bases of communal continuity. These ties are structural as well as cultural; they reflect deeply embedded forms of family, educational, job, and residence patterns, reinforced by religious and ethnic-communal behavior, cemented by shared lifestyles and values.

We review in this chapter the highlights of our data analysis, pulling together the themes which mark Jewish social change and continuity.

JEWISH COHESION AND THE "MARGINALS"

Our focus on Jewish cohesion involved the examination of the contexts of interaction between Jews and non-Jews. In general, modern American Jews have been described in terms of increasing levels of social contacts with non-Jews and therefore high rates of intermarriage, residential integration, and marginality to the Jewish community. College education and geographic mobility were assumed to be the mechanisms generating greater contact between Jews and non-Jews and increasing alienation from the community. These patterns were thought to be the consequence of the desire for assimilation and the move toward non-Jewish circles—spouses, neighbors, and friends. In turn, those who intermarried, those who lived in less Jewish neighborhoods, and young migrants were assumed to be less attached to the community and less Jewish in their behavior.

The evidence we present suggests a somewhat different picture. An analysis of attitudinal data revealed that there has been increasing acceptance of the intermarried within the Jewish community. No deep-rooted ideological base was uncovered which favors out-marriages among Jews, nor is there any evidence that intermarriage reflects values emphasizing assimilation. Younger Jews in their late teens and early twenties see little connection between intermarriage and total assimilation and express less alarmism over it and greater acceptance of the intermarried. Consistent with the analysis of marriage patterns, the data seem to support the argument that social-structural factors are more important than cultural values in accounting for intermarriage patterns.

Perhaps the most important aspect of intermarriage examined relates to the links between intermarriage and Jewish continuity. Not surprisingly, the intermarried are less Jewishly identified than those born Jewish. Nevertheless, differences in the extent of Jewishness and the observance of religious rituals between the intermarried and nonintermarried have narrowed among the younger age cohorts. The religious and ethnic-communal dimensions of religiosity and Jewish identification among young intermarried couples do not imply disaffection from Judaism and the Jewish community. Strong Jewish communal bonds and identificational networks link the intermarried to the Jewish community. When these patterns are placed in the context of the increasing levels of acceptance of the intermarried by the Jewish community, it becomes clear that marriage between Jews and non-Jews is not necessarily the final step toward total assimilation.

One of the continuing sources of Jewish communal cohesion is residential concentration. The location of Jews within neighborhoods which are disproportionately Jewish implies greater interaction among Jews, the development of institutions directed at servicing the Jewish population, the reinforcement of Jewish networks, and the emergence of a common lifestyle and general norms which characterize a community. The general argument has been that communities anchored geographically are higher in cohesion than dispersed communities. The greater the geographic dispersal of Jews and residential integration with non-Jews, the weaker their ties with other Jews. Similarly, the more Jews are geographically mobile, the weaker are their local community roots, and the less their community can serve as a source of ethnic-religious continuity.

These general arguments need to be qualified. First, residential concentration is only one form of cohesion. While high levels of Jewish density may enhance Jewish cohesion, low Jewish density is not necessarily associated with the absence of all forms of cohesion. The extent to which there are alternative sources of cohesion in the absence of residential concentration is an empirical issue, not necessarily to be inferred from the geographic distribution of Jews. Second, while migration reduces local community roots, it is not clear whether these are long-term effects. Nor is there a clear relationship between migration and Jewish density. People can migrate to areas of higher, as well as to areas of lower, Jewish density.

The evidence we presented shows a relatively high residential concentration of Jews in Boston. Clearly, the distribution of Jews is not random within the metropolitan area. Nor is residential concentration limited to the older, foreign-born generation. Residential concentration is linked more to structural conditions of housing markets, family life cycle, and economic constraints than to assimilation. Local, ecological, income, and ethnic-racial factors are prime determinants of Jewish residential densities. The legacy of the "old world," the desire to live in Jewish areas, and values associated with residential concentration do not appear to be the causes of Jewish population distribution.

When Jews live in areas of low Jewish density, formal community ties (e.g., synagogue membership or organizational linkages) tend to be weaker. But other ethnic and identificational sources of cohesion are not directly related to residential clustering. Thus, while living in areas of high Jewish density represents an additional basis of Jewish cohesion, living in areas of low Jewish density does not result in the decline of all forms of Jewish continuity.

Indeed, as with intermarriage, the movement to areas of low Jewish density is not linked to any desire to assimilate or to the search for residential integration with non-Jews. Most Jews express norms in support of high levels of residential concentration; most Jews prefer Jewish neighbors. Even among Jews living in areas of low Jewish concentration, two-thirds express these values and want more Jewish neighbors. Thus, the reason for living in areas of low Jewish density must be sought in the structural constraints of housing markets and economic factors, not in the desires to assimilate. It is not the preference for residential integration, but costs and availability.

What emerges from the data is that the community defined geographically is not the sole source of Jewish continuity. Generally, living in areas of high Jewish density implies high levels of interaction among Jews and a stronger form of community cohesion. Nevertheless, there are alternative sources of social ties and networks among Jews, linked to family, social class, and religion, which often transcend residential locations.

These findings on the effects of residential concentration on Jewish cohesion fit with the higher rates of geographic mobility among Jews. In turn, these are particularly associated with their educational, occupational, and marriage patterns. The Boston metropolitan area is attractive to young Jews because of the large number of universities and the wide range of technologically sophisticated industries located there.

The evidence linking migration and Jewish continuity shows that geographic mobility does not uproot and alienate Jews from their Jewishness. Migration does not automatically lead to disassociation from the community. Except for short-term effects (for the first several years after entering a community) on formal ties to the community (e.g., organizational ties, synagogue membership), migration is not empirically associated with declining Jewishness. When the age and educational selectivity of migration is taken into account, no significant links are found between family ritual and ethnic-community dimensions of Jewishness and migration status. Hence, most of the association between migration and Jewishness reflects patterns characteristic of young educated Jews, with the net effects of migration per se weak. Together, the evidence on the behavior of the "marginals"—the intermarried, the migrants, and those in neighborhoods of low Jewish density—does not reveal any desire for assimilation or alienation and disengagement from the Jewish community.

MARRIAGE, FAMILY, AND CHILDREN

Perhaps no area of social change has been studied, discussed, and interpreted as much as the family. Families and children are the links between generations, involve the socialization of the young, and are the sources of elementary demographic forms of survival and continuity. Family remains a powerful basis of community, although not the only one. It is related to other bases of cohesion, and is one of the major sources of group continuity.

To study the Jewish family often means to encompass everything. Jewish family becomes a semantic substitute for Jewish people, the Jewish community, or Jews generally. Here, we use the family in its narrower meaning of family processes. In particular, we focus on selected aspects of family formation, marriage, and reproduction to investigate (1) whether family processes among Jews differ from those among non-Jews; (2) sources of Jewish family variation and change; and (3) the implications of Jewish family patterns for group continuity.

Overall, the extent of marriage is similar for Jews and non-Jews. The higher rate of marriage among younger non-Jews probably reflects issues of timing, not longer-term nonmarriage, among Jews. Indeed, after age 30, few Jews remain unmarried. The higher proportion married among middle-aged Jews reflects their greater family stability compared to non-Jews. Lower divorce rates continue to characterize Jews, despite increasing levels. It is a pervasive group characteristic, distinctive at all educational levels. High educational attainment, therefore, does not mean nonmarriage but only some delayed marriage among Jewish women; it also does not lead to higher rates of marital instability.

Most Jewish women are not delaying marriage beyond their childbearing period, nor are they particularly marrying at later ages compared to women of other ethnic and religious groups. Jewish men, however, marry at distinctively later ages, a pattern tied not to education but more broadly to socioeconomic status, occupation, and economic resources. All together, age at marriage shows few direct links to group continuity. The timing of marriage does not seem to be particularly problematic in this regard. The marriage probabilities of the currently nonmarried cannot be determined from the data available. Viewed in another way, there is no evidence available to suggest high rates of permanent nonmarriage among single Jewish men or women.

The attainment of high levels of education is one source of the later marriage of Jewish (as well as non-Jewish) women, but Jewish men of all educational levels marry later. The response of Jewish women to the potential conflict between marriage, educational attainment, and childbearing seems to be to marry relatively early and to delay childbearing within marriage. Thus, neither socioeconomic level nor higher education interferes with relatively early marriage and eventual childbearing.

Jewish marriage patterns, including the extent, stability, and timing of marriage, confirm the family-oriented nature of the Jewish community. The only evidence indicating nonfamily orientation relates to the youngest cohort examined (age 18–29), where delayed marriage rather than permanent nonmarriage seems more likely.

The relationship between religious values and marriage patterns is not clear. There are no systematic differences among Orthodox, Conservative, and Reform Jews in the timing or extent of marriage. There is a positive relationship between later age at marriage and nonaffiliation, but the causal direction is not clear: Does nondenominational affiliation lead to delays in marriage age (as an extreme form of communal alienation), or does late age at marriage result in delayed identification with religious denominations (which will become more crystallized when children are old enough to be enrolled in Jewish-related schools)? Both are probably factors, but only longitudinal data can untangle their relative weight.

Marriage and family patterns appear not to be related to religious or particularly ethnic values but to reflect the structural conditions of the marriage market (the number of "eligible" men and women). Variations among Jews and differences between Jews and non-Jews reflect market and socioeconomic constraints to marriage, remarriage, and out-marriage rather than cultural features particular to Jews.

The empirical demonstration of the continuing centrality of family life for American Jews sharpens our focus in isolating the contents of family life. In large part, we argue that the centrality rests with the generational linkages and family networks which bind Jews together as a community. We have inferential evidence on this conclusion but no empirically based data. We do know that family orientation does not mean living in extended households. In the trade-offs between family centrality-control and independence-autonomy, most younger and older Jews are not incorporated into nuclear households. Young Jews move away from family even when they do not marry, mainly for school and to live independently of parents. Most older Jews who do not themselves constitute a nuclear family live alone.

Variations in household structure by family life cycle and gender indicate the strong structural basis of living arrangements. In large part, the Jewish household pattern is the consequence of education and marriage relationships. Young Jews, men and women, leave the parental home significantly earlier than non-Jews. When not forming new nuclear households, young non-Jewish women are three times more likely than Jewish women to live with relatives.

But family-kinship ties measured in terms of the residential household are particularly strong among older Jewish women. That is not a general Jewish pattern, since it does not apply either to men or to younger women. Nor is it a question of income, for it characterizes a variety of income levels. It seems unlikely that Jewishness relates to living arrangements and household structure in any simple sense, or that the greater incorporation of older Jewish women into extended households and the greater probability of older Jewish men living alone are the consequences of Jewish values which are gender-specific. Empirically, the data show no systematic relationship between the identification with a particular denomination and living arrangements. Perhaps more-generalized Jewish values are operative, although it seems more reasonable to argue that issues of family relationships and the role of older women as sources of household and child assistance are more important.

Living away from family does not result in the deterioration of attachments to Judaism or Jewishness. Hence, living alone (among younger and older nonmarrieds) does not seem to have major consequences for Jewish continuity. In turn, the structural changes away from extended family residences are probably not related to a decline and weakening of the Jewish community.

Jewish family centrality also does not mean larger size. Confirming cumulative evidence in the United States for over a century, the Boston data show lower Jewish than non-Jewish fertility. Expected family size

among younger Jewish women barely will replace the previous generation. While the importance of the family is not translated into the number
of children, several findings provide important clues about factors associated with Jewish fertility.

The most educated among Jewish women have larger family size expectations than those with lower educational levels. This relationship is important, because it does not characterize Protestants or Catholics, where
there is a clear and consistent inverse relationship between education and
fertility. The distinctiveness of Jewish fertility extends not only to size of
family but to patterns of associations as well. As a result, there appears to
be no necessary contradiction between postgraduate education and childbearing among Jewish women.

Given the very high levels of educational attainment among younger
Jewish women, this finding takes on particular significance. One obvious
implication is that any inference from the generally low Jewish fertility of
all educational levels to even lower levels as Jewish women become more
educated (an expectation based on the non-Jewish empirical pattern)
would be misleading. While an analysis of non-Jewish fertility patterns is
necessary to study Jewish exceptionalism, it is a misleading basis for assessing patterns or relationships to particular explanatory variables among
Jews.

An additional implication is less obvious. The inverse relationship between education and non-Jewish fertility and the positive relationship between education and Jewish fertility imply fertility convergence between
Jews and non-Jews at the highest educational level. If these patterns of
expected family size are carried out behaviorally, then the unique pattern
of lower Jewish fertility at all educational levels may be disappearing.
Such convergence needs to be examined more systematically and would
be most fruitfully investigated in the broad context of changing women's
roles and family patterns rather than within an assimilation framework.

Supporting findings about the higher fertility of the most-educated Jewish women are the conclusions about the relationship between labor force
participation of women and their fertility. The general conflict between
work and childbearing roles and the lower fertility of working women
characterize only Protestants and Catholics. Among Jewish women, the
data show a weak relationship between working and fertility and the reverse of the expected—working Jewish women have somewhat larger family size expectations.

Although the Boston evidence is the first data set to allow the examination of this critical issue, it is nevertheless problematic because of the
cross-sectional nature of the data.

In part, the differential patterns of Jewish and non-Jewish women may
reflect the type and nature of jobs, level of socioeconomic status of husbands, and related differences. Nevertheless, there is no support in these
data for the argument that the work patterns of young, educated, career-

oriented Jewish women pose a threat to Jewish demographic continuity by their particularly low fertility behavior.

There are few patterns which link family size and religiosity among Jews. That suggests that religious values per se are not among the primary determinants of low Jewish fertility or a source of major fertility variation. Two qualifications are needed. First, the Boston study, like many other community studies, did not include a sufficient number or representative sample of Orthodox Jews. In particular, Orthodox Jews in closed communities are underrepresented. They probably have larger families; the conclusion relating to the nonrelationship between religiosity and fertility applies only to acculturated segments of the Jewish community.

A second qualification relates to the finding that those who do not identify denominationally (i.e., did not identify themselves as Orthodox, Conservative, or Reform) have the smallest family size expectations. Here the causal connection is again difficult to establish. It appears, however, that nondenominationalism is associated more with life cycle patterns than with long-term nonreligious commitments. That is clearly evident in the links between nondenominational affiliation and other ethnic and religious forms of Jewishness. It also is evident in the analysis of marriage and family patterns. Hence, it is reasonable to argue that the absence of children among nondenominational Jews is not the result of their lower Jewish commitments but one of its determinants. Children reinforce religious commitments, particularly formal ones associated with type of synagogue membership and affiliation, as well as family-related religious rituals.

The quantitative analysis of fertility is based on the fertility expectations of Boston married women in the mid-1970s. The data point to the conclusion that below-replacement fertility will characterize only a small minority of these married Jewish women. They are the farthest removed from the Jewish community and would be least receptive to policies to encourage childbearing. Most important, they also have the smallest impact on the community and its continuity. The evidence suggests that future marriage patterns are of greater concern for Jewish population replacement than the reproductive behavior of the currently married. The quantitative issue of the future of American Jewry seems to revolve around the proportion of young singles in their twenties who will marry, since the fertility expectations of those who are married are adequate for population replacement.

It is of course not reproduction alone which determines population growth. Other factors are of central importance—particularly net losses due to intermarriage (i.e., intermarriage minus conversions to Judaism, plus the extent to which the children of intermarriages are raised as Jews and continue to identify as Jews as they become adults) and, at a local level, net migration. Unfortunately, no new data on intermarriage levels or quantitative losses due to the combination of out-marriages and replacement-level fertility can be inferred from the Boston studies. The quantitative impact of intermarriage on Jewish continuity has yet to be systematically researched. Until comprehensive data on intermarriages, conversions, socialization, and subsequent Jewish identification of the children of the intermarried and nonintermarried are collected and analyzed in a wide range of contexts, the quantitative implications cannot be evaluated fully.

STRATIFICATION AND SOCIAL-CLASS NETWORKS

The occupational and educational stratification of the American Jewish community is one of its unique features. The distinctive concentration of Jews in high white-collar jobs and in the upper levels of education marks the Jewish community relative to other ethnic religious groups. Clearly, the increasing disparities between Jews and non-Jews in educational attainment and occupational achievement cannot be understood in the simplistic context of "assimilation." The occupational concentration of Jews goes beyond the crude categories of professionals or managers. Not only are between 75 and 85 percent of Jews below age 50 in these upper-white-collar positions, but they are concentrated in a narrow range of occupations within these categories.

We argue that these high levels of concentration have important consequences for the structure of the Jewish community as a whole and for the lifestyle of the Jewish group. No less important are the consequences of occupational concentration for the development and reinforcement of ethnic communal networks. The centrality of the occupational linkage to institutions, networks, family, neighborhood, social class, and political interests emerges clearly from the evidence. Not only has the occupational mobility of Jews not resulted in the occupational assimilation of Jews, but it has become a powerful base of ethnicity and ethnic continuity. In this context, ethnic cohesion finds its primary source in the structural conditions of job and social class, not in the "search" for ethnic identity or in the "desire" for group survival. Socioeconomic underpinnings of ethnicity are major sources of group continuity and the primary contexts of the values which sustain group cohesion. The occupational transformation of the Jews over time from low to high occupational status can therefore be viewed as a structural support for ethnic cohesion, not as a source of group assimilation.

The occupational concentration of Jews is linked to their very high levels of educational attainment. The educational differences between Jews and non-Jews have widened, as has the occupational distribution. At the same time, educational and occupational differences have narrowed among Jews. The transformation over time in both educational and occupational dimensions implies more than extensive and intensive change. It means that the entire population shifted, thoroughly and rapidly, in socioeconomic levels. One implication of this transformation for younger

Jews is the reduction of generational conflict. Since high levels of education and occupation have emerged for two generations of Jews, one potential source of generational conflict has lessened within the Jewish group.

As with occupation, educational concentration has resulted in the development of networks and bonds among Jews in the same age cohort. Generational continuity in occupational and educational levels further links the young to kin and community.

These transformations were documented clearly in the analysis of generational transfers. The very high levels of generational continuity among professionals characterize both Jews and non-Jews. However, Jewish sons of managers not inheriting their father's occupational status move up; non-Jews move down. Among workers, the contrasts are even sharper: two-thirds of the Jewish workers had sons who were professionals; two-thirds of the non-Jewish workers had sons who were workers. Similarly, the proportion of fathers with a high-school education whose sons also had a high-school education is 5 percent among Jews, 36 percent among Protestants, and 55 percent among Catholics in Boston.

The stratification system—managers and professionals at college and graduate, professional-school levels—emerging among Jews has led to the crystallization of socioeconomic distinctiveness.

The interpretation of these changes only in the context of occupational change, mobility, and assimilation misses a major dimension of continuity at high socioeconomic levels. It also places too little emphasis on the networks, ties, and linkages which similarities in occupation and education imply. If one of the major features of ethnic continuity revolves around the overlap of ethnicity and social class, then the Jewish community is characterized by a powerful source of structural continuity.

A detailed examination of occupations and in particular patterns of self-employment reinforces these conclusions. Very high levels of self-employment have characterized Jews for several generations. Changes over time in the structure of economic opportunity and in the educational-occupational distribution of Jews have resulted in changes in the level and type of self-employment. Nevertheless, there have been no convergences between levels of self-employment of Jews and non-Jews. Indeed, generational analyses show a widening of differences. These differences are not simply the result of the socioeconomic characteristics of Jews and others. Nor do overall Jewish values on economic independence account for variations over time and among places. Self-employment patterns appear to be related to ethnic structural dimensions, particularly ethnic networks and kin linkages. As with socioeconomic levels—occupation and education—self-employment patterns link Jews with other Jews to form economic and family bonds.

The evidence on Jewish women adds important dimensions to this analysis. Jewish women have distinctive work patterns and occupational concentration. These reflect longer schooling, delayed childbearing, concentrated childbearing, fewer children, and higher socioeconomic status among Jews compared to non-Jews. Hence, the distinctive pattern for Jewish women relates to these structural features, not to Jewish values per se.

As with men, there have been occupational and educational divergences between Jewish and non-Jewish women. Similar patterns emerge when self-employment of Jewish women is examined. Unlike the pattern for males, the self-employment of women is tied more to occupational and educational concentration. Yet continuing Jewish–non-Jewish differences in self-employment are not solely a consequence of their distinctive socioeconomic characteristics.

The specific labor force, self-employment, and educational characteristics of Jewish women suggest that their socioeconomic transformation also is tied to kin and community networks. Self-employment is less disruptive of family and other roles; occupational concentration results in the formation of linkages among Jewish women outside family and neighborhoods. Hence, the work patterns of Jewish women reinforce the ethnic network rather than result in ethnic discontinuity.

Overall, the evidence leads to the conclusion that social class and ethnic interests are becoming embedded in the community. The commonality of class and status among Jews is distinctive and results in social bonds, economic networks, and common lifestyles and interests. High socioeconomic status—class, occupation, education—among Jewish women and men for at least two generations cements the basis of Jewish cohesion. The stratification system ties generations together, linking networks of family and community across time and often across space, establishing continuing bonds within the broader Jewish community.

RELIGION AND ETHNIC FACTORS

Religion and ethnic factors are particularistic features of the Jewish community. They are the defining quality of American Jewish life and the source of communal consensus. The secularization of Judaism and Jews has long been observed in America. The critical issue, however, is whether alternative sources of group cohesion have emerged as religious centrality has declined. Religious and ethnic forms of Jewishness have changed in America. Interpreting these changes and understanding their link to the future of the American Jewish community are a key analytic concern.

The data from the Boston surveys document the changing manifestation of religious forms of cohesion. They also clearly indicate how forms of religious and ethnic cohesion provide a wide range of options for Jews at different points in the life cycle. For some, religion in its Americanized form is of central importance in their Jewishness; for most Jews, social, communal, ethnic, and religious dimensions of Jewishness are combined.

It is most problematic to specify and measure the "quality" of Jewish life, since there is no theoretical or empirical consensus about it. Nevertheless, it is clear that the decline in religiosity per se must be viewed in the context of the emergence of these alternative forms of Jewishness. Secularization in the religious sense is not necessarily equal to the decline of the Jewish community, to its assimilation or demise. By treating Jews as members of a community in the broad sense, we recognize religion as one dimension of the total array of factors, but not as equivalent to the whole.

Despite the evidence of secularization, there remains a strong sense of religious identification among Jews. Fully three-fourths of Boston Jewry define themselves denominationally, attend synagogue sometimes during the year, and observe some personal religious rituals. This high level of religious identification is not matched by formal membership in religious institutions. Hence, membership per se is not an adequate indicator of religious identification. Life cycle- and family-related factors determine membership patterns. Nonmembership does not seem to imply the lack of commitment to Jewish continuity.

These patterns characterize the younger as well as the older generations, men and women, and appear to be a pervasive feature throughout the Jewish community. In particular, there are no clear relationships between educational level and religiosity or between other social class indicators and Jewishness. Hence, neither the attainment of high levels of education nor upward mobility can be viewed as a "threat" to Jewish continuity.

For recent generations, there are high levels of religious denominational continuity, albeit in less traditional and usually less intense forms. Similarities in affiliation across generations forge bonds of interaction and reduce conflict over religious issues. Even those not affiliated denominationally are similar in background to the denominational, thereby not splitting them from their age peers. The increasing generational homogeneity in religious denominational affiliation, in which three-fourths of the younger generation have the same denominational affiliation as their parents, while three-fourths of the older generation were "downwardly" religiously mobile, is an additional source of cohesion in the community.

This generational continuity in religious denominational affiliation parallels the continuity in social class and family life. Over and above the effects of religious affiliation on Jewish continuity, generational continuity per se has become an additional basis of Jewish cohesion. This socioeconomic, family, and religious continuity implies high levels of consensus between generations in lifestyle, interests, kin networks, economic linkages, values, and norms. It also implies fewer sources of generational conflict. Again, we argue that the more the bases of cohesion, the stronger the community and the firmer the anchors for continuity. This continuity takes on particular significance, since it characterizes the young and most-educated, the future of the American Jewish community.

These indicators of religious continuity and the importance of religion as one distinguishing feature of Jewish communal life are reinforced by ethnic-communal forms of Jewish cohesion. Jewish networks have emerged which are based not on traditional modes of behavior but on lifestyle, jobs, residence, education, and family ties—cemeted by religious observance and identification. The new forms of Jewishness are family- and community-based. While religion has lost its centrality and dominance in the Jewish world, it continues to play a supportive role in linking educational, family, economic, and lifestyle issues to broader communal issues.

Among those who are religiously anchored and who share family, social-class, and residential ties with other Jews, the issues of continuity are not problematic. In this context, the question of the future of the non-denominational, those not affiliated or identified religiously, has been raised. Most of the conclusions in previous research about the non-denominational have been inferential: if Jews do not identify religiously, they are lost to the community. Nondenominationalism is an indicator of (or a first step toward) total assimilation.

The evidence does not confirm this inference. The causal connections between nondenominationalism and other social processes are difficult to establish. In particular, nondenominationalism is linked to life cycle changes. Hence, higher rates among the young do not necessarily imply generational decline, but life cycle effects which will change as the young marry and have children. Most important, there is no systematic relationship between nondenominationalism and the variety of communal and ethnic ties characteristic of the Jewish community.

The incomplete and limited data which we have analyzed together with the body of previous cumulative research lead to the overall conclusion that there is much greater cohesiveness in the Jewish community than is often portrayed. It is consistent with the data (although beyond its power to confirm fully) that the Jewish community is characterized by multiple bases of cohesion. On both quantitative and qualitative grounds, the American Jewish community of the late twentieth century has a variety of sources of continuity. The changes and transformations over the last several decades have resulted in greater ties and networks among Jews. These connect Jews to each other in kinship relationships, jobs, neighborhoods, lifestyles, and values. Change—whether referred to as assimilation or acculturation—has reinforced ethnic-communal identification. The modernization of American Jews has been so far a challenge, not a threat, to continuity.

The longer-range question is whether these social networks and the emerging constellation of family, ethnic, and religious ties will persist as bases of cohesion for the Jewish community in the twenty-first century. How much secularization and erosion of traditional religious practices can occur without having a major impact on the Jewishness of the younger generation? Are the new forms of Jewish ethnicity able to balance secularization? Will the "return" to Judaism or the development of creative expressions of Jewish religious fellowship become the new core of generational continuity? These questions emerge from our study, although they cannot be addressed with any data available.

Nevertheless, the response to modernization as threatening, as the road to total assimilation and the end of the Jewish people, is not consistent with the evidence. The Jewish community in America has changed; indeed has been transformed. But in that process, it has emerged as a dynamic source of networks and resources binding together family, friends, and neighbors, ethnically and religiously. As a community, Jews are surviving in America, even as some individuals enter and leave the community. Indeed, in every way the American Jewish community represents for Jews and other ethnic minorities a paradigm of continuity and change in modern pluralistic society.

References

Angel, R., and Tienda, M. 1982. "Determinants of Household Structure: Cultural Pattern or Economic Need?" *American Journal of Sociology* 87 (May): 1360–83.

Axelrod, Morris; Fowler, Floyd; and Gurin, Arnold. 1967. *A Community Survey for Long Range Planning: A Study of the Jewish Population of Greater Boston*. Boston: Combined Jewish Philanthropies of Greater Boston.

Bachi, Roberto. 1976. *Population Trends of World Jewry*. Jerusalem: Hebrew University.

Barth, Frederik, ed. 1969. *Ethnic Groups and Boundaries: The Social Organization of Culture Differences*. Boston: Little, Brown and Co.

Bell, Daniel. 1975. "Ethnicity and Social Change." In N. Glazer and D. Moynihan, eds., *Ethnicity: Theory and Experience*. Cambridge, Mass.: Harvard University Press.

Bergman, Elihu. 1977. "The American Jewish Population Erosion." *Midstream* (October).

Billings, John S. 1890. "Vital Statistics of the Jews in the United States." *Census Bulletin*, no. 19, 30 December.

Blake, Judith. 1979. "Structural Differentiation and the Family: A Quiet Revolution." In A. Hawley, ed., *Societal Growth: Processes and Implications*. New York: Free Press.

Blau, Peter, and Duncan, O. D. 1967. *The American Occupational Structure*. New York: Wiley.

Bock, Geoffrey. 1976. "The Jewish Schooling of American Jews." Unpublished doctoral dissertation, Graduate School of Education, Harvard University.

Bonacich, Edna. 1973. "A Theory of Middlemen Minorities." *American Sociological Review* 38 (October): 583–94.

Bulka, Reuven. 1982. "The Jewish Family: Reality and Prospects." *Jewish Life* 6 (Spring–Summer): 25–36.

Bumpass, L., and Presser, H. 1973. "The Increasing Acceptance of Sterilization and Abortion." In C. Westoff, ed., *Toward the End of Growth*. Englewood Cliffs, N.J.: Prentice-Hall.

Burch, T. K. 1970. "Some Demographic Determinants of Average Household Size: An Analytic Approach." *Demography* 7: 61–70.

Carliner, G. 1975. "Determinants of Household Headship." *Journal of Marriage and the Family* 37: 28–39.

Cherlin, Andrew. 1981. *Marriage, Divorce, Remarriage*. Cambridge, Mass.: Harvard University Press.

Cherlin, Andrew, and Celebuski, Carin. 1983. "Are Jewish Families Different?: Some Evidence from the General Social Survey." *Journal of Marriage and the Family* 45 (November): 903–910.

Cheskis, R. 1980. "Jewish Identification and Fertility: An Analysis of Subgroup Fertility Differentials." Unpublished Master's thesis, Brown University.

Cohen, Steven M. 1982. "The American Jewish Family Today." *American Jewish Yearbook*, 136–54.

————. 1983. *American Modernity and Jewish Identity*. London: Tavistock.

Cohen, S. M., and Ritterband, P. 1981. "Why Contemporary American Jews Want Small Families." In P. Ritterband, ed., *Modern Jewish Fertility*. Leiden: Brill.

DellaPergola, Sergio. 1980. "Patterns of American Jewish Fertility." *Demography* 17 (August): 261–73.

Elazar, Daniel. 1976. *Community and Polity: The Organizational Dynamics of American Jewry*. Philadelphia: Jewish Publication Society.

Farber, Bernard, and Gordon, Leonard. 1982. "Accounting for Jewish Intermarriage: An Assessment of National and Community Studies." *Contemporary Jewry* 6 (Spring/Summer): 47–75.

Farber, Bernard; Gordon, L.; and Mayer, A. J. 1979. "Intermarriage and Jewish Identity: Implications for Pluralism and Assimilation in American Society." *Ethnic and Racial Studies* 2: 222–30.

Farley, Reynolds; Bianchi, S.; and Colasanto, D., 1979. "Barriers to the Racial Integration of Neighborhoods." *Annals of The American Academy of Political and Social Science* 441: 97–113.

Fein, L. et al. 1972. *Reform Is a Verb*. New York: Union of American Hebrew Congregations.

Ford, K. 1978. "Contraceptive Use in the United States, 1973–76." *Family Planning Perspectives* 10, no. 5 (September/October): 264–69.

Fowler, F. J. 1977. *1975 Community Survey: A Study of the Jewish Population of Greater Boston*. Boston: Combined Jewish Philanthropies of Greater Boston.

Freedman, R.; Whelpton, P. K.; and Smit, J. 1961. "Socio-Economic Factors in Religious Differentials in Fertility." *American Sociological Review* 26 (August): 608–14.

Glazer, Nathan. 1971. "Blacks and Ethnic Groups: The Difference and the Political Differences It Makes." *Social Problems* 18: 444–61.

Glazer, N., and Moynihan, P. 1970. *Beyond the Melting Pot*. 2d ed. Cambridge, Mass.: M.I.T. Press.

Glazer, N., and Moynihan, P., eds. 1975. *Ethnicity: Theory and Experience*. Cambridge, Mass.: Harvard University Press.

Glick, Paul. 1960. "Intermarriage and Fertility Patterns among Persons in Major Religious Groups." *Eugenics Quarterly* 7: 31–38.

———. 1977. "Updating the Life Cycle of the Family." *Journal of Marriage and the Family* 39: 5–14.

Glick, Paul, and Norton, A. 1977. *Marrying, Divorcing, and Living Together in the U.S. Today*. Washington, D.C.: Population Reference Bureau.

Goldberg, Nathan. 1945–46. "Occupational Patterns of American Jews." *Jewish Review* 3.

———. 1948. "Jewish Population in America." *Jewish Review* 5: 36–48.

———. 1962. "Demographic Characteristics of American Jews." In Jacob Fried, ed., *Jews in the Modern World*, vol. 2. New York: Twayne Publishing Co.

———. 1968. "The Jewish Attitude toward Divorce." In Jacob Fried, ed., *Jews and Divorce*. New York: KTAV Publishing.

Goldscheider, Calvin. 1965a. "Ideological Factors in Jewish Fertility Differentials." *Jewish Journal of Sociology* 7 (June): 92–105.

———. 1965b. "Nativity, Generation, and Jewish Fertility." *Sociological Analysis* 26 (Fall): 137–47.

———. 1965c. "Socioeconomic Status and Jewish Fertility." *Jewish Journal of Sociology* 7 (December): 221–37.

———. 1966. "Trends in Jewish Fertility." *Sociology and Social Research* 50 (January): 173–86.

———. 1967. "Fertility of the Jews." *Demography* 4: 196–209.

———. 1971. *Population, Modernization, and Social Structure*. Boston: Little, Brown and Co.

———. 1973. "Childlessness and Religiosity: An Exploratory Analysis." In *Papers in Jewish Demography, 1969*, Institute of Contemporary Jewry. Jerusalem: Hebrew University.

———. 1974. "American Aliya: Sociological and Demographic Perspectives." In M. Sklare, ed., *The Jew in American Society*, pp. 335–84. New York: Behrman House.

——. 1978. "Demography and American Jewish Survival." in M. Himmelfarb and V. Baras, eds., *Zero Population Growth—for Whom?* pp. 119–47. Westport, Conn.: Greenwood Press.

——. 1982. "The Demography of Jewish Americans: Research Findings, Issues, and Challenges." In M. Sklare, ed., *Understanding American Jewry*. New Brunswick, N.J.: Transaction Books.

——. 1983. "Contraceptive Usage among American Jewish Families." *Jewish Population Studies*. Jerusalem: Hebrew University.

——. ed. 1983. *Urban Migrants in Less Developed Nations: Patterns and Problems of Adjustment*. Boulder, Colo.: Westview Press.

Goldscheider, Calvin, and Goldstein, S. 1967. "Generational Changes in Jewish Family Structure." *Journal of Marriage and the Family* 29 (May): 267–76.

Goldscheider, Calvin, and Kobrin, F. 1980. "Ethnic Continuity and the Process of Self-Employment." *Ethnicity* 7: 256–78.

Goldscheider, Calvin, and Zuckerman, Alan. 1984. *The Transformation of the Jews*. Chicago: University of Chicago Press.

Goldstein, Sidney. 1969. "Socioeconomic Differentials among Religious Groups in the United States." *American Journal of Sociology* (May), pp. 612–31.

——. 1971. "American Jewry, 1970: A Demographic Profile." *American Jewish Yearbook*, pp. 3–88.

——. 1973a. "Sources of Statistics of Jewish Vital Events and Migration in the United States." In *Papers in Jewish Demography: 1970*, Institute of Contemporary Jewry. Jerusalem: Hebrew University.

——. 1973b. "Completed and Expected Fertility in an American Jewish Community." In *Papers in Jewish Demography, 1969*, Institute of Contemporary Jewry. Jerusalem: Hebrew University.

——. 1979. "A Demographic View of the Jewish Community in the 1980's." A JWB Greater Northeast Convention paper, 20 April.

——. 1981a. "Jewish Fertility in Contemporary America." In Paul Ritterband, ed., *Modern Jewish Fertility*. Leiden: Brill.

——. 1981b. "The Jews in the United States: Perspectives from Demography." *American Jewish Yearbook*, pp. 3–59.

——. 1982. "Population Movement and Redistribution among American Jews." *Jewish Journal of Sociology* 24 (June): 5–23.

Goldstein, Sidney, and Goldscheider, Calvin. 1968. *Jewish Americans*. Englewood Cliffs, N.J.: Prentice-Hall.

Good, Dorothy. 1959. "Questions of Religion in the United States Census." *Population Index* 25: 3–16.

Gordon, Milton. 1964. *Assimilation in American Life*. New York: Oxford University Press.

Greeley, A. 1974. *Ethnicity in the United States*. New York: Wiley.

——. 1976. *Ethnicity, Denomination, and Inequality*. Sage Research Papers in the Social Studies (Studies in Religion and Ethnicity, vol. 4, no. 90,029). Beverly Hills: Sage Publications.

Hecht, A. 1976. "Trends in the Size and Structure in Europe, 1960–1970 and the Outlook for the Period 1970–2000." Paper presented at the Annual Meeting of the Population Association of America.

Hechter, Michael. 1975. *Internal Colonialism: The Celtic Fringe in British National Development, 1536–1966*. Berkeley and Los Angeles: University of California Press.

Hendershot, Gerry, and Placek, P., eds. 1981. *Predicting Fertility: Demographic Studies of Birth Expectations*. Lexington, Mass.: Lexington Books.

Herberg, Will. 1960. *Protestant, Catholic, Jew*. New York: Anchor Books.

Himmelfarb, Harold. 1982. "Research on American Jewish Identity and Identification." In M. Sklare, ed., *Understanding American Jewry*. New Brunswick, N.J.: Transaction Books.

Jarret, Charles. 1978. "The Impact of Geographical Mobility on Jewish Community Participation: Disruptive or Supportive." *Contemporary Jewry* 4 (Spring/Summer): 9–20.

Kantrowitz, Nathan. 1973. *Ethnic and Racial Segregation in the New York Metropolis*. New York: Praeger.

Kluegel, J. R. 1978. "Causes and Cost of Racial Exclusion from Job Authority." *American Sociological Review* 43: 285-301.

Kobrin, Frances E. 1976a. "The Fall in Household Size and the Rise of the Primary Individual in the United States." *Demography* 13, no. 1: 127–38.

———. 1976b. "Leaving the Nest: A Dual Life Cycle Variable." Annual Meeting of the Southern Regional Demographic Group. New Orleans, Louisiana.

———. 1976c. "The Primary Individual and the Family: Changes in Living Arrangements in the United States since 1940." *Journal of Marriage and the Family* 38: 233–40.

———. 1981. "Family Extension and the Elderly: Economic, Demographic, and Family Cycle Factors." *Journal of Gerontology* 36: 370–77.

———. "Family Patterns among the Yiddish Mother-Tongue Subpopulation: U.S. 1970." In S. Cohen and P. Hyman, eds., *The Evolving Jewish Family*. Forthcoming.

Kobrin, Frances, and Goldscheider, Calvin. 1978. *The Ethnic Factor in Family Structure and Mobility*. Cambridge, Mass.: Ballinger Press.

———. 1979. "Primary Individuals and Family Extension." Paper presented at the Population Association of America Meetings in April, in Philadelphia.

———. 1983. "Family Extension or Non-family Living: Life Cycle, Economic, and Ethnic Factors." *Western Sociological Review*.

Kramer, Judith, and Leventman, Seymour. 1961. *Children of the Gilded Ghetto*. New Haven: Yale University Press.

Kupinsky, Stanley, ed. 1977. *The Fertility of Working Women*. New York: Praeger.

Laslett, Peter. 1972. "Introduction: The History of the Family." In P. Laslett, ed., *Household and Family in Past Time*. London: Cambridge University Press.

Lazerwitz, Bernard. 1973. "The National Jewish Population Study: Sample Design." In *Papers in Jewish Demography, 1970*, Institute of Contemporary Jewry. Jerusalem: Hebrew University.

———. 1973. "Jewish Identification and Jewish Fertility in the Chicago Jewish Community." In *Papers in Jewish Demography, 1969*, Institute of Contemporary Jewry. Jerusalem: Hebrew University.

———. 1978. "An Estimate of a Rare Population Group: The United States Jewish Population." *Demography* 15 (August): 389–94.

Leifer, Eric. 1981. "Competing Models of Political Mobilization: The Role of Ethnic Ties." *American Journal of Sociology* 87 (July): 23–47.

Lenski, Gerhard. 1961. *The Religious Factor*. Garden City, N.Y.: Doubleday and Co.

Levy, Marion. 1965. "Aspects of the Analysis of Family Structure." In A. J. Coale et al., *Aspects of the Analysis of Family Structure*. Princeton: Princeton University Press.

Lieberman, Samuel, and Weinfeld, M. 1978. "Demographic Trends and Jewish Survival." *Midstream* (October), pp. 9–19.

Lieberson, Stanley. 1963. *Ethnic Patterns in American Cities*. New York: Free Press.

———. 1980. *A Piece of the Pie*. Berkeley and Los Angeles: University of California Press.

Light, Ivan. 1972. *Ethnic Enterprise in America*. Berkeley and Los Angeles: University of California Press.

Lipset, S. M., and Bendix, R. 1959. *Social Mobility in Industrial Society*. Berkeley and Los Angeles: University of California Press.

Massarik, Fred. 1973. "The United States National Jewish Population Study: A Note on Concept and Reality." In *Papers in Jewish Demography, 1970*, Institute of Contemporary Jewry. Jerusalem: Hebrew University.

Massarik, Fred, and Chenkin, A. 1973. "United States National Jewish Population Survey: A First Report." *American Jewishyear Book*, pp. 264–306.

Matras, Judah. 1975. *Social Inequality, Stratification, and Mobility*. Englewood Cliffs, N.J.: Prentice-Hall.

Modell, John; Furstenberg, F. Jr.; and Strong, D. 1978. "The Timing of Marriage in the Transition to Adulthood." In J. Demos and S. Boocock, eds., *Turning Points*, Chicago: University of Chicago Press.

Mosher, William, and Hendershot, Gerry. 1984. "Religion and Fertility: A Replication." *Demography* 21: 185–91.

Mueller, Samuel, and Lane, Angela. 1972. "Tabulations from the 1957 Current Population Survey on Religion." *Journal for the Scientific Study of Religion* 11 (March): 76–98.

Newman, William, and Halvorson, Peter. 1979. "American Jews: Patterns of Geographic Distribution and Change, 1952–1971." *Journal for the Scientific Study of Religion* 18 (June): 183–93.

Nielsen, Francois. 1980. "The Flemish Movement in Belgium after World War II: A Dynamic Analysis." *American Sociological Review* 45 (February): 76–94.

O'Connell, Martin, and Moore, M. 1977. "New Evidence on the Value of Birth Expectations." *Demography* 14: 255–64.

Pearl, R. 1939. *The Natural History of Population*. New York: Oxford University Press.

Ritterband, Paul, and Cohen, S. M. 1979. "Religion, Religiosity, and Fertility Desires." *Papers in Jewish Demography*, Institute of Contemporary Jewry. Jerusalem: Hebrew University.

Robinson, R., and Kelley, J. 1979. "Class as Conceived by Marx and Dahrendorf." *American Sociological Review* 44 (February): pp. 38–58.

Rosenthal, Erich. 1961. "Jewish Fertility in the United States." *Eugenics Quarterly* 8 (December): 198-217.

———. 1963. "Studies of Jewish Intermarriage in the United States." *American Jewish Yearbook*, vol. 64, pp. 3–53.

———. 1975. "The Equivalence of United States Census Data for Persons of Russian Stock or Descent with American Jews: An Evaluation." *Demography* 12 (May): 275–90.

Ross, H., and Sawhill, I. 1976. *Time of Transition*. Washington, D.C.: Urban Institute.

Ryder, N., and Westoff, C. 1971. *Reproduction in the United States: 1965*. Princeton: Princeton University Press.

Schmelz, U. O. 1969. "Evaluation of Jewish Population Estimates." *American Jewish Yearbook*, pp. 273–88.

———. 1981. "Jewish Survival: The Demographic Factors." *American Jewish Yearbook*, vol. 81, pp. 61–117.

Shryock, Henry, and Siegel, J. 1973. *The Methods and Materials of Demography*. Washington, D.C.: U.S. Bureau of the Census.

Sklare, Marshall. 1971. *America's Jews*. New York: Random House.

———, ed. 1982. *Understanding American Jewry*. New Brunswick, N.J.: Transaction Books.

Sklare, Marshall, and Greenblum, J. 1967. *Jewish Identity on the Suburban Frontier*. New York: Basic Books.

Smelser, Neil. 1969. "Mechanism of Change and Adjustment to Change." In W. Faunce and W. Form, eds., *Comparative Perspectives on Industrial Society*. Boston: Little, Brown and Co.

Soldo, B. 1977. "Demographic Composition and Source of Temporal Variation in the Living Arrangements among the Elderly." Paper presented at the Annual Meeting of the Population Association of America, St. Louis, Mo.

Steinberg, Stephen. 1981. *The Ethnic Myth*. New York: Atheneum.

Stix, R. K., and Notestein, F. 1940. *Controlled Fertility*. Baltimore: Williams and Wilkins Co.

Stone, J., ed. 1979. *Internal Colonialism*. Special issue of *Ethnic and Racial Studies*, vol. 2, no. 3, July.

Sweet, J. 1972. "The Living Arrangements of Separated, Widowed, and Divorced Mothers." *Demography* 9: 143–59.

Tienda, M., and Angel, R. 1982. "Headship and Household Composition among Blacks, Hispanics, and Other Whites." *Social Forces* (December).

United Nations. 1973. *The Determinants and Consequences of Population Trends*. New York.

U.S. Bureau of the Census. 1958. "Religion Reported by the Civilian Population of the United States: March, 1957." *Current Population Reports*, series P-20, no. 79 (February).

Waite, Linda, and Spitze, G. 1981. "Young Women's Transition to Marriage." *Demography* 18 (November): 681–94.

Waite, Linda, and Stolzenberg, Ross. 1976. "Intended Childbearing and Labor Force Participation of Young Women." *American Sociological Review* 41 (April): 235–51.

Waxman, Chaim. 1981. "The Fourth Generation Grows Up: The Contemporary American Jewish Community." *Annals* 454 (March): 70–85.

———. 1982. "The Family and the American Jewish Community on the Threshold of the 1980s." In M. Sklare, ed., *Understanding American Jewry*. New Brunswick, N.J.: Transaction Books.

Westoff, C., and Jones, E. 1977. "Contraception and Sterilization in the United States, 1965–75." *Family Planning Perspectives* 9, no. 4 (July/August): 153–57.

———. 1979. "The End of 'Catholic' Fertility." *Demography* 16 (May): 209–217.

Westoff, C.; Potter, R.; Sagi, P.; and Mishler, E. 1961. *Family Growth in Metropolitan America*. Princeton: Princeton University Press.

Westoff, C., and Ryder, N. 1977. *The Contraceptive Revolution*. Princeton: Princeton University Press.

Wirth, Louis. 1928. *The Ghetto*. Chicago: University of Chicago Press.

Wright, E., and Perrone, L. 1977. "Marxist Class Categories and Income Inequality." *American Sociological Review* 42: 32–55.

Yancey, W. et al. 1976. "Emergent Ethnicity: A Review and Reformulation." *American Sociological Review* 41: 391–402

Zuckerman, Alan S. 1982. "New Approaches to Political Cleavage: A Theoretical Introduction." *Comparative Political Studies* (July).

Index

Age. *See also* Intergenerational transfers
  and denominational identification, 26, 154–56, 161–65, 182
  and educational attainment, 116–18, 131–32
  and fertility patterns, 95–101, 103–105
  and household structure, 75–88
  and income, 119
  and intermarriage, 11, 14–16, 18–27
  and Jewishness measures, 165–69
  and marital stability, 63–64
  and marital status, 60–62
  and marriage, age at first, 58, 66–69
  and migration, 41, 43–57
  and occupational concentration, 111–14
  and residential concentration, 33–37
  and self-employment, 137–40, 142, 144, 147–49
  of women in labor force, 126–32
Anti-Semitism, 135, 143, 171

Birthplace. *See* Migration
Blacks, and Jews compared, 29
  in age at first marriage, 65–67, 70
  in fertility patterns, 95–97, 99–100
  in self-employment, 137, 144
Boston Study, introduction to, xii–xiii, 7–9

Catholics, and Jews compared
  in age at first marriage, 65–69, 70
  in educational attainment, 115–16, 123–24, 132
  in female participation in labor force, 127–31
  in fertility patterns, 93, 95–98, 102–103
  in household structure, 79
  in income, 118–19
  in marital status, 60–62
  in migration patterns, 42, 48–50
  in occupational concentration, 110–11, 113–14
  in self-employment, 136, 144, 145

Childbearing, timing of. *See also* Fertility
  and fertility, 91–92, 177
  Jewish/non-Jewish differences in, 69–71, 77, 78, 80, 82
  and work patterns, 102, 126
Clerical-sales positions
  Jewish men in, 109–10, 113, 120, 122
  Jewish women in, 128, 130, 148
  self-employed, 145, 146, 148
Cohesion of Jewish community, problem of, stated, 1–9
Community-ethnic activities, and Jewishness, 26, 152, 166–69
Conservative Judaism
  and age at first marriage, 71–72, 175
  changes in identification with, 153–63
  and fertility, 103–105
  and household structure, 85, 86
  and intermarriage, 20, 23–24, 26
  and migration, 55
  and residential concentration, 38
Contraception, 69, 70, 92
Conversions to Judaism, 11, 12, 24
Current Population Survey, 11, 58

Denominations, Jewish. *See* Religious denominations, of Jews
Detroit study, 136
Discrimination. *See* Anti-Semitism
Divorce, 58, 59, 61–64, 97

Educational attainment
  and age, 116–18, 131–32
  and fertility, 92–93, 99–101, 106, 177
  and household structure, 80–85
  intergenerational outflows in, 123–25, 132–34
  and intermarriage, 17, 19–23
  Jewish/non-Jewish patterns of, 108–109, 115–19, 123, 172, 179
  of Jewish women, 131–34
  and marriage, age at first, 58–59, 69–70, 175
  and marriage stability, 62–64
  and migration, 42, 48–50, 55–57

191